"This book is a 'must read' for those who want to understand how the church entered into the lives of its people in El Salvador after Vatican II and Medellín through the ministry of Rutilio Grande, SJ. When you begin with Rutilio, his life, his ministry, and his death, then you can understand the period of suffering endured by the prophetic church of El Salvador."

—Jon Sobrino
Author of *Jesus the Liberator* and *Witnesses to the Kingdom*

"Catholic theology walks the dusty roads of history, the same roads where Jesus walked and his first followers first met him. At its most elemental, Catholic theology is biography. Just so, the life of Rutilio Grande, beautifully narrated and interpreted in these pages by Professor Thomas Kelly, is more than a life: it is a dogmatic theology that shows us where and how the Gospel grows feet."

—Kevin F. Burke, SJ
Jesuit School of Theology of Santa Clara University

When the Gospel Grows Feet

Rutilio Grande, SJ, and the Church of El Salvador

An Ecclesiology in Context

Thomas M. Kelly

A Michael Glazier Book

LITURGICAL PRESS
Collegeville, Minnesota

www.litpress.org

A Michael Glazier Book published by Liturgical Press

Cover design by Jodi Hendrickson. Cover images: Thinkstock. Rucksack image courtesy of the author.

Excerpts from documents of the Second Vatican Council are from *Vatican Council II: The Basic Sixteen Documents*, by Austin Flannery, OP, © 1996 (Costello Publishing Company, Inc.). Used with permission.

Papal encyclicals and exhortations are from the Vatican's digital archives, accessible at http://www.vatican.va/holy_father/index.htm.

Scripture texts in this work are taken from the *New Revised Standard Version Bible* © 1989, Division of Christian Education of the National Council of the Churches of Christ in the United States of America. Used by permission. All rights reserved.

1   2   3   4   5   6   7   8   9

Library of Congress Cataloging-in-Publication Data

Kelly, Thomas M., 1969–
    When the gospel grows feet : Rutilio Grande, SJ, and the church of El Salvador : an ecclesiology in context / Thomas M. Kelly.
        pages   cm
        "A Michael Glazier book."
        ISBN 978-0-8146-8077-3 — ISBN 978-0-8146-8086-5 (ebook)
    1. Grande, Rutilio, 1928–1977.   2. Catholic Church—El Salvador—History—20th century.   3. El Salvador—Church history—20th century.   I. Title.

    BX4705.G61759K45   2013
    271'.5302—dc23   2012048196

This book is dedicated to the women, men, and children who lost their lives in the civil war of El Salvador and those who continue to mourn them.

Contents

Acknowledgments

I would like to thank many people for their help in making this book possible. I begin with Maria Teresa Gaston who first invited me to El Salvador, John Giuliano, the Tamarindos, and the community of Guarjila in Chalatenango, especially the family of Casimiro and Esperanza and in particular Luis, Gio, Cobra, and Chele who kindly hosted travel courses from Creighton for five years. There I learned about the church of El Salvador from the people who lived through the war and who were accompanied by the church.

For the academic research aspect of this book I want to thank the University of Central America, especially the late Dean Brackley, SJ. Fr. Brackley was instrumental in providing me access to so much in El Salvador and he is sorely missed. I would also like to thank Kevin and Trena Yonkers-Talz of Santa Clara's *Casa de la Solidaridad* program for both inviting me to teach in their program as well as making my family a part of their lives; thank you for the community and friendship over those six months. I would also like to thank John Thiede, SJ, who helped in numerous ways during the final month of my sabbatical in El Salvador—from the interview with Monsignor Urioste to the access of the UCA archives—you were instrumental. I would like to thank two professors at the Maryknoll Language Institute in Cochabamba, Bolivia, for carefully checking this translation during June and July 2012. Wilma Rocha Montecinos and Karla Rojas Cuba offered invaluable assistance and ensured that this translation was accurate to both the content and spirit of Rutilio Grande.

I would like to thank Creighton University for allowing me to teach summer courses in Latin America, and especially my dean, Robert Lueger, PhD, who has been generous in his support of my sabbatical, this book, and the theology which grounds all of it. I want to thank Kate Macan, Ben McCann, Caitlin Malone, Tim Leacock, and Effie Caldarola for being my readers who gave great feedback. Finally, I want to thank my wife of twenty years, Lisa, and our children Andrew, Michael, and Catherine for being willing to move to El Salvador and live for the six months of research—without you, none of this would have been possible.

Abbreviations

ANDES	National Association of Educators of El Salvador
ANEP	National Association of Private Enterprise
ARENA	Nationalist Republican Alliance
CELAM	Latin American Bishops Conference
CEB	Christian Base Community
CISPES	Committee in Solidarity with the People of El Salvador
CONAMUS	National Coordination of Salvadoran Women
CONSALCOA	Salvadoran buying cooperative used by peasants
ECA	*Estudios Centroamericanos*
FDR	Democratic Revolutionary Front
FAPU	United Popular Action Front of El Salvador
FARO	Landowner Organization against Land Reform
FECCAS	Federation of Christian Peasants of El Salvador
FENASTRAS	National Federation of Salvadoran Workers
FMLN	Farabundo Marti National Liberation Front
FPL	Popular Liberation Forces
GAM	Mutual Support Group
IMF	International Monetary Fund
IPLA	Latin American Pastoral Institute (Quito Ecuador)
OAS	Organization of American States
ORDEN	Paramilitary Force of the Salvadoran Government and Landowners
PCN	National Conciliation Party of El Salvador
PCS	Salvadoran Communist Party
UCA	Central American University
UTC	Union of Rural Workers
UNTS	National Union of Salvadoran Labor

Introduction

On March 12, 1977, shortly after five o'clock in the afternoon, a Volkswagen Safari left a small town in El Salvador known as Aguilares. In the vehicle were three people—an elderly man named Manuel Solorzano, a fifteen-year-old boy named Nelson Lemus, and a Roman Catholic priest named Fr. Rutilio Grande, SJ. On the way out of town, near the train tracks, the vehicle stopped to give three small children a ride. They were leaving Aguilares, a small dusty town roughly an hour north of the capital of San Salvador. Their destination was the town of El Paisnal, roughly three miles away, where Fr. Grande was travelling to continue a novena in celebration of the town's feast day. As the bell was tolling to gather the people near the small church situated in the central plaza of El Paisnal, Fr. Grande and his entourage made their way along the narrow dusty road that connected Aguilares and El Paisnal. "Rutilio liked the people already gathered when he arrived."[1] As they passed the small village of Los Mangos, the children recall seeing groups of two or three men located on the banks of the small canals on either side of the road. Behind the VW was a small pickup truck that had followed them from Aguilares. In a low voice, Fr. Grande is quoted as saying, "We must do what God wants."[2] As the pickup came closer to the VW, a hail of bullets fell from the sky, impacting the car. Later, a doctor who examined the bodies indicated that Fr. Grande was killed by bullets coming from both the front and rear of the vehicle. The weapons and ammunition used were common to the local police. The bullets from the front of the vehicle hit Fr. Grande's jaw and neck and penetrated his skull. From the rear and left, he was shot through the lower back and pelvis. Altogether, he was killed by twelve bullets.[3] When the bodies were found it appeared that seventy-two-year-old Manuel Solorzano tried, in

---

[1] Rodolfo Cardenal, *Historia de una Esperanza: Vida de Rutilio Grande*, Colección Teología Latinoamericana 4 (San Salvador: UCA Editores, 2002), 573, translation mine.
[2] Ibid.
[3] Salvador Carranza, ed., *Una Luz Grande nos Brilló: Rutilio Grande, SJ* (Comisión de la Compañía de Jesús, 2007), 96.

vain, to protect Fr. Grande, as his body completely covered him. "Nelson sat quietly in his seat with a bullet in his forehead."[4] The three children who had been given a ride were screaming in the far back of the vehicle. A man whom they recognized ordered them to leave, which they did, full of panic. They passed by the bodies of the three others, not even seeing them. As they ran down the road toward El Paisnal, they heard one final shot.[5] Covered in blood and dirt, they did not stop running until they had arrived in El Paisnal.

Immediately, the news of these murders was transmitted to Archbishop Oscar A. Romero of San Salvador as well as to the provincial of the Society of Jesus, who also resided in the capital. Three Jesuits from the provincial office, Archbishop Romero, and his auxiliary Bishop Rivera y Damas all travelled to El Paisnal. At seven o'clock President Arturo Molina called the archbishop to offer his condolences and promise a thorough investigation. Later, the newspapers would say that the archbishop had called the president first.[6] This discrepancy between the government and church accounts of what occurred continued to be a developing theme throughout the period of violence that followed (1977–92).

The three bodies were placed in front of the altar in the church of El Paisnal and the Jesuit provincial asked that a liturgy be offered that "gives hope to the community and avoids the temptations to hatred or revenge."[7] At ten-thirty that same evening, Archbishop Romero presided over Mass, which lasted until midnight. The next morning, responding to a radio announcement by the archbishop, streams of peasants began walking into El Paisnal for a nine o'clock memorial Mass. They came from near and far to mourn the death of their beloved priest and his friends. The next Sunday, Archbishop Romero declared a "single Mass," a memorial Mass for Rutilio Grande, as the only Mass to be offered in the country. During the final funeral procession, one that would ultimately inter these bodies in the floor of the church in El Paisnal directly in front of the altar, the slogan could be heard: "Rutilio's walk with El Paisnal is like Christ's journey with the cross."[8]

The reality of Fr. Rutilio Grande's death, as described in detail in the preceding paragraphs, leaves the reader with some very serious questions.

---

[4] Cardenal, *Historia de una Esperanza: Vida de Rutilio Grande*, 574.
[5] Ibid.
[6] Carranza, ed., *Una Luz Grande nos Brilló: Rutilio Grande, SJ*, 100.
[7] Cardenal, *Historia de una Esperanza: Vida de Rutilio Grande*, 575.
[8] Carranza, ed., *Una Luz Grande nos Brilló: Rutilio Grande, SJ*, 104.

How could powerful forces within the overwhelmingly Catholic country of El Salvador both plan and carry out the execution of a Roman Catholic priest and two innocent people in broad daylight in front of witnesses? Why would this same government deepen its confrontation with the Catholic Church until thousands of lay ministers, dozens of priests, and even the archbishop of San Salvador, Oscar Romero, were murdered? What was so threatening about the church and its ministry? Why would the government, and the oligarchy that supported it, believe it necessary to repress the church in such a brutal manner?

To gain insight to even provisional answers to these questions, it is necessary to start at the beginning, with what the Roman Catholic Church used to be, in order to understand what it became—at least in El Salvador. Only then can we understand the extraordinary transformation of the Roman Catholic Church in Latin America. Part of this transformation came from a method of doing theology officially sanctioned by both the Vatican and the bishops of Latin America. What follows is the story of how this method became real in the country of El Salvador through the life, ministry, and death of the first Jesuit killed there, Rutilio Grande. To be "church" in the manner realized by Rutilio Grande was to give one's life in the effort to build the kingdom of God.

This work is organized more or less chronologically. The first two chapters begin with an illustration of the church's identity and mission during the colonial period (1500–1820) as it participated in the conquest of Latin America. As that period is considered, it is important to understand the theological presuppositions which framed the church's understanding of its identity and mission to the world it inhabited. Chapters 3 and 4 touch upon the transformative impact of Vatican II (1962–65) and how the Latin American bishops appropriated the teachings of that Council in their own context. Chapters 5 through 9 introduce Rutilio Grande, his life, his formation, his transformation, his ministry, his martyrdom, and his impact on Archbishop Oscar Romero. Finally, chapter 10 will ask, "What can Rutilio Grande and the church of El Salvador teach the Roman Catholic Church of North America?" This is especially pertinent if "church" is considered, according to Vatican II, as "the people of God."[9]

---

[9] Austin Flannery, ed., *Lumen gentium* in *Vatican Council II: The Basic Sixteen Documents* (Northport, NY: Costello Publishing Co., 1996), no. 9.

Part 1

Colonialism and Conquest

Chapter 1

Church and State in Colonial Times

Since its arrival [to Latin America] in the early sixteenth century, the institutional church has been marked by its wealth, power and privilege. As centuries passed, the church did little to change the daily hardships faced by the poor and powerless. During the conquest, millions of indigenous inhabitants suffered untold misery from war, disease, and slave-like conditions under Spanish conquistadores who claimed the name of Christ.[1]

The Catholic Church played an important role in the colonization of the peoples of Latin America.[2] At first glance, this statement may appear too strong; surely the church was not responsible for the suffering and enslavement that occurred because of European colonization! How could it preach the Gospel of Jesus Christ and not see what was happening as native peoples were slaughtered or enslaved? In order to even partially answer this question, we first have to study how the church understood itself and its role in the world, how it related to the broadly conceived "state," and, more importantly, how it stood to benefit from this relationship. Only then can we put the church's actions in context.

It is important to remember that the conquest of what is today called "Latin America" began after a war between Christian Spain and Muslim North Africa, which lasted over seven hundred years. Of course, to those involved, that conquest was not merely a war but also an epic struggle between two worldviews, religions, and cultures. The church understood

---

[1] David Tombs, *Latin American Liberation Theology* (Boston: Brill Academic Publishers, Boston, 2002), xi.

[2] With other scholars, I mean by "the church" "a message, an institution and its relationship to the Universal church and the state." See Emilio Betances, *The Catholic Church and Power Politics in Latin America* (Plymouth, UK: Rowan & Littlefield Publishers, 2007), 15, note 1. Unless otherwise specified, any time a reference to "church" is made I intend to signify the Roman Catholic Church.

the Spanish victory over the Muslims of North Africa as a validation and instantiation of Christianity as the one true religion on earth. With that zeal and vindication of its own superiority, the church turned its attention to new lands and expansion. Hoping to spread its power and influence, as well as "save souls," members of the church accompanied the conquistadores of both Spain and Portugal to what was then termed the "New World."

One need only read the first few pages of Christopher Columbus' diary (and underline each time the world "gold" is used) to see that the main motive for European exploration and colonization was not to spread the Christian faith but to profit from what they could and did take from indigenous peoples. Bartolomeo de las Casas, an early settler who became a Dominican priest, clearly stated what he thought was the foundational cause of oppression in the New World: "The cause for which the Christians have slain and destroyed so many and such infinite numbers of souls has been simply to get as their ultimate end, the Indian's gold of them, and to stuff themselves with riches in a very few days."[3] The church would directly benefit from this new source of wealth. Recall that the Vatican controlled lands and armies and participated in the political world in ways similar to any other nation-state at the time. If gold was not discovered immediately in a particular conquered area, each indigenous man, woman, and child was required to pay a quota to the Spanish. Failure to pay this quota resulted in the amputation of limbs, torture, and even death. Hispaniola, the first island to be exploited and devastated by conquistadors, lost nearly its entire population of roughly five hundred thousand Taíno people during the first fifty years of Spanish presence. Similar effects were recorded throughout Latin America.

It appears, from the various accounts of the Dominican friar Fr. Bartolomeo de las Casas, that the church not only condoned the violent takeover of native peoples and their lands in the pursuit of wealth but actually blessed it and participated in it. Prior to becoming a friar, las Casas himself was given land and slaves upon his arrival in Cuba. He benefitted from the very system he would later critique with so much determination. Shortly after arriving in the Caribbean, he began to study for the priesthood. Although he lived comfortably from the encomienda system in the New World, five years after his studies for the priesthood, las

---

[3] Bartolomeo de las Casas, *An Account, Much Abbreviated, of the Destruction of the Indies*, ed. Franklin W. Knight, trans. Andrew Hurley (Indianapolis: Hackett Publishing Company, 2003), 8.

Casas experienced a conversion that made him the most ardent defender of indigenous peoples during his lifetime:[4] "In 1514, as he prepared his sermon for Pentecost, the words of Ecclesiasticus 34:18-22 struck him with full force. The judgment of those who make sacrifice and other religious rituals before God and yet oppress their fellow human beings, spoke directly to his feelings about the ill-treatment of the Indians. He set free his Indian workers and prepared a special sermon for the Feast of the Assumption on August 15, 1514."[5]

Las Casas was a bright light in what was otherwise a dark chapter for the church. While those who denounced the practices of the conquering Spanish and Portuguese conquistadores were almost always people of the church, it was never the church as a whole that denounced the injustices and actively struggled against them. Why was this so? It was partly due to the fact that the church had violated its own earlier reforms (the Gregorian Reform) through the arrangement with the Spanish and Portuguese crowns that ensured its participation in the conquest. Gregory VII (1028–1085) introduced a ban on the practice of lay investiture near the turn of the millennium. Lay investiture was the practice that allowed temporal rulers (kings, queens, etc.) to appoint abbots of monasteries or bishops of the church in their area of political control (i.e., to invest them with an office and the power that went with it). Gregory VII knew that allowing secular rulers to appoint church offices both undermined the independence of the church and affected its cohesion.

Nevertheless, the practice of allowing secular leaders to appoint church leaders was the cost of the church's participation in the conquest. Spain, for example, allowed priests and other church officials to accompany the voyages to the New World in exchange for the power to appoint bishops in the newly discovered lands. These arrangements made it nearly impossible for the church to critique or denounce the brutality it witnessed as the state clearly had appointed (i.e., given great power and wealth to) those very church officials who should have been more critical of Spanish cruelty. A letter from King Philip II (1558–1598) to his governor in the Philippine Islands made it very clear who held and exercised power.

---

[4] David Tombs, *Latin American Liberation Theology*, 14, note 33. The encomienda system granted free labor (indigenous slaves) to Spaniards of appropriate social status. Las Casas was granted this free labor in both Cuba and Hispaniola prior to his conversion.

[5] Ibid., 21.

The King. To our viceroy of Nueva España, or the person or persons who shall, for the time being, be exercising the government of that country: As you know, the right of ecclesiastical patronage belongs to us throughout the realm of the Yndias—both because of having discovered and acquired that new world, and erected there and endowed the churches and monasteries at our own cost, or at the cost of our ancestors, the Catholic Sovereigns; and because it was conceded to us by bulls of the most holy pontiffs, conceded of their own accord. For its conservation, and that of the right we have to it, we order and command that the said right of patronage be always preserved for us and our royal crown, singly and in solidum, throughout all the realm of the Yndias, without any derogation therefrom, either in whole or in part; and that we shall not concede the right of patronage by any favor or reward that we or our successors may confer. . . .

We desire and order that no cathedral church, parish church, monastery, hospital, votive church, or any other pious or religious establishment be erected, founded, or constructed, without our express consent for it, or that of the person who shall exercise our authority; and further, that no archbishopric, bishopric, dignidad, canonry, ración, media-ración, rectorial or simple benefice, or any other ecclesiastical or religious benefice or office, be instituted, or appointment to it be made, without our consent or presentation.[6]

Because of the obvious benefits, this arrangement was willingly agreed to by the church; nevertheless, the moral cost was steep. "The royal patronage brought great benefits to both the monarchy and the institutional church, but it severely limited the church's potential to oppose the state's power. It meant that Rome would not have direct contact with the Latin American church, but would have to go through the mediation of the Spanish and Portuguese monarchs."[7] Even when the highest levels of the church denounced the treatment of indigenous peoples, it was helpless to enact its own decrees in a substantive manner. For example, Pope Paul III issued the following pronouncement in 1537, a "papal bull," which clearly affirmed the rationality, and hence the humanity, of indigenous peoples. Recall the Greek definition of a human being as a body inhabited by a rational soul.

[6] King Philip II, "Royal Instructions to Gómez Pérez Dasmariñas Regarding Ecclesiastical Affairs," in *Religion in Latin America: A Documentary History*, ed. Lee M. Penyak and Walter J. Petry (Maryknoll, NY: Orbis Books, 2006), 66.

[7] Tombs, *Latin American Liberation Theology*, 18.

The enemy of the human race, who opposes all good deeds in order to bring men to destruction, beholding and envying this, invented a means never before heard of, by which he might hinder the preaching of God's word of Salvation to the people: he inspired his satellites, who, to please him, have not hesitated to publish abroad that the Indians of the West and South, and other people of whom We have recent knowledge should be treated as dumb brutes created for our service, pretending that they are incapable of receiving the catholic faith.

We, who, though unworthy, exercise on earth the power of our Lord and seek with all our might to bring those sheep of His flock who are outside, in to the fold committed to our charge, consider, however, that the Indians are truly men and that they are not only capable of understanding the catholic faith, but, according to our information, they desire exceedingly to receive it.[8]

This pronouncement, without hesitation, "affirmed the rationality of the Indians and the importance of their evangelization."[9] Contrary to the opponents of las Casas who simply wanted to use these "animals" for free labor, Pope Paul III viewed the indigenous inhabitants of Latin America as fully human. It is for this reason that the papal bull was suppressed by Spain: they simply refused to promulgate it. Since Spain appointed local church leaders who depended on the state for status and power, only scattered opposition in the form of letters came from that quarter.

The problem deepened with the incapacity of the church to enforce the view of Pope Paul III. The church had given up its moral voice at the cost of inclusion. Some, though, did protest loudly. Going even further than the pope, the bishop of Santa Marta (located in the modern day Yucatan Peninsula in southeastern Mexico) stated the following in a letter to the Spanish crown in 1541:

Wherein Your Majesty will clearly see how those who rule over these parts deserve to be stripped of their ranks so the republics may have some relief. And if this be not done, it is my belief their sicknesses shall have no cure. It is also meet that Your Majesty know that there are no Christians in these parts, but rather demons, that there are no men who serve God or the king but only traitors to their law and their king. For it is true that the greatest obstacle I find, to turning

---

[8] Pope Paul III, *Indians Are Men*, in Penyak and Petry, eds., *Religion in Latin America: A Documentary History*, 15.

[9] Tombs, *Latin American Liberation Theology*, 21.

the warring Indians to peace and bringing those at peace into the knowledge of our faith, is the harsh and cruel treatment that the Indians of peace receive from the Christians.[10]

Societas perfecta

Why was the church impotent to change the situation in relation to the conquest? Partly this resulted from how it understood itself and its realm of operation in relation to the state. For many centuries the church had embraced a model of church-state relations known as *Societas perfecta*. Under this vision, two perfect societies correspond to two very different realities: the church and state. One society, the church, is responsible for the care of the divine or spiritual dimension of human beings. The other society, the state, is responsible for the earthly material dimension of human beings. Each society is the highest of its kind; each has certain limits within which it moves. Both maintain boundaries that emerge from the nature and purpose of each of the two areas of responsibility.[11] Later, this understanding of *Societas perfecta* would be formally instantiated by Pope Leo XIII in 1885.

Many scholars indicate that this understanding accurately captures the relationship between the governments of Spain and Portugal and the Catholic Church throughout the conquest. The church's primary role was to represent the concerns of the spiritual and divine, while the state had full control of the temporal order in the "secular" world. This manner of dividing up the world and understanding it from two (nearly) separate domains is called dualism. In the next chapter we will explore how such a dualism marked the church's involvement with the conquest—the church as the overseer of all things "spiritual," with the state as the overseer of all things "material." Additionally, we will explore some of the consequences that resulted from such division. But first, it is necessary to understand some of the cultural legacies left behind by the church-state conquest of the New World. These colonial attitudes and practices resulted in cultural preferences and patterns that are critical to understanding contemporary Latin America.

---

[10] Bartolomeo de las Casas, *An Account, Much Abbreviated, of the Destruction of the Indies*, 55–56.

[11] Until the Second Vatican Council, the doctrine of the two perfect societies of Leo XIII was held to be official in theological studies. During the Council itself, as well as in the new Code of Canon Law, the doctrine is no longer explicitly mentioned. In modern Catholic post-conciliar theology, it hardly has any role at all. Its abandonment was somewhat controversial.

The Cultural Legacy of Conquest

The cultural values and social mores imposed upon the peoples of modern-day Latin America by the conquering European powers continue to have incredible force.[12] This is true not only in Latin America but in Africa and Asia as well. Social and economic patterns inherited from the time of the conquest continue to deeply affect the social reality of Latin America. Of the many legacies from this period of history, it is worth noting three particular patterns that emerged as a result of European conquest. First, there was colonial disdain for physical labor and a preference for exploiting native lands and peoples to do work. This disdain emerged from social and racial attitudes. Such attitudes are still prominent today. Second, there was an attitude that conquered peoples and lands existed to serve the needs of distant European (or other) peoples, especially by providing the conquering nation complete and total access to natural resources and minerals. While the exploitation has changed, this attitude continues to influence how wealthy contemporary Latin Americans both perceive and encourage outside intervention in their countries. Third, the conquest left behind a system of land distribution that created, or at least contributed to, the vast inequality of wealth and access to land among the peoples of Latin America. One way to understand these social mores is to compare and contrast them to attitudes formative of North American culture.

Poverty and Race in Latin America

Contrary to the North American spirit, admired and promoted by folklore, about the equality of all people (though contradicted for many years in the slave-owning South), owners of land and industry in Latin America rarely worked alongside those who produced for them. Working with someone implies a basic equality, and from the beginning of the European conquest, the humanity of the indigenous peoples had always been suspect. Due to the vast differences in language, culture, and religion, European settlers were slow to view the indigenous in terms of equality, which is an issue even today.

Bartolomeo de las Casas spent the majority of his life arguing for and defending the humanity of indigenous peoples in Latin America within the civil and ecclesiastical (church) courts of Europe. Promoting the idea that native peoples possessed rationality and, thus, a soul, was difficult in a

---

[12] The main points of this are drawn from David Tombs, *Latin American Liberation Theology*, 13–14, and related illustrations come from personal experiences of the author.

Europe so separated by language, culture, and distance. Even as recently as the mid-1700s the church in South America allowed the indigenous peoples only the sacraments of baptism and marriage. Until their status as human or sub-human was determined finally, Eucharist was generally withheld.

Most contemporary Latin American countries have an oligarchy, or upper class, with traditional Spanish or European racial characteristics, while those in the lower economic and social levels tend to look more like indigenous Latin Americans or Africans (depending on the country). It is not difficult to find shopping centers in Peru or entertainment establishments in the Dominican Republic that do not permit the entrance of someone who is darker or who appears indigenous. It is true that, from Haiti to Bolivia, distinctions of race still create and maintain deep economic and social divisions. Anecdotally, I have been introduced to country clubs in Latin America where membership is open to anyone, but one must be from Spain to sit on the governing board. This continued preoccupation with pura sangre, or "pure blood," is reflective of concrete attitudes about racial and socioeconomic classification.

It is interesting to note the difference in how people in the lower classes of Latin America are perceived by the wealthy of their countries in contrast to North American attitudes. Of course, we have to generalize here, but (correctly or incorrectly) in North America many today believe that regardless of race or birth, people can, or should, try to work their way up and out of poverty through a combination of responsibility, hard work, and luck. Some would call this our greatest myth, while others would call it an achievable dream. Whether such opportunity exists or not in North America, its contrast with Latin American attitudes is stark. The lower class in Latin America is perceived to exist in order to serve the upper class—whether one is referring to *restavecs* (child slaves) in Haiti or *indiginas* (indigenous female house employees) in Bolivia. I have personally witnessed the prevalence of this phenomenon throughout Latin America. In many countries, *indiginas* are perceived as less than human by their employers. In Central America specifically, domestic helpers are often referred to as *muchachas* (girls), when they are often poor older women who work, out of necessity, in the homes of the wealthy. These linguistic titles reveal societal attitudes toward the poor, which understand them as being of value but only insofar as they serve the rich. As a result of this attitude, we will see in a later chapter that when the poor reclaimed their own dignity as human beings, it shocked the wealthy.[13]

---

[13] For an interesting and informative discussion of how poor *campesinos* (rural peasants) are perceived by wealthy city dwellers in Guatemala, see *I Rigoberta Menchu, An*

Whose Land? Whose Resources?

The attitude that the poor exist to serve the rich leads to a second cultural pattern established during colonization: Latin America exists to serve the needs of distant countries and, if strong enough, other peoples and countries can and should take what they want. Originally this began as a battle over colonies in the New World. For example, the island of Hispaniola (modern-day Haiti and Dominican Republic) was occupied by no less than five separate nations throughout its tumultuous early history. Unfortunately, this attitude has extended itself into recent history as well. US intervention in Latin America, ostensibly behind the Roosevelt corollary of the Monroe Doctrine, is the practical fruit of this attitude. In theory, this doctrine would prevent a European (and later, Soviet) intervention in Latin America while the latter began its movements for independence from Spain, et al.

In practice, the United States was delineating Latin America as being within its sphere of influence and control in the context of the Cold War with the Soviet Union. It was determining who could and could not have influence over *other sovereign* countries. This was particularly true in relation to debt repayments and military intervention by the United States in the Caribbean and Latin America throughout the twentieth century. The Monroe Doctrine, initially welcomed by many Latin American countries, would later prove to be the rationale for countless US interventions. Most of these interventions were justified as responses to the meddling of foreign powers, while in actuality they were about preserving US economic interests.[14]

In nearly every case of US intervention in Latin America during the twentieth century, from Haiti to Chile, those in each respective nation's oligarchy (wealthy political elites) cooperated with outside powers to maintain and strengthen their positions of power and wealth within their own countries. Oligarchies are systems of governance managed by those with the wealth and power to determine how a country is governed. Anticommunism or threats to national security usually functioned as the justification for outside intervention. The oligarchy understood that the key to their own survival was to cooperate with those who saw their own

---

Indian Woman in Guatemala, ed. Elisabeth Burgos-Debray, trans. Ann Wright, chap. 5 (London: Verso Press, 1994).

[14] For an interesting overview of US intervention in the twentieth century, see Stephen Kinzer, *Overthrow: America's Century of Regime Change from Hawaii to Iraq* (New York: Times Books, 2006).

nation as a place which served the interests of greater foreign powers, whether in terms of economics (antinationalization) or global politics (the Cold War).

This was particularly true when Latin American countries began to nationalize the industries and natural resources of their own land. An industry is nationalized when a state seizes a private, and usually foreign, business. After compensating its owner(s) for its publicly declared tax value, the state makes it a public company owned by, and therefore benefiting, the citizens of that country. Many of these businesses are involved with cultivating and exporting natural resources such as agriculture, mining, oil, and gas.

Many Latin American nations implemented nationalization programs in the twentieth century. These were viewed as necessary for the public good as young nations emerged weak and in debt from their colonial histories. During the colonial period, conquered peoples had no control over, and little direct benefit from, the use of their own natural resources.[15] A brief overview of the history of US intervention reveals some startling facts about US resistance to nationalization programs in various Latin American countries.

For example, when the United Fruit Company (a US-owned company) was threatened with nationalization in 1954, the United States staged a coup to oust the democratically elected leader of Guatemala, only ten years into that country's experiment with democracy. The justification was that while the Guatemalan president Arbenz had no communists in his government, he did have "friends" who were communists.[16] When Bolivia was going to nationalize oil in 1970, the United States helped overthrow President Juan Jose Torres. The coup to overthrow Torres was led by US-trained officer and Gulf Oil beneficiary Hugo Banzer, who had support from Washington. When Banzer's forces had a breakdown in radio communications, US Air Force radios were placed at their disposal. In addition, the United States invaded the Dominican Republic twice (to guarantee debt repayment): once before and once after the reign of Dominican dictator Gen. Rafael Trujillo, whom the United States supported.

---

[15] It has been claimed, for example, that over approximately three hundred years, enough silver left the mines of Potosi, Bolivia, to construct a physical bridge from Potosi to Madrid, Spain.

[16] For an excellent and easily accessible commentary on this, see the CNN *Cold War* series which has interviews with CIA station chiefs who explain the goal and rationale for US action.

Nicaragua was also invaded and occupied numerous times. When the openly socialist but democratically elected president of Chile, Salvador Allende, threatened a US company named ITT with nationalization (part of a program for nationalizing the entire telecommunications of the country) he was killed in a CIA-supported coup and replaced by the Chilean dictator General Augusto Pinochet, a military man who faithfully protected US interests in that country. The pattern was clear and consistent. The United States did not hesitate to protect its own economic interests—even when democracy and human rights had to be sacrificed in order to do so.

Land Distribution in Colonial Latin America

The third and final cultural legacy that the conquest bequeathed to the peoples of Latin America was the pattern of land distribution adopted in the "New World." The distribution of land during the conquest was modeled on the method used by the Spanish government when it reclaimed most of the Iberian Peninsula from the Muslims during their seven hundred–year war. Those who were most powerful and successful militarily in winning back land were rewarded with large tracts of liberated territory. When this method was applied to the New World, it resulted in a small group of conquistadors receiving vast amounts of conquered land. In some places, this actually created the entrenched oligarchy that continued to have power well into the latter decades of the twentieth century.[17]

Land and its distribution have been at the center of many conflicts in Latin America. Civil wars, civil unrest, and even military action between countries in this region can often be traced back to the availability of land. Land reform has been attempted with varying degrees of success, but mostly failure, in Haiti, Bolivia, Brazil, the Dominican Republic, Chile, El Salvador, Nicaragua, and other Latin American countries. Land was certainly a cause of El Salvador's civil war as close to 90 percent of the land was owned and managed by fourteen families descended from the original conquistadores.

Recall that until recently, the key to wealth and social mobility throughout the Americas was land. One either had land or worked on someone else's land. What one's land produced was, and still is, in many cases, the key to wealth. Contrast this reality with the North American history of land rushes and homesteading where pioneers were assured a piece of

---

[17] We will see this as true in future chapters relating to the social and economic inequalities in El Salvador.

land. Though the land had been forcibly taken from Native Americans, it became available to many people in North America. With so much land for the taking, people moved west and established farms or ranches, which allowed for wealth to be more broadly distributed. In Latin America, all of the territory had been claimed shortly after the original conquest, leaving many indigenous people without land.

From Conquest to Democracy: The Church and Change

Throughout the first three hundred years of European presence in Latin America and until approximately 1820, the Catholic Church constituted one of the three pillars of colonial society alongside oligarchic commercial interests and colonial governments. Recall that oligarchies are systems of governance managed by those with the country's wealth and power. In many contemporary Latin America towns, one can still find the mayor's office (or another government building), the cathedral, and usually a major business on most town squares or plazas. It is important to realize that the church not only participated in the colonial power structure but benefitted from it was well.

Prior to the national independence movements of the early 1800s inspired by Simon Bolívar, the church (after the state) was the second largest landholder in all of Latin America. The church benefitted from indigenous labor through the *encomienda* system—a system that allotted a certain amount of indigenous slave labor to each person of a certain social class. In some cases, even religious orders ran *encomiendas* and enslaved the native peoples for the profit they generated.[18] This system made it possible to take and manage *haciendas* (large ranches) set up to benefit European invaders. Thus, the colonial church was a highly conservative force, supporting and sustaining the status quo and firmly on the side of the powerful. Despite some prophetic exceptions (e.g., Fr. Antonio de Montesinos, Fr. Bartolomeo de las Casas, and Fr. Juan de Zumarraga), the church usually served as an uncritical chaplain to colonial power and encouraged its exploitive practices.

Nevertheless, the church in Latin America has always been an institution that has conferred legitimacy—directly or indirectly, actively or

---

[18] It seems that religious orders, including the Franciscans and Jesuits, had a proclivity toward this arrangement, at least in South America. See Jeffrey Klaiber, *The History of the Jesuits in Latin America, 1549–2000: 450 Years of Inculturation, Defense of Human Rights, and Prophetic Witness* (Saint Louis: The Institute of Jesuit Sources, 2009), 22, 89.

passively—upon individuals, groups, and governments.[19] Over the past four hundred years, legitimacy from the church came either by way of tradition, by legal means, or, most recently, by embracing the fight for justice championed by the Second Vatican Council (1962–65). According to noted Latin American and church historian Jeffrey Klaiber, SJ, at different times throughout the history of the church in Latin America, various understandings of church-state relations were envisioned and encouraged. The three that deserve further discussion here include Christendom, integralism, and liberalism.[20]

Christendom

Christendom is an understanding of the church-state relation that emerged during the late Middle Ages. It is one in which the church acts as the senior partner and the state, essentially, does the former's bidding. Clergy wielded significant political power, from the pope down to the local parish priest. In medieval Christendom, issues such as whom one could marry, where one could both work and be buried, and whether one could own land or be permitted to worship in church were all decided by church authorities. Under this arrangement the church and the state should be one, unified, but always with clergy in positions of power or the church as the senior partner. Early in the conquest, certain regional leaders of the church in Latin America harbored ambition toward a Christendom-type model where the church would serve as the leader and wield considerable influence and power. Quickly this ceased to be a real possibility.

> First, the rise of absolute monarchies in Western Europe from the fifteenth to the nineteenth centuries increasingly subjected the exercise of the church's mission to state control. By the nineteenth century, the time when popes would speak and emperors and monarchs would do their bidding had long passed. Christendom had come to an end and the medieval harmony (maintained in theory if not in practice) between church and state gave way to suspicion and controversy. The emergence of stronger nation-states led their monarchs to place more restrictive limits on the activity of the church within the boundaries of their state.[21]

---

[19] Jeffrey Klaiber, *The Church, Dictatorships and Democracy in Latin America*, chap. 1 (Maryknoll, NY: Orbis Books, 1998).

[20] These three arrangements are put forth by ibid.

[21] Richard Gaillardetz, *The Church in the Making:* Lumen Gentium, Christus Dominus, Orientalium Ecclesiarium (New York: Paulist Press, 2006), 3.

In the midst of this time period, the expulsion of the Jesuits from South America in 1767 put to rest any ambitions of the church as senior partner in the New World and established, quite forcefully, who was the power broker in Latin America.

Integralism

Integralism understands the church and state as separate but envisions a privileged place for the church within the system and practice of national governance. For example, the Catholic Church would be the only national religion, church property would be exempt from taxes, and fees from the state would support numerous church projects, including hospitals, schools, and orphanages. From the original conquest and establishment of controlled regions to the Bolivarian revolution that swept through Latin America in the 1820s, integralism had been the dominant model for church-state relations. The benefits to the church as a socio-political institution were enormous: "The church became the wealthiest institution and the largest landowner in Spanish and Portuguese America. Tithes paid to the state and reapportioned to the church plus fees charged for services represented important income."[22] The church's status and wealth, of course, depended on European rulers and their particular policies. For this reason, the institutional church (though, not always individual church representatives) sided with the colonial government against nearly all movements for independence. This privileged relationship with the state allowed the church to acquire an enormous amount of wealth.

Liberalism

According to Klaiber, "In the eighteenth and nineteenth centuries liberalism emerged as a new and powerful political force and it constituted a new source of legitimacy. The church, which did not learn to change with the times, lost a measure of its own legitimacy in the eyes of liberals, positivists, and other reformers of advanced thinking. The church symbolized the old colonial order, while liberalism represented modernity and progress."[23]

Liberalism is primarily characterized by a suspicion of centralizing power in one person or institution. Historically, this is the latest arrange-

---

[22] Penyak and Petry, eds., *Religion in Latin America: A Documentary History*, 83. A "tithe" is a percentage of income given to a particular religious denomination.

[23] Klaiber, *The Church, Dictatorships and Democracy in Latin America*, 5.

ment of the relationship between church and state in Latin America. Deeply entrenched in the colonial order, the church did not embrace the diffusion of political power and economic activity for the greatest number of people until the middle of the twentieth century. Under this arrangement the church would wield little or no political *power*, but it could exercise great moral *authority* toward its own vision of how human society should be shaped in light of the Gospel.[24] The struggle between liberalism and Catholicism was really the struggle between both democracy and human rights and the old oligarchic colonial order that depended on real or imagined class distinctions. The church came dangerously close to irrelevance for its continued embrace of the older order.

> Throughout the nineteenth century the church steadily lost influence among the upper classes, and in the twentieth it began losing influence among the popular classes as well. With industrialism, migrations from the country to the city, and an increased level of political consciousness among both peasants and workers, the popular classes soon fell under the influence of the new populist and Marxist doctrines. The church came seriously close to finding itself marginalized in the wake of these great changes, which were sweeping over Latin America.[25]

During the time between conquest and modernity, the church was always a purveyor of legitimacy. First it gave legitimacy to the colonial powers by upholding the status quo of church, state, and oligarchic domination. This "traditional" legitimacy would emerge from an understanding of history as static (unchanging) and the social order as divinely ordained. Later the church would legitimize peoples and institutions with a more democratic orientation as it emerged from its own colonial past. In the past fifty years, with a new commitment to peace and social justice, it has also offered legitimacy to marginalized groups who are challenging civil authority. Often these groups have been oppressed by dictators appointed by the oligarchy—traditional allies of the church hierarchy. By supporting these groups over and against their oppressors, the church paid a substantial price in terms of its own rights, as well as increased persecution and oppression of its people and institutions.

---

[24] If power is the ability to force people to do one's will, authority is the ability to inspire others to do one's will.

[25] Klaiber, *The Church, Dictatorships and Democracy in Latin America*, 5.

Two Churches: One Latin America

There is an interesting contrast in what the Catholic Church represents if one visits the main cathedral in the Archdiocese of San Salvador, El Salvador. On the main level is a traditional cathedral constructed in the shape of a cross with huge side altars and a main altar some distance away from the front pews. The seat for the archbishop is situated as far back toward the rear wall as possible.[26] Liturgies in the main cathedral tend to be very traditional, with little input or participation from people in the pews.

In the basement of this cathedral is a place of worship referred to as the "Romero Chapel." Situated near the tomb of martyred Salvadoran Archbishop Oscar Romero, there is a raised altar in the middle of a circular configuration of folding chairs set up every Sunday. The archbishop presides over the liturgy above on the main level, while below a volunteer priest from another part of the country says Mass every Sunday of the year. Upstairs the distance between the archbishop and the congregation allows for a solemn Mass with very little participation outside of the traditional parameters. Downstairs the homily is usually interactive, with parishioners engaging in dialoguing with the priest and each other as the meaning and application of the gospel is worked out between them. "Participatory" homilies, where multiple parishioners may stand and contribute to the reflection on the readings, are the order of the day.

In many ways, these two Masses within the one church epitomize contradicting ecclesiologies (understandings of the mission and identity of "church"). They also represent the two Catholic churches of Latin America and have coexisted for quite some time. The understandings of "church" are lived out differently in style, mission, and substance.

> The two central events in recent Latin America church history were Vatican II and Medellín. Put somewhat simplistically, ecclesiastical leaders were guided by two different ecclesiologies or views of the church. Many bishops and priests in Latin America may be considered conservatives, because they still follow a pre–Vatican II ecclesiology. For them the church is essentially a spiritual monarchy that functions along hierarchical and paternalistic lines, from top to bottom. According to this model the bishops, who represent the magisterium (the teaching power) of the church, see themselves as teaching authorities commissioned to teach the truth to the faithful. The duty

---

[26] This was true as of 2009.

of the faithful is to listen to these teachings. Generally, *conservative bishops* and priests work closely with tradition-minded *cultural elites*. By way of contrast, the Vatican Council proposed the model of the church as community, which, without ceasing to be hierarchical, aims to encourage intercommunication, spontaneous participation, and fraternal dialogue. Bishops, priests, religious and laity who opt for this model see themselves more as pastors called to help the faithful to grow in maturity and to assume leadership roles.[27]

The differences between these two churches do not end there. Conservatives in the Latin American church strongly believe that faith and spirituality are individual, vertical, and ultimately personal realities that manifest themselves socially by worshiping with fellow Catholics. Progressives embrace the new Vatican II teaching that calls the faithful to actively work for the kingdom of God in and through the transformation of political, economic, and social realities. They believe the purpose of the church is to encourage societal transformation in a manner consistent with the ministry of Jesus and his preference for the marginalized, evident throughout the gospels. "For conservatives, unity and religious uniformity are positive values,"[28] which manifest themselves in unquestioning acceptance of abstract doctrine relating to faith and spirituality. This acceptance is concretized or contextualized through personal moral decision making. The type of education that both conservatives and progressives promote, while both Catholic, are markedly different as well.[29]

Progressive Catholics seek to understand and embrace religious and cultural pluralism and try to understand the Gospel and its demands in the actual world of men and women *where they live—socially, economically, and politically*. Context becomes the lens through which the Gospel is understood; it is part of how one reads and integrates one's Christianity. If one

---

[27] Klaiber, *The Church, Dictatorships and Democracy in Latin America*, 15, emphasis mine.
[28] Ibid.
[29] See Jeffrey Klaiber, "The Catholic Church, Moral Education and Citizenship in Latin America," *Journal of Moral Education* 38, no. 4 (December 2009): 407–20. "On a formal educational level, the church runs private schools for the wealthy, the middle class and the poor. In some schools for the wealthy, such as those run by Opus Dei, a pre–Vatican II mindset prevails and emphasis is placed on individual advancement. But in others, especially those run by the Jesuits, solidarity with the poor is emphasized. On the popular level, the Fe y Alegría schools for the poor stress civic participation and commitment to building the local community. The same divisions may be found in Catholic universities: some incorporate the ideals of social responsibility in their programs, but others simply foster an individualism that is more in tune with neoliberalism" (407).

is poor and indigenous, will he or she see and understand the Gospel in the same way as someone wealthy and from the cultural elite? Progressive Catholicism in Latin America—that is, Catholicism in the spirit and tone of Vatican II—believes that context deeply affects how one appropriates religious faith. This question of context and how it is addressed has seriously challenged the unity and message of the Catholic Church in Latin America.

The differences between conservatives and progressives go even deeper on other levels. Early in the colonial enterprise, bishops and other church leaders were almost always wealthy Europeans. It is true that the church had some Creole bishops (from the upper class of the colonial caste system), *mestizo* priests (mixed-race), and a few indigenous missionaries in the frontier areas, but the church was fundamentally a foreign and largely Spanish institution.[30] After the initial conquest, priests who came from mixed or indigenous ancestry were mainly formed and trained in their own country where they shared very similar conditions with those whom they served. Thus, the leadership came to be defined by its Roman or European ancestry (and later training), while the priest and his parishioners were perceived to share the same context. Bolivia, for example, has only recently had a cardinal-archbishop from Bolivia; the Vatican used to import them from Italy. Conversely, most diocesan priests from the lower classes were trained in their own country when seminaries began to form. The lower classes, in general, would come to participate in what would later be characterized as "popular" Catholicism, a blending of Christianity with certain indigenous beliefs.[31] These two types of Catholicism, "official" and "popular," have existed side by side for centuries.

Popular Catholicism tends to emphasize the intersection of the human and divine in everyday life in ways that would appear magical to the North American or European imagination. Intercession of the Virgin Mary and the saints, for example, is central to many people's faith in this area even today. God works in and through nature, and in other noninstitutional ways. As some would say, the highway between heaven and earth is very busy.[32] Conversely, official Catholicism focuses on the institution as the exclusive conduit between the human and divine, which is centered on sacramental practice—particularly Sunday Mass and frequent confes-

---

[30] For a more in-depth analysis of this topic, see Phillip Berryman, *Stubborn Hope: Religion, Politics and Revolution in Central America*, chap. 1 (Maryknoll, NY: Orbis Books, 1997).

[31] For some interesting examples of this, see Menchu, *I Rigoberta Menchu, An Indian Woman in Guatemala*.

[32] Berryman, *Stubborn Hope: Religion, Politics and Revolution in Central America*, 6.

sion—and a clearly defined set of ethical demands. One's soul and its spiritual state are the main concerns here, not one's material state of being or even the suffering one may encounter in this world.

It is important to note how the division between a popular church and an official church emerges from two separate and distinct cultures interacting. Usually, this does not happen between two cultures of equal power. "This is what is meant by *transculturation* or the imposition of one culture over another whereby one culture considers its way of life superior to the others."[33] The abstract and traditionally Latin formulated "truths" of the faith were imported by the Roman Catholic Church and uniformly imposed on a plethora of cultures, peoples, and indigenous religions in a way that made their acceptance nearly impossible. The still unfinished task of the church is "to participate in the Holy Spirit's work of *enculturation* where the local church makes the Catholic faith its own." This means that the local church needs "to embrace the pain and the joys of the process of *acculturation* in meeting a new culture on a playing field that is never fully equal, accepting some of its premises, rejecting or resisting many others and finally, coming into a fuller acceptance of it with its strengths and weaknesses."[34]

The division between official and popular Catholicism has resulted in deep divisions within the church, and its consequences are far-reaching. One can only generalize here, but the official church is usually comprised of members of the cultural elite (oligarchy) and senior clerical leadership (bishops, archbishops, and cardinals), who embrace an institutional Catholicism concerned with cultic obligation and doctrinal orthodoxy. Popular Catholicism comprises "the people" (poor) and clerics who emerge from this under-class who embrace a form of religiosity which addresses the very real and direct challenge of living life in an oppressive, dangerous environment. "These two ecclesial models are, of course, stereotypes; in between there are many variations and nuances. The important point is that differing theological orientations must be taken into account in order to understand the divisions that existed in many Episcopal conferences."[35]

---

[33] Address by Stephen P. Judd, "Acculturation and Leaning a Second Language in a Missionary Context at the Maryknoll Language Institute," Cochabamba, Bolivia, March 2005. The Maryknoll Order is visionary in its respectful engagement with diverse peoples and cultures.

[34] Ibid.

[35] Klaiber, *The Church, Dictatorships and Democracy in Latin America*, 16.

Conclusion

What is at the root of these ecclesial divisions? One could argue that whether or not one takes into account the context in which Christianity is lived really depends on the importance one assigns to the world. Imagine the complexity involved in bringing a particular religious faith to different peoples and cultures in languages that are totally different from one's own, not to mention bringing this faith to those who are radically poor. Is not Christianity simply a disembodied truth which hovers over the world and is valid throughout history regardless of where or when? Isn't God to be found most reliably only through the cultic practices of the sacraments and in a formal church setting? Do Christians have an obligation to challenge the world when human society causes suffering and death? It is toward these theological questions that we now turn.

Questions for Discussion:

1. What is lay investiture and what consequences did it have on the prophetic role of the church in the "New World?"

2. What was *Societas perfecta* and how did it concretely affect the role of the church in the conquest?

3. Why did the church react to independence movements in the manner it did?

4. Explain the various systems of Christendom, integralism, and liberalism.

5. Why were there "two" churches within the Catholic Church of Latin America throughout the colonial period?

Chapter 2:

Theological and Philosophical Roots of the Conquest

Although some church clerics took pity on the suffering of Indians and even questioned the moral rights of the Spanish to treat them so harshly, these were usually seen as separate from the theological issues that should concern the church. Because the church sought to claim the souls of the inhabitants for the glory of God, their concern for the Indians was often exclusively for the state of their disembodied souls, rather than the conditions of their life under colonial rule. God's glory was seen in terms of the number of conversions, rather than the survival of the converts.[1]

In 1891 Pope Leo XIII published *Rerum novarum*, the first social encyclical of the church. Following this, the magisterium of the Catholic Church began to author a series of documents explicitly extending the essence of the Christian gospel into the social, economic, and political structures of the world in a very concrete manner. Various popes addressed, for example, the notion of fair wages, the benefit of labor unions, the private ownership of property, and the role of the state in relation to the individual. Until the Second Vatican Council (1962–65) called by Pope John XXIII, many of these documents, collectively known as Catholic social teaching, continued to embrace charity as the preferred model for church engagement with social problems. Charity, the satisfaction of an immediate material need, sought to address the needs of the marginalized while saying very little about the *causes* of that marginalization. This model for world engagement changed radically after Vatican II.

---

[1] David Tombs, *Latin American Liberation Theology* (Boston: Brill Academic Publishers, 2002), 16.

It is a legitimate question to ask why it took so long for the Catholic Church to enter into active debate about how to socially transform the world. Why was it not until the late 1800s, after Karl Marx and his system of thought had become firmly entrenched in the lives of working-class movements in Europe and the United States, that the church deigned to speak formally about the troubling conditions of humans throughout the world? Of course the church had always been concerned with the poor, but what took it so long to begin addressing the structures that created suffering? Why did it take almost two millennia before it addressed the importance of changing its mission to the world? In order to understand why, we need to look closely at some philosophical and theological presuppositions that grounded the church's self-understanding in relation to the world between the Council of Trent (1554–63) and Vatican II.

What perspective on the relationship between faith and the world did the church have? What could make it possible for the church to collaborate with, assist, and, in some cases, participate in the colonial oppression of native peoples during the European conquest of Latin America? How is it even possible to make sense of this, while maintaining some degree of intellectual integrity and commitment to the church itself? It could be argued that dominant approaches to three critical topics were essential for supporting a worldview that permitted the church to participate in something it could never condone today. First was the preferred method for understanding "reality," as well as what is most important within human beings; second was the method of how the church practiced evangelization in the world; third was how the church understood history and its own capacity for change. It becomes evident that the church's former stances on these issues resulted in a preference for the spiritual world divorced from the material world, a preference for evangelization through persecution rather than persuasion, a preference for a static view of human history over a dynamic one, and, finally, a preference for charity over people's right to justice.

What Is the True and the Real?

To understand how the church could perceive itself as faithful to its mission, even as it accompanied the conquistadores in their efforts at domination and subjugation, it is necessary to digress a bit and understand how people thought and perceived the world during the age of conquest. Throughout Western intellectual history, there has been a variety of methods for arguing for the existence of, or the reality of, something.

Two of these methods can be referred to, in shorthand, as the inductive and deductive methods.

The study of how human beings understand is called hermeneutics. German in origin, hermeneutics roughly translates as, "the art of understanding." In the first method, one can begin with material reality and argue toward an immaterial conclusion that may not be immediately evident in that reality. Essentially, one can glean from empirical evidence around oneself information that leads to an assertion defensible by the data. This is called the inductive method.

Another method by which to argue for the reality of something is to begin with a pre-given, perfect ideal or immaterial exemplar that is only partially reflected in the material world around us. This is called the deductive method. Both methods will become clearer in the brief examples that follow. At different times in intellectual history, one of these methods has usually dominated—and at times they have been used together. In the last two hundred years, a variety of approaches have created whole new methods of intellectual understanding that, due to the nature of our study, we will not discuss.

Recall that both models (inductive and deductive) for how human beings understand the world and what matters are concerned with finding the "universal," the "true," or the "real." Thinkers have always sought to declare that "this is so," everywhere and always. The inductive method argues for the "universal" through particular things, and from these particular things philosophers make general or universal claims. Through observation and analysis of a particular material or spiritual reality, one can induct something greater—a universal, something true for everyone. Conversely, the deductive method begins with that "something greater" or "whole" which we can call a prototype or exemplar—an ideal. The difference between these methods is very important. The inductive method will enter into an analysis of this world (because it moves through particular things) and how it works in order to confirm a universal truth. The deductive approach will begin outside the material world (i.e., rise above it, abstract from it) in order to confirm a pre-given exemplar or universal that may be represented in the material world. In both ways of thinking, human beings search for the "universal," the "true," or the "real," but in very different ways.

The inductive approach begins with what one knows and builds a case to posit something that may not be immediately verifiable. For example, one could look at human beings and their insatiable appetite for knowledge, love, friendship, etc., and argue that we are made for something greater than material fulfillment. Aristotle called it happiness. Since we certainly do not seem content with what we have, it is reasonable to posit that we were created for the enjoyment of something greater than all the particulars we encounter in this existence. This doesn't mean we do not experience happiness on a daily basis, but it does mean that although we all yearn for such happiness, none of us experiences ultimate happiness in more than a momentary sense. Could we really yearn for something that doesn't exist? Philosophically, we could posit the totality toward which we move as this "other" for which we yearn. Theologically we named that other "God." So, I have a made a general claim (we all move toward a unified whole that is greater than ourselves for ultimate happiness) by examining the particulars in this world (our constant yearning for more knowledge, more love, more hope, etc.).

The deductive method perceives created reality as a diminishment or lesser representation of a particular exemplar or universal ideal located *outside* of time and space. This ideal exists apart from or outside of material reality. For example, Absolute Truth is encountered in diminished smaller "t" truths here in one's existence. There is mathematical truth, scientific truth, and poetic truth, which all descend from Absolute Truth. One explanation for all of the varied, partial truths one encounters in this world is a single, unified, absolute Truth. This Truth from which all other truths come is from another realm outside of existence.

Plato's Allegory of the Cave is the perfect example to help us understand this concept. Plato proposed that people in the material world are like inhabitants chained to a wall in a cave with the sun shining outside. They can see and understand some of reality from the shadows that play on the wall of this cave. These shadows (partial truths) exist because the sun (Truth) outside the cave partially illuminates what those in the cave (life in this world) can see and know. Becoming unchained from the cave (death) will permit us to finally look upon the full light of the sun—and thus be able to perceive the "really real"—without any filters or intermediary shadows (our bodies and other material limitations).

Plato called the light from the allegory of the cave, a "Form." This form is the really real; everything else is but a shadow, a diminished reflection of it in time and space. Forms are perfect because they exist outside the limitations of time, space, and matter. For example, Beauty as a Form is reflected in "beauty" in a sunset, "beauty" in a flower, and "beauty" in a piece of art. But the source of all these "beauties" is Beauty (the Form outside of all reality which exudes its diminished reality into the material world). The really real is *outside* of space and time, not inside of it. What can be known of the really real is only knowable in partial and imperfect ways. For example, there is balance between two people on a see-saw and there is balance between animals and plants in a given environment. Both "balances" are reflections of Balance (the Form).

One does not have access to a Form without filters (like a physical, limited brain and the five senses) that diminish the ability to see it. The five senses were considered examples of such filters. Whether we speak of balance, proportion, or equality, for example, with regard to insects or planets or weights and measures, the reality of those terms never change— even when the examples that embody them do. Equality is always equality whether in reference to people or quantity. Forms do not change. They *are* the real. To see that truth and understand it was to participate, however deficiently, in the Form of something.

Material, Spiritual, and Why It Matters

Many thinkers in the Western intellectual tradition have used a combination of the inductive and deductive methods for understanding and arguing for what is True. By arguing from both what one knows and what one posits as an ideal, one can posit "the Truth." This is where we get to the crux of our concern here.

For many philosophers in the Platonic school (deductive), created things are rightly perceived as always changing, while pre-given ideals are perceived as unchanging. Things that changed were understood to be corrupt because, like the human body upon death, they break down and diminish. Things that did not change were considered incorruptible. The Greeks had a preference for that which was unchanging and so they argued that eternity was real while time, which always changed, was simply a moving image of eternity. Infinity was real, while finitude, which changed, was its diminishment. Soul was real, while the body and all the knowledge gleaned through the changing senses, was its diminishment. Consider the following illustration, as it may help make this concept more concrete. The following quote is from "The Phaedo," one essay in *The Five Dialogues of Plato*. In it, Socrates is trying to give an explanation to his fellow philosophers for why he does not fear death but rather embraces it. Pay careful attention to how the body, as part of the material world, is perceived in various sections of this monologue.

> All these things will necessarily make the true philosophers believe and say to each other something like this: "There is likely to be something such as a path to guide us out of our confusion, because

as long as we have a body and our soul is fused with such an evil we shall never adequately attain that which we desire, which we affirm to be the truth. The body keeps us busy in a thousand ways because of its need for nurture. Moreover, if certain diseases befall it, they impede our search for the truth. It fills us with wants, desires, fears, all sorts of illusions and much nonsense, so that, as it is said, in truth and in fact no thought of any kind ever comes from the body. . . .

It has really been shown to us that, if we are ever to have pure knowledge, we must escape from the body and observe matters in themselves with the soul by itself. . . .

While we live, we shall be closest to knowledge if we refrain as much as possible from association with the body or join with it more than we must, if we are not infected with its nature but purify ourselves from it until the god himself frees us. . . .

'And if this is true, my friend,' said Socrates, 'there is good hope that on arriving where I am going, if anywhere, I shall acquire what has been our chief preoccupation in our past life, so that the journey that is now ordered for me is full of good hope, as it is also for any other man who believes that his mind has been prepared and, as it were, purified.'"[2]

The argument of Socrates in "The Phaedo" is beautifully simple. Released from time and the limitations of the material world (especially the body) one is free to contemplate the truth without any irritating mediation (or distortion) by the physical senses. Thus, aspects of our humanity which change (e.g., the body) are perceived as corrupt, an "impure" influence on this quest for pure Truth. The aspects of our humanity that do not change (e.g., the soul) are considered higher, more noble, even "pure."

Material and Spiritual in Early Christianity

Reflecting on what has just been presented, can we imagine how absurd Greek thinkers must have found the fundamental teachings of early Christianity? Early Christians believed their savior, Jesus Christ, was fully human, fully divine, and one integrated person. From the perspective of Greek thought, as discussed in the previous section, this was simply idiotic. St. Paul's references to Christian truth as "foolishness to Gentiles" in the First Letter to the Corinthians (1 Cor 1:20) provides evidence that this opinion prevailed in the age of early Christianity. It is obvious in the

---

[2] Plato, *The Five Dialogues*, trans. G.M.A. Grube (Indianapolis: Hackett Publishing Company, 1981), 102–3.

Acts of the Apostles (17:18-32) that thinkers from the Greek philosophical tradition completely rejected the idea of the resurrection of the body. So, why is this short detour into intellectual history important? Why have we gone through all of this to understand the colonial church?

The basic dualism of Greek thought, understanding the human person as the uneasy coexistence of the material and spiritual, affirms that human beings are comprised of a body and a soul that do not mix. This philosophical perspective has *always* been in tension with the Christian belief that human beings are "whole" persons made up of body and soul and that one does not diminish the other. Convinced that "rationality" could not contradict itself, many early Christian thinkers simply tried to mesh the two worldviews: Platonism and Christianity. Some still do.

For Christianity (not originally of Greek origin), human beings are united, whole—"holy" just as they are. Creation is fundamentally good even if it is "fallen." Furthermore, Christians have always believed in the resurrection of the body at the end of time. This concept is very important. Christianity has always maintained that the body, with all of its limitations, is still good. Thus, we exist as a unity of body and soul. How do we know this? Jesus of Nazareth inhabited a body, lived with the same limitations we have, and suffered a physical death. For Christians, Christ represents what it means to be both fully human and fully divine. Of course, this doctrine was not always this clear when early Christians began to record the basic tenets of the faith. There were periods of history when it also remained unclear, as will become evident when we look at the colonial church. An integration of the care for soul and body was not accomplished by the church upon its arrival in the New World, and the root of this failure was a dualism that did not permit such integration.

Consequences of Dualism

One widespread belief of early Christians was a school of thought called *Gnosticism*. Gnostics believed in a dualistic universe similar to Platonism where all that was "spiritual" was good and all that was "material" was bad. Simply put, Gnostics basically understood Christianity through strict Platonic categories. They believed that Christ left the good or spiritual world and descended into the evil, material world in order to reveal to some elect individuals the divine spark within them. This special knowledge imparted to some by Christ was thought to be the key to salvation. Because nothing good could assume a material existence according to the Gnostics, Christ only *appeared* to be human. And note what saves in this system of thought—special knowledge. *Docetism* was the name of the belief that Jesus of Nazareth only appeared to be human but never truly had bodily substance.

It is clear how this understanding of Jesus and his ministry followed if one took Platonic philosophy as a point of departure. Nothing truly good comes from matter. In these approaches, the human spirit, disconnected from earthly corporeal existence, was valued. This disconnection included the social, economic, and political world. Thus, a preference for disembodied "truth" or "knowledge" prevailed. Contrary to these beliefs, some early Christians argued that Jesus of Nazareth was fully human and fully divine and that he was one person. His divinity was framed in terms of his capacity for absolute Love, which he embodied perfectly (1 John 4:7-21). It was *not* special knowledge that saved human beings. Christians espoused that what saved human beings was the presence of Jesus through the Holy Spirit in the living out of self-sacrificial love, always in the context of a community.

How did this tension between dualism and Christianity make its way into medieval theology and then to the colonial church? Later in the Middle Ages, the well-known theologian St. Thomas Aquinas (1225–1274) incorporated the ideas of Aristotle, a pagan philosopher, into his efforts to better understand and articulate Christian theology. Aristotle was an inductive thinker. The works of Thomas Aquinas helped Christian theology balance out its heavily Platonic leaning. Prior to Aquinas, a very influential approach to Christology came from a theologian heavily influenced by Platonic thought, St. Anselm of Canterbury (1033–1109). Anselm wrote what became a very influential text in the study of Christology for nearly nine hundred years: *Cur Deus Homo*, or *Why God Became Man*.

Recall that Christology is the study of Jesus Christ in his messianic identity—fully human, fully divine, and one person. Thus, not only is any Christology declaring what true *divinity* is; it is *also and always* declaring what true *humanity* is at the same time! Anselm's task was to write an understanding of Jesus of Nazareth as the Christian savior for missionaries leaving for foreign, mainly Muslim, lands at the turn of the millennium (AD 1000). What was important for Anselm was not how Jesus Christ was fully human and fully divine but *why*. Explaining why the incarnation was necessary for human salvation was the focus of Anselm's Christology. Anselm, of course, always affirmed the humanity of Jesus Christ, but his work became problematic in framing the relationship between the human and divine within the unified person of Jesus Christ. Note how Anselm framed the humanity and divinity in Christ in the following passage from his famous work:

For we affirm that the Divine nature is beyond doubt impassible, and that God cannot at all be brought down from his exaltation, nor toil in anything which he wishes to effect. But we say that the Lord Jesus Christ is very God and very man, one person in two natures, and two natures in one person. When, therefore, we speak of God as enduring any humiliation or infirmity, we do not refer to the majesty of that nature, which cannot suffer; but to the feebleness of the human constitution which he assumed. And so there remains no ground for objection against our faith. For in this way we intend no debasement of the Divine nature, but we teach that one person is both Divine and human. In the incarnation of God there is no lowering of the Deity; but the nature of man we believe to be exalted.[3]

Anselm's final sentence adequately captures the early medieval sense of which realities are most important—the spiritual, the divine, the otherworldly. Our world merely represents the "feebleness of the human condition." Anselm resolves the tension of Platonic dualism by strictly separating the divine from the human throughout his book. The implication is that the "divine" and the "world" exist in separate realms. For example, Anselm argues that Jesus does not really "grow in wisdom" as indicated by the Gospel of Luke (Luke 2:52), by stating that this assertion in Scripture is "not really the case, but that he deported himself as if it were so."[4]

Under a Platonic conception of body and soul, there is no other way to resolve this seeming dichotomy. While Jesus Christ was truly God and truly human for Anselm, the human suffering Jesus experienced never touched the divine reality of Christ. One is left to wonder exactly how this "person" constitutes a unity in any contemporary sense.[5] For Anselm, there was full divinity and full humanity, but there was no vocabulary to adequately demonstrate real unity.

What results is an argument similar to the following: physical abuse only hurts your body, not your spirit—because they are separate. We know this is false under any understanding of modern psychology or physiology.[6] We also know that without this deeper sense of "unity," we are not

---

[3] Anselm of Canterbury, *St. Anselm Basic Writings*, trans. S. N. Deane, 2nd ed. (La Salle, IN: Open Court Publishing Company, 1962), 204–5.

[4] Ibid., 209.

[5] The inability to "connect," in a humanly adequate manner, the divinity and humanity of Jesus Christ is the heresy known as *Nestorianism*.

[6] I would argue here that Anselm puts forth a "functional Nestorianism," even though he uses language to avoid this heresy, in a strict sense; nevertheless, it exists in

discussing a human being. Nevertheless, this is the dualism employed by Anselm and it has remained dominant in the church for centuries—and even still today.[7] Throughout this very important work of Christology the "divine" in Christ is exalted while the "human" in Christ is diminished to a corollary only necessary for the incarnation to save human beings and restore God's original plan.[8] The consequences of this overwhelming preference for, and separation of, the spiritual over and against the material will be profound when the church encounters the people of the "New World."

Body and Soul in the Conquest

Let us fast-forward to a story from Bartolomeo de las Casas and see if we can make a connection between the modes of thinking which have been described and the actions of some in the church during the conquest. In his book, *An Account, Much Abbreviated, of the Destruction of the Indies,* las Casas recounts in graphic detail precisely how the Spanish conquerors caused so much suffering to those in the "New World." At one point, he describes a priest baptizing the natives as they descended into the mines where many died that day. The purpose of this baptism was, of course, to save the souls of the natives. But what of the bodies and the communities comprised of those bodies? Why were the bodies perceived as separate, less important, even disposable? Why were souls *not connected* to bodies? While there was general sympathy for the suffering of native peoples, one's earthly existence, to be honest, was not all that important. In multiple stories from las Casas' recollection of the Spanish conquest, priests always seemed to be present when people were being tortured and killed but ostensibly only to save their souls, for no doubt they considered themselves powerless to change the situation that caused such suffering.

---

his thought. Nestorianism essentially argued that Christ possessed two persons—neither of which interacted with the other. Anselm holds to the one-person, two-natures view, but those two natures don't seem to interact. While Anselm convincingly argues that humanity is elevated through the incarnation, he fails to show how the divinity is affected by the humanity of Christ.

[7] While contemporary students of theology have little difficulty framing the divinity of Christ, they struggle to take seriously his humanity.

[8] What one means by "divine" and "human," of course, has changed over time. Likewise, the understanding of "unity" adequate for intellectual acceptance of the incarnation has changed as the study of psychology has progressed. It goes without saying that Christology is essential to how Christians perceive the world, its value, and its demands of the faithful.

The following is one of many exchanges where those representing the church emphasize the next life over the present:

> This cacique [chief] and lord was constantly fleeing from the Christians, from the moment they came to that island of Cuba, being one who knew them well, and he would defend himself when he came upon them, but at last they captured him. And for no reason but that he fled such iniquitous and cruel people, and defended himself from those who wished to slay him and oppress him until the death of him and all his people and the succeeding generations, they burned him alive. And when he was bound to the stake, a friar of the order of Saint Francis, a holy father who was thereby, spoke some things to him concerning God and our faith, which he had never heard before—or as much as what that friar was able in the short time that the executioners gave him—and the friar asked if the lord wished to believe those things that he told him, for if he did he would go to sky (that is, heaven), where there was glory and eternal rest, but if not, he would certainly go to hell and suffer perpetual torments and sufferings. And thinking a while, the lord asked the holy father whether Christians went to the sky. The priest replied that they did, but only those who were good. And the cacique then said without thinking on it any more, that he did not desire to go to the sky, but rather down to hell, so that he would not be where *they* were and would not see such cruel people.[9]

It is not true to say that the church thought only souls had value and bodies were worthless; that is too superficial. Rather, one could argue that when the spiritual is overemphasized without the positive inclusion or connection to the corporeal, we have diminished the human being and all human beings. This diminishment, in turn, has real-world consequences. Such a move also diminishes what it means to "save" a human being. This dualistic view of the human person emerges from a dualistic understanding of Christ made popular by the Platonic influences in the thought of Anselm. It will nearly always disdain the earthly in favor of the heavenly and the body in favor of the soul.

One could speculate that the church was so concerned with abstract, idealized human beings (their *abstracted* instead of *embodied* souls), that it missed the suffering of human beings. They missed this because if souls were the focus of salvation, bodies and their sufferings were not as

---

[9] Bartolomeo de las Casas, *An Account, Much Abbreviated, of the Destruction of the Indies* (Indianapolis: Hackett Publishing Co., 2003), 19.

important. This belief and the practices that resulted from it were only possible through the embrace of a strong dualism where body and soul were seen as connected, only out of necessity, here on earth. Truly, only the soul was the object of salvation.

This understanding leads to a diminishment of the importance of this world and the relevance of the conditions in which human beings live. While this reduction in the importance of the material world is consistent with Greek thought, it deeply contradicts the teachings and ministry of Jesus of Nazareth. It also led Christianity to apathy or at least a kind of passivity about transforming the world in which it inhabited until only recently (the last 150 years). When this passivity was combined with an understanding that human history is settled, the result became deadly.

Perceptions of History and Social Change

> The social principles of Christianity preach the need of a dominating class and an oppressed class. And to the latter class they offer only the benevolence of the ruling class. The social principles of Christianity point to heaven as the compensation for all the crimes that are committed on earth. The social principles of Christianity explain all the viciousness of oppressors as a just punishment either for original sin or other sins, or as trials that the Lord, in infinite wisdom, inflicts on those the Lord has redeemed. The social principles of Christianity preach cowardice, self-hatred, servility, submission, humility—in a word, all the characteristics of a scoundrel.[10]

This quotation from Karl Marx stands as an indictment of the social apathy perceived in the Christian faith by those who refused to address the injustice of certain economic systems in Europe during the industrial revolution (1850s). If social transformation was needed during this epoch, it was *not* toward the church that one turned. It is interesting to ponder whether the church's apathy toward the world actually created the possibility for atheistic humanism to succeed as it did in the line of Karl Marx.[11] Had the church extended its spiritual quest for perfection into the structures and relationships of human society earlier, one wonders what would have and would not have been possible in terms of social transformation.

[10] Karl Marx, *MEGA* 1, no. 6 (1847), 278.
[11] Michael J. Buckley, *At the Origins of Modern Atheism* (Yale University Press, 1992). I speculate here, but a recurring thesis in this work on atheism is that bad theology often gave openings to the critiques of Christianity that came to be quite powerful in their own right.

It is difficult for the modern Western person to think of the future in any way other than as the possibility for improvement, upward mobility, progress, and evolution. But what if none of these things were perceived to be possible or even good? Remember, the ideal form of Christian discipleship throughout the majority of Christian history was *not* to help build the kingdom of God on earth through cooperation with God's grace (an idea recovered from the gospels only recently) but instead to move *away* from the world into the monastery or convent.[12]

From roughly AD 300 to AD 1400, the highest or most noble form of Christian discipleship according to the church was the monastic life. Indeed, Yale historian Jaroslav Pelikan argues that a dominant image for Jesus of Nazareth throughout much of Christian history was "the Monk who ruled the world."[13] "[Monasticism] is endowed with such prestige and standing that practically the entire church seems to be governed by monks."[14] This probably emerged as an application of the dualist tension already mentioned. Monastic life was idealized in contrast to life "in the world." It justified itself through Jesus' resistance to the temptations in the desert in Matthew (4:8-10). Pelikan states, "Yet by his denial of the world he had conquered the world and established his everlasting kingdom, in which he invited his followers to share by also denying the world, taking

---

[12] The amount of literature on this topic is vast, but the following are concrete references which, in one way or another, support this thesis. David Brakke, *Demons and the Making of the Monk: Spiritual Combat in Early Christianity* (Cambridge, MA: Harvard University Press, 2006), 51–52, 62, 133, 136, 200; James Goehring, *Ascetics, Society, and the Desert: Studies in Early Monasticism* (Harrisburg, PA: Trinity Press International,1999), 15, 41, 45, 47, 51; William Harmless, *Desert Christians: An Introduction to the Literature of Early Monasticism* (Oxford: Oxford University Press, 2004), 417, 429; Daniel Caner, *Wandering, Begging Monks: Spiritual Authority and the Promotion of Monasticism in Late Antiquity* (Berkeley: University of California Press, 2002), 5, 71; Marilyn Dunn, *The Emergence of Monasticism: From the Desert Fathers to the Early Middle Ages* (Malden, MA: Blackwell Publishing, 2003), 19, 38, 124, 134; Thomas Merton, *Pre-Benedictine Monasticism: Initiation into the Monastic Tradition 2*, ed. Patrick F. O'Connell (Kalamazoo, MI: Cistercian Publications, 2006) 54, 87–89, 96, 128, 130–31, 282–83, 295, 299–300, 307. Do not confuse this tendency in early or medieval monasticism with all forms of monasticism today. Many monasteries and convents are deeply engaged with the world through direct service, colleges, universities, etc.

[13] Jaroslav Pelikan, *Jesus through the Centuries: His Place in the History of Culture* (New York: Harper & Row, 1985), 109. This in spite of that fact that according to the gospels Jesus neither lived in isolation from the world nor encouraged his followers to do so.

[14] Ibid., 115. This quote is from a letter written by Symeon of Thessalonica in his fifteenth-century work, *On the Priesthood*.

up their own cross, and following him."[15] Now, the temptations in Matthew and the world are seen as equivalent. The only good in the world is discovered in a flight *from* it.[16] Celibacy was preferred over marriage insofar as bishops had to be celibate, while secular priests could be married. Contemplation in pursuit of spiritual perfection was preferred over action in the world. In this way, "commandments" and "spiritual perfection" became one and the same. Pelikan continues, "Thus there was introduced into the life and teachings of the church a double standard of discipleship, based on a bifurcation of the ethical demands of Jesus into 'commandments,' which 'imply necessity' and which were taken to be binding upon everyone, and 'counsels of perfection' which were 'left to choice' and which ultimately were binding only upon the monastic athletes."[17]

It was a common phrase to refer to the monastery as a ship on the stormy seas of the world. The purpose of the ship was to keep one safe from the turbulent ocean, lest one drown in it. Once the early persecution of Christians, commonly known as the "red martyrdom," had passed, zealous believers looked for a new way of living and dying for their faith. Hence, what was referred to as the "white martyrdom" of monasticism was embraced as a higher level of true discipleship. This way was characterized by self-denial, avoidance of the world, prayer, contemplation, and work to sustain a life in community.

In his work, *A Concise History of the Mediaeval Church*, Isnard Frank argues that the basic motive at the foundation of Western monasticism "was an ascetic flight from the world: separation from the 'world.'"[18] Frank insists that we take this flight seriously: *"The ascetic content of monasticism and its concern to flee from the world must be emphasized.* Here was hostility to the world which was sometimes heightened to become the view that all those who were entangled in 'worldly things' had no chance of attaining eternal salvation."[19] Later, of course, the monastery was very involved in the generation and accumulation of wealth that allowed for and sustained monastic life. According to Frank, "The early mediaeval proprietary church system controlled monastic institutions as proprietary monasteries; as

---

[15] Ibid., 110.

[16] No mention is made by early monks that following this temptation in the desert Jesus returned to Galilee and began an active public ministry deeply engaging the world in which he lived.

[17] Jaroslav Pelikan, *Jesus Through the Centuries*, 114.

[18] Isnard Wilhelm Frank, *A Concise History of the Mediaeval Church* (New York: Continuum, 1996), 30–31.

[19] Ibid., 31, emphasis mine.

royal abbeys they had been integrated into the church of the realm. In each case the monasteries were given control of property and were drawn into the process of acting as lords. So what has been said about the bishop as lord of the proprietary church and a royal official can equally be said of the head of a propertied monastery."[20] While it is impossible to go into an extensive history of monasticism here, it is important to note that increasingly there developed "a growing symbiosis between the nobility and monasticism."[21] The great irony, of course, is that in fleeing from the world, many monasteries became wealthy.[22]

Of greater importance for our purposes here is the separation of contemplation from action in Christian life that some monastic orders actually promoted. Nicholas Gallicus, prior-general of the Carmelites (1266–1271), was skeptical of "the value of preaching" as opposed to "the Carmelite tradition of solitary contemplation."[23] This division of the Christian life into strict domains of action *or* contemplation was problematic for emerging religious orders such as the Dominicans, Franciscans, and later the Jesuits. According to Gallicus, "In the context of the Carmelite Rule and the order's origins, it is an impossible combination. Contemplative life cannot be diluted with the work of public ministry."[24]

Why did exemplary Christians in monasteries believe that "public ministry" was a dilution of the contemplative life? There are two elements of intellectual history that converge here and provide some insight. The first was the prioritizing of the spiritual over the worldly (as if they can or should be separated), as already discussed. This prioritization effectively led to a disconnection of the spiritual from the worldly in any meaningful sense. The second was an understanding of human history as essentially closed and complete (i.e., already written) as we will explore next.

Imagine if there were no great change that human beings are to work for and nothing toward which to progress. With this worldview, both a faithful patience anticipating the end times and an acceptance of one's place in life as willed by God become necessary. In some ways, walking into the monastery and leaving the outside world behind was a deep

---

[20] Ibid., 30.

[21] Ibid., 31.

[22] For more on this, see John McManners, *Church and Society in Eighteenth-Century France: The Clerical Establishment and Its Social Ramifications*, vol. 1 (Oxford: Oxford University Press, 1999).

[23] Andrew Jotischky, *The Carmelites and Antiquity: Mendicants and their Pasts in the Middle Ages* (Oxford: Oxford University Press, 2002), 93.

[24] Ibid.

affirmation of this opinion. For the medieval mind, why was the world as it was? God willed it to be so. Why did God will it to be so? God's plan is beyond human understanding but nevertheless demands human acceptance. Narrow and literal interpretations of certain scriptural passages also encouraged this understanding. For example, consider Romans 13: "Let every person be subject to the governing authorities; for there is no authority except from God, and those authorities that exist have been instituted by God. Therefore whoever resists authority resists what God has appointed, and those who resist will incur judgment" (Rom 13:1-2). Changing societal structures is close to impossible if leaders rule by divine right.

When the Jesuits embarked upon the creation of missions in South America, they were inspired, in part, by St. Thomas More's book *Utopia*. More wrote of an imaginary island country named Utopia where people owned land in common, men and women were educated in an equal manner, and there was a healthy degree of religious toleration. Published in 1516, this work inspired others to imagine new societies throughout the Renaissance (1300–1650), Enlightenment (1650–1800), and so on. Although this work was about an imaginary community, it inspired questions regarding what can be done to change society in the here and now.

For many in the church, the idea that human beings could or should change society (i.e., social structures) was considered arrogant. The prevailing belief was that only the author of human history could change human history. This history included the social levels and societal structures which were understood to have been established by divine will (as in the previous quote from the Letter of Paul to the Romans). How else can one explain the passive (and active) acceptance of slavery by Christianity for nearly nineteen hundred years? How can the church explain that Catholic social teaching did not formally develop until the late nineteenth century? Historically, why has there been so much resistance by the church to new developments in "non-sacred" sciences, philosophy, and art?

The state of peoples and human society, generally what we call "history," was understood by the church as a static reality with the incarnation at its center. Time was divided between, before, or after Jesus of Nazareth. God created the world and human society had been established. If God wanted social reality to be different, God would initiate such a change. Human beings were seen as weak, sinful, and utterly dependent on God. They could do nothing on their own to change what had been established. Theologically speaking, life was perceived as a vale of tears. God ordained both fixed social positions and an inseparable obedience to God, the church, and the colonial order. Ordinary believers were left to find solace in their prayers for charity and their hope for a better life in the *next* world.

How, then, does one live in relation to a world full of suffering and want? When one cannot change the world but must patiently wait for the end times (in theological terms, the *eschaton*), this does not mean that human misery or want is ignored. The way of addressing human misery and desire was through charity.[25] While they never intended or hoped to change the world, many monasteries and other forms of cloistered life were the source of incredible amounts of charity.

Charity, Not Justice . . . Yet

According to historian Peter Hatlie, monasteries were the main sources of charity throughout the early church.[26] Palestinian monks probably began this commitment with their houses for pilgrims who wished to visit the Holy Land. In the late fifth century, monks and monasteries were known to manage everything from hotels to almshouses, as well as other charitable institutions. According to Hatlie, as monks provided more charity to outsiders, "they also became more consistent in their defense of suffering and vulnerable populations." Additionally, monks served as counselors, teachers, and arbitrators of disputes, and, most importantly, "monks prayed for people. By doing so they were thought by contemporaries to do much good in the world."[27]

At the same time, this service to the poor was oddly divorced from the material needs of the people who wanted to live humane lives. A humane life would be one where the material necessities for human growth and development were always present. This divorce between the material lives of people and the ordering of social reality continued into medieval times.

> Inherent in the writings of John Chrysostom, Basil, Jerome, and Augustine of Hippo is contempt for wealth, a sense that the individual could strive for God only by rejecting the material. Their injunctions to aid the poor thus reflected a spiritual motivation quite divorced

---

[25] This word "charity" is not to be confused with the theological virtue of "caritas." The word "charity," as it is understood today, refers to meeting the immediate needs of people but not the cause of those needs.

[26] Peter Hatlie, *The Monks and Monasteries of Constantinople, c. 350–850* (Cambridge: Cambridge University Press, 2007), 43–47.

[27] Ibid., 44.

from the economic and social realities of poverty. While a genuine concern for human suffering must have played some role in patristic thought, nonetheless, this attitude lent a ritualistic character to charity in the early Middle Ages. For example, cathedral churches and, later, monasteries would support poor persons, often called the *matricularii*, who frequently were fixed in number at the apostolic twelve. Monastic hospitality, too, developed its own ritual in the form of the welcome, the washing of the feet, the provision of hospitality (i.e., food and shelter), and the presentation of a farewell gift. Such folk were treated more as symbols than as real people because the monks viewed themselves as the real 'poor of Christ,' having voluntarily laid aside the accoutrements of power for a life of humility. Those assisted did not represent any particular economic group or class because this was a society of serfs and tenant farmers where most people by any sort of objective standard could be labeled as poor. Instead, charity focused on travelers, rich and poor alike, whose distress was of a temporary and transient nature.[28]

Interestingly, in the history of monasticism one sees a real concern for the spiritual work of caring for the poor. The problem is that this actual care was abstracted from the poor and made to signify religious obligation over the contextual needs of human beings. Serving the poor was necessary to fulfill a religious obligation. And changing the context of the poor was beyond the scope of Christian charity. What would change, and change drastically in the twentieth century, was the traditional church emphasis on charity. For the global church, the new model of interaction with the world became one of justice.

Evangelization and Persecution

Evangelization, or the attempt to educate and convert people to Christianity, has always been deeply tied to how one understands the church. In the second century, for example, Justin Martyr argued that any adherence to "truth" among pagan philosophers was actually an affirmation of the great Truth exemplified by Christianity—since truth cannot contradict itself (note the deductive Platonism in this approach). Logos, the reason that runs throughout the universe (in Greek philosophy) is personified in Jesus Christ—so any affirmation of truth, anytime, is an affirmation of

---

[28] James William Brodman, *Charity and Welfare: Hospitals and the Poor in Medieval Catalonia*, chap. 1 (Library of Iberian Resources Online, 1998), http://libro.uca.edu /charity/cw1.htm; accessed September 10, 2009.

Christianity. Recall that in the second century, Christianity had no political or social power to speak of, so congruency with other thought systems and a desire to discover common ground characterized early attempts at Christian evangelization. Justin Martyr looked for ways to connect to non-Christian audiences, namely, through an appeal to reason as it was understood in the Greek philosophical world.

The Christian religion was legalized by Constantine through the Edict of Milan in AD 313. It later became the official religion of the Roman Empire under Theodosius in AD 380. With this new legal status, a new and stronger understanding of the salvific necessity of the official church followed. Becoming a Christian also became necessary in order to conduct business in the empire. Cyprian of Carthage stated the well-known phrase that outside the church, there is no salvation. This has been interpreted in a number of ways throughout the history of the church, but in all cases it could never be confused with the approach of Justin Martyr. If Christ is the key to salvation, and the church represents Christ on earth, then the church actually preached *itself* as the key to salvation—and with no apologies. Pope Boniface VIII stated as much in his papal pronouncement *Unam sanctam* (1302):

> We are compelled in virtue of our faith to believe and maintain that there is only one holy Catholic Church, and that one is apostolic. This we firmly believe and profess without qualification. Outside this Church there is no salvation and no remission of sins, the Spouse in the Canticle proclaiming: "One is my dove, my perfect one. One is she of her mother, the chosen of her that bore her" (*Canticle of Canticles* 6:8); which represents the one mystical body whose head is Christ, of Christ indeed, as God. And in this, "one Lord, one faith, one baptism" (Ephesians 4:5). Certainly Noah had one ark at the time of the flood, prefiguring one Church which perfect to one cubit having one ruler and guide, namely Noah, outside of which we read all living things were destroyed. . . We declare, say, define, and pronounce that it is absolutely necessary for the salvation of every human creature to be subject to the Roman Pontiff.[29]

There is little doubt that this church-centered evangelization was central to the approach of missionaries who travelled to Latin America with the conquest. This was actually encouraged by the nations of Spain and

[29] Pope Boniface VII, *Unam sanctam* (Promulgated November 18, 1302). For a translation available online, see http://www.fordham.edu/halsall/source/B8-unam.asp.

Portugal. As Phillip II stated so boldly in 1573, "The Indians should be brought to an understanding of the position and authority which God has given us and of our zeal in serving Him by bringing to His Holy Catholic Faith all the natives of the Western Indies."[30]

Because of their internal structure and discipline, members of religious orders were seen as "especially apt to undertake evangelization during the first decades of colonialism."[31] Jeffrey Klaiber, SJ, goes so far as to claim "that evangelization increasingly became an instrument of social control."[32] These religious orders, contrary to diocesan bishops and priests, operated outside the patronage system (they were not subject to government rule or the temptation for power). Eventually they had to be reined in by the state: "As the colonial period matured, the Habsburg monarchs of Spain sought to curb the influence of regular orders. The Crown had needed the organizational skills and dedication of the regulars during the initial, precarious phase of colonialism, but once royal authority was firmly established it feared their strong presence and growing influence."[33] "Regular" orders such as the Franciscans, Dominicans, Augustinians, Jesuits, and others were placed under the supervision of local bishops who eventually replaced these orders with diocesan clergy answering directly to the bishops.

What was the method of colonial evangelization? How did it take shape? How was it executed? The following is an excerpt from a Jesuit priest, Anthony Pires, SJ, who wrote about his efforts to evangelize indigenous peoples in Brazil in 1558. While this is not representative of all evangelization, it does reveal the challenges, the approaches, and some attitudes about what was taking place in the "New World."

> All these are losing their habit of eating human flesh; and if we learn that some are about to eat flesh, we order them to send it to us. They send it, as they did several days ago, and they bring it to us from a long distance so that we can bury or burn it. In this way they all tremble with fear of the Governor, a fear which, although it may not last a lifetime, is enough so that we can teach them; it serves us so

---

[30] "Rationalizing Imperialism," in *Religion in Latin America: A Documentary History*, ed. Lee M. Penyak and Walter J. Petry (Maryknoll, NY: Orbis Books, 2006), 68.

[31] Ibid., 32.

[32] Jeffrey Klaiber, *The Jesuits in Latin America, 1549–2000: 450 Years of Inculturation, Defense of Human Rights and Prophetic Witness* (Saint Louis: Institute of Jesuit Sources, 2009), 67.

[33] Ibid., 33.

that we can tell them of Christ, and the kindness which our Lord will show them will cause all human fear to flee so that they will remain a strong and stable people. The fear makes them more capable of being able to hear the word of God. Their children are instructed; the innocent ones about to die are all baptized; they are forgetting their habits and exchanging them for good ones. Proceeding in this way, a noble Christianity will be inculcated at least among the youngsters.[34]

Years later, Toribio de Benavente, OFM, wrote a letter to Spain's Charles I criticizing the work of Bartolomeo de las Casas and his perspective on missionary activity. A telling sentence concludes one of the sections of his letter: "Thus it is your majesty's mission to give haste to the preaching of the holy gospel through all these lands, and with those who will not willingly hear the holy gospel of Jesus Christ, let it be by force, for here one can apply the proverb 'better good forced on you than the bad you desire.'"[35] It seems that from these few excerpts, the church did not hesitate to use either fear or force in preaching the Gospel of Jesus Christ.

Clearly there was frustration by early missionaries who knew that "conversion," in many cases, was not authentic. How could a missionary know whether new converts were praying to Catholic saints, for example, or merely changing the names of their own gods and goddesses? Missionaries often struggled with the demands of multiple languages, terrible living conditions, and misunderstandings inevitable in cross-cultural encounters. Combined with the perceived superiority of European culture, there was often conflict. At times this resulted in violence between groups of missionaries and the souls they were sent to convert. Suffice it to say that church and state both contributed to the domination of indigenous peoples. This occurred first through the imposition of Spanish and Portuguese subjugation in economic, social, and cultural terms. It occurred

---

[34] Antonio Pires, from E. Bradford Burns, "Introduction to the Brasilian Jesuit Letters," *Mid-America: An Historical Review* 44, no. 3 (July 1962): 182–83. Quoted from a section titled "Rigorous Evangelization of Adult Amerindians," from *Religion in Latin America: A Documentary History*, 44.

[35] Toribio de Benavente, *Colección de documentos inéditos relativos al descubrimiento, conquista y colonización de las antiguas posesiones españoles (sic) en America y Oceanía*, 7: 254–89, in *Letters and Peoples of the Spanish Indies: Sixteenth Century*, trans. and ed. James Lockhart and Enrique Otte (London: Cambridge University Press, 1976), 221–24, 230–32, 237–38. This was likewise asserted by José de Acosta according to Jeffrey Klaiber in *The Jesuits in Latin America, 1549–2000: 450 Years of Inculturation, Defense of Human Rights and Prophetic Witness*, 30.

secondly through the church's imposition of Christianity over indigenous beliefs.[36] In a word, the conquest was total and destructive.

At the same time, evangelization was not uniform over time or by different religious orders. The Jesuit missions in modern-day Bolivia, Brazil, Paraguay, and Argentina were quite effective at protecting indigenous peoples from the Spanish and Portuguese slave trade. Conversely, other religious orders assisted slave traders and benefitted economically from that collaboration: "With the exception of the Dominicans, most churchmen during this period supported the practice of enslaving Indians under the guise of the just war doctrine."[37] Therefore, whether the indigenous people truly accepted the Christian faith (however that is ascertained) is debatable.

Overall, "successful" evangelization was evaluated in three ways. First, it was evaluated by whether or not it subdued native peoples; second, whether or not it taught religious orthodoxy; and third, whether or not it resulted in the cessation of certain practices found repugnant by the missionaries (i.e., cannibalism). Today there is an important debate about the level of enculturation that Catholicism has achieved among native peoples. How much syncretism (mixing of two or more religions) is possible or acceptable for a person to be or remain a Christian? These issues and others like it will be taken up much more directly by the Catholic Church after the sea change of the Second Vatican Council.

Conclusion

The way we think about reality affects what we value and how we interact with the world. Thought systems that emphasize the spiritual as more noble, while neglecting or diminishing its connection to the material or corporeal, lead to a neglect of human beings in this world. Without an integrated unity of body and soul, it is impossible to address social and economic structures that result in so much suffering. Such structures will always be perceived as merely temporary while heaven will remain the

---

[36] For an amazing example of this, see *The Devil's Miner: The Story of a Child's Survival*, an excellent documentary outlining the religious and cultural beliefs embraced by miners, including children in Potosí, Bolivia.

[37] Jeffrey Klaiber, *The Jesuits in Latin America, 1549–2000: 450 Years of Inculturation, Defense of Human Rights and Prophetic Witness*, 89. The rationale could have been that if overwhelming force was not necessary to subdue them, slavery was a better alternative to death.

permanent focus. The consequence of this worldview is a preference for charity over justice (changing unjust structures).

A perspective on history as static and unchangeable promotes a passive approach or even resistance toward change or development. Conversely, a perspective on history as evolutionary or dynamic understands Christians as capable of significant social change when they collaborate with the ever-present grace of God. With an evolutionary mind-set, the question then becomes how human agency can collaborate with God's agency in the transformation of human history.

As discussed in the final part of this chapter, the forced imposition of a foreign belief system resulted in evangelization through persecution rather than through persuasion. And while there were exceptions to this, such as the successful and peaceful Franciscan missions in northern Mexico, this does not represent the norm. All of these perspectives characterize presuppositions shared by the colonial rulers and the church that accompanied them. Finally, while this does not explain away the actions or attitudes of the church, it does give some insight into how the church could have partnered with colonial powers in this very un-Christian enterprise known as the conquest. It was thought to be an opportunity to save souls who otherwise were believed to suffer eternal torment because they never had the opportunity to come to Christ. What occurred at the Second Vatican Council reversed centuries of intellectual and theological presuppositions. We will now consider Vatican II and its effects on Latin America.

Questions for Discussion:

1. What is the difference between deductive and inductive reasoning? Provide a concrete example.

2. How would a dualistic understanding of human beings contribute to the exploitation of indigenous peoples during the conquest?

3. How did the church aid the state in the domination of native peoples?

4. How did monasteries in the early church embody charity?

5. What were some factors that made real evangelization difficult, from both the native and missionary standpoints?

Part 2

Vatican II and a New Mission

Chapter 3

A New Mission of the Church for the World

The alms we gathered going house to house were put in a vase with flowers. There were some houses where there was no husband, just a single mother or a widow. Poor things, with their clothes all torn and dirty . . . . Then, when we'd arrive, the little boy would come out hanging on to his mother's skirt and crying, "Mommy, I'm hungry! Mommy, I'm hungry!" You know, the children are always demanding when they're hungry. And since we were there with the statue and the bell, the mother would say, "Hush! Don't behave so badly!" But children don't understand these things. For them, it's "I'm hungry," that's that.

And there, right in the middle of such total misery, we'd follow the same formula, telling her that the Virgin had come to visit her. . . . And this woman, who didn't even have 5 centavos, what could she do?

Once, after we'd made the presentation of the Virgin, and after the woman had adored the statue, the woman, feeling badly, said, "You'll forgive me, but as the Virgin well knows. . . . unless you could settle for an egg."

"But Senora, we accept everything: a little rice, a few beans, some corn, a bit of money, eggs. . . . whatever people give us. . . ."

Then, the woman said to her young child, "Go over there in the corner and see if the hen has laid an egg."

"No! No!," said the boy. "No!"

"Don't act like that. Go and see. . . ." And then the boy threw himself on the ground, rolling around in the dirt and crying. And we said it was because he was ill-behaved. . . . Then, the mother went and hit him across the behind, so that he'd get up. And then the child, weeping, went and put his hand under the hen, removed the egg and came toward us.

"Okay, here it is. My egg!"

It was the only hope he had. It was maybe eleven A.M., and he hadn't had any breakfast and that little egg was his hope. And we had taken it from him

*to give it to the mayor, the judge, the comandante, and the priest, who had a
big belly from having stuffed himself so much. . . . I get angry when I think
of that, you know![1]*

On October 11, 1962, Pope John XXIII opened the Second Vatican
Council to reinvigorate and redirect a church that had become increasingly
distant from the modern world. Three years and sixteen formal documents
later, it would close under Pope Paul VI on December 8, 1965. Over 2,500
men took part in the opening session, including a global representation of
bishops, superiors of religious orders, theological consultants, and observ-
ers from various denominations of Christianity and other world religions.
The Second Vatican Council was significantly different from Vatican I
(1868), which included around 750 men, the vast majority European.

John XXIII emphasized the need for *aggiornamiento* in the church, which
roughly translates as a "bringing up to date." Increasingly, the church
found itself in a world with pressing social, economic, and political challenges that it was incapable of addressing. From the Council of Trent in
1545 until Vatican II in 1962, the church had increasingly collapsed in
upon itself. It condemned new developments in intellectual thought and
resisted the modern age which was characterized by democracy and the
diffusion of political and economic power (liberalism). The noted ecclesiologist Dr. Richard Gaillardetz explains:

> A rather polemical and defensive account of the church would appear,
> an account that would stress its institutional features. Ecclesiology
> during this period gave little attention to the church's spiritual ori-
> gins in the Trinitarian missions of Word and Spirit. Defense of the
> legitimacy of church office and ordained ministry led to an emphasis
> on the sacrament of holy orders over the sacraments of initiation. In
> the following centuries, this defensive posture was directed not just
> against the churches of the Reformation but against other external
> forces perceived as threats to the church's mission and very existence.[2]

Vatican II was the church's evaluation of its capacity to respond to
massive changes in the world, including those technological, political, and
developmental challenges which had been slowly emerging over time. The
Council began a deep reflection on what it means to be a church in and for

---

[1] Maria Lopez Vigil, *Don Lito of El Salvador* (Maryknoll, NY: Orbis Books, 1990), 14–15.
[2] Richard Gaillardetz, *The Church in the Making:* Lumen Gentium, Christus Dominus,
Orientalium Ecclesiarium (New York: Paulist Press, 2006), 2.

this world. There were a variety of topics addressed at the Council, such as how the church perceived itself in relation to other Christian denominations, other religions, and especially the suffering present throughout the world. In *Nostra aetate*, for example, the Declaration on the Relation of the Church with Non-Christian Religions, the church acknowledged that God is present and active even *outside* of the Catholic Church. Previously, the church had acknowledged God as present within only Christianity. Thus *Nostra aetate* stated, "The Catholic Church rejects nothing of what is true and holy in these religions. It has a high regard for the manner of life and conduct, the precepts and doctrines which, although differing in many ways from its own teaching, nevertheless often reflect a ray of that truth which enlightens all men and women."[3]

While a full and comprehensive history of Vatican II is neither necessary nor possible here, there is one document written prior to Vatican II and two documents from the Council that deserve special attention. *Lumen gentium*, the Dogmatic Constitution of the Church, put forth how the church at Vatican II understood itself in a new light. In order to fully appreciate the content of this document, it is necessary to reference *Mystici corporis Christi* written by Pope Pius XII in 1943. This document by Pius XII outlined how the church understood itself prior to Vatican II. It will become evident that *Lumen gentium* represented a significant departure from its recent past, most notably *Mystici corporis Christi*. The second document from Vatican II necessary to consider is *Gaudium et spes*, the Pastoral Constitution on the Church in the Modern World. In this document, the final document of the Council, the church put forth how it understood the world and the church's mission in service to the world and its people. This signified a radical departure and movement beyond the "charity" model formerly embraced by the Catholic Church. This departure has not been fully accepted by many, including some in the magisterium, even fifty years after the document was approved.

An important consideration for understanding the significance of *Lumen gentium* is the fact that it offers a self-understanding put forth for the entire church, not just the hierarchy.[4] For this reason, *Lumen gentium* will frame its understanding of the entire church in a way that is a significant departure

---

[3] Austin Flannery, ed., *Vatican Council II: Constitutions, Decrees, Declarations* (Northport, NY: Costello Publishing Co., 1996), 570–71. Unless otherwise noted, all subsequent references to Vatican II documents are from this source.

[4] Brian Gleeson, "Commemorating *Lumen gentium*: A Short History of a Groundbreaking Charter," in *The Australian EJournal of Theology*, no. 3 (2004).

from previous formulations. There are three essential contributions from *Lumen gentium* that need to be emphasized. First, the overall image used to understand the church changed significantly. Prior to Vatican II, the church had understood itself through the image of the "Mystical Body of Christ." Vatican II changes this image of church self-understanding to the "people of God." This new image characterized not only the laity but the entire church, prior to any division of hierarchy and faithful. Second, in *Lumen gentium* the status and function of the laity changed significantly. Prior to Vatican II, the laity was encouraged to worship, contribute, and obey the magisterium. Following Vatican II, they were encouraged to take the social teaching of the church and transform the world in the direction of the kingdom of God. Third, there was a new recognition of how *all* members of the church, from layperson to pope, have a universal call to holiness. Prior to Vatican II, holiness resided in holy orders and the laity was considered spiritually inferior.

Mystici corporis Christi

In June 1943, Pope Pius XII promulgated an encyclical titled *Mystici corporis Christi*, the Mystical Body of Christ. Within it, he put forth his vision of how the church understood itself and its internal governance, as well as its relation to its founder (Jesus Christ) and to the world mired in the Second World War. He began:

> The doctrine of the *Mystical Body of Christ*, which is the Church, was first taught us by the Redeemer Himself. Illustrating as it does the great and inestimable privilege of our intimate union with so exalted a Head, this doctrine by its sublime dignity invites all those who are drawn by the Holy Spirit to study it, and gives them, in the truths of which it proposes to the mind, a strong incentive to the performance of such good works as are conformable to its teaching.[5]

Pius XII went on to refer to the church, at various points in this document, as the "mystical body of Christ," the "spotless bride" or "bride" of Christ, and "Holy Mother Church."[6] This emphasis on the close relation-

---

[5] Pope Pius XII, *Mystici corporis Christi*, no. 1 (The Vatican, 1943), accessed from http://www.vatican.va/holy_father/index.htm. Unless otherwise noted, all subsequent references to papal encyclicals and exhortations are from this source.

[6] Ibid., "mystical body of Christ" is used fifty-six times; the "spotless bride" is used in paragraph no. 106, while "bride" is used in no. 86 and no. 96. "Holy Mother Church" is used in nos. 3, 92, 105, and 109.

ship between God and the hierarchy of the Catholic Church was notable in response to what the pope termed "popular naturalism." Popular naturalism understood the church to be seen as "nothing but a juridical and social union."[7] In contrast to this natural institution perspective, Pius XII emphasized the relationship between hierarchical Catholicism and God. Some modern commentators on this encyclical argue that Pius XII tried to correct the opinion that limited "the Church to a hierarchical institution." In fact, the church is largely understood by Pius XII to be the hierarchy.[8]

Compare this with how the church, twenty-one years later at Vatican II, framed its own self-understanding. This change was not only linguistic but substantive as well.

> Christ instituted this new covenant, the new covenant in his blood (see 1 Cor 11:25); he called a people together made up of Jews and Gentiles which would be one, not according to the flesh, but in the Spirit, and it would be the new people of God. For those who believe in Christ, who are reborn, not from a corruptible but from an incorruptible seed, through the word of the living God (see 1 Pet 1:23), not from flesh, but from water and the holy Spirit (see Jn 3:5–6), are finally established as "a chosen race, a royal priesthood, a holy nation, a people for his possession . . . who in times past were not a people, but are now the people of God." (LG 9)

How does the image of the church as the "the people of God" differ from the image of the church as the "Mystical Body of Christ"? Why is this difference so significant? The difference is important, for it reaches deeply into what is meant by "church" and how we understand ourselves within it.

The first image used in the 1943 encyclical, "the Mystical Body of Christ," presents a very "high" ecclesiology. A high ecclesiology will emphasize the church's relationship to God, its spiritual purity, its uniqueness, and its elevation above all else—especially the world. The mission to the world, over and against how it is defined, thus becomes secondary. This is not done indirectly but rather quite bluntly. In effect, the church considers itself "Christ in the world," in a very literal sense.

---

[7] Ibid., no. 9.

[8] John Gavin, "'True Charity Begins Where Justice Ends': The Life and Teachings of St. Alberto Hurtado," *Studies in the Spirituality of Jesuits* 43, no. 4 (Winter 2011): 25. Gavin makes the argument that "the Pope sought to correct two problems in contemporary ecclesiology: the tendency to limit the Church to a hierarchical institution and the newer tendency to view her as a mystical entity that required no visible structures." This thesis is contradicted by the document itself, at least on the first point.

As Bellarmine notes with acumen and accuracy, this appellation of the Body of Christ is not to be explained solely by the fact that Christ must be called the Head of His Mystical Body, but also by the fact that He so sustains the Church, and so in a certain sense lives in the Church, that she is, as it were, another Christ. The Doctor of the Gentiles, in his letter to the Corinthians, affirms this when, without further qualification, he calls the Church "Christ," following no doubt the example of his Master who called out to him from on high when he was attacking the Church: 'Saul, Saul, why persecutest thou me?' Indeed, if we are to believe Gregory of Nyssa, the Church is often called simply "Christ" by the Apostle; and you are familiar Venerable Brethren, with that phrase of Augustine: "Christ preaches Christ."[9]

Similar to how we have seen Christology already presented, at least by Anselm, there is a high and low aspect of this reality, and while the church will acknowledge its low reality (the church in the world), it will always emphasize its spiritual connection to the divine as it did in the following:

Hence, this word in its correct signification gives us to understand that the Church, a perfect society of its kind, is not made up of merely moral and juridical elements and principles. It is far superior to all other human societies; it surpasses them as grace surpasses nature, as things immortal are above all those that perish. Such human societies, and in the first place civil Society, are by no means to be despised or belittled; but the Church in its entirety is not found within this natural order, any more than the whole man is encompassed within the organism of our mortal body. Although the juridical principles, on which the Church rests and is established, derive from the divine constitution given to it by Christ and contribute to the attaining of its supernatural end, nevertheless that which lifts the Society of Christians far above the whole natural order is the Spirit of our Redeemer who penetrates and fills every part of the Church's being and is active within it until the end of time as the source of every grace and every gift and every miraculous power. *Just as our composite mortal body, although it is a marvelous work of the Creator, falls far short of the eminent dignity of our soul, so the social structure of the Christian community, though it proclaims the wisdom of its divine Architect, still remains something inferior when compared to the spiritual gifts which give it beauty and life, and to the divine source whence they flow.*[10]

---

9 Pope Pius XII, *Mystici corporis Christi* (1943), no. 53.
10 Ibid., no. 63, emphasis mine.

This understanding of the church appeared to be an extension of the Christology put forth by Anselm. And similar to that Christology, "The former theology of perfect society offered a static vision of the church unrelated to peoples and history, as an entity isolated and alone in the universe."[11] There is a reluctantly acknowledged "human" side, but this is always minimized. It never diminished the divine as the overriding principle of its existence: "Of course, in practice there were always involvements, but they were seen as defects and proof of the frailty of human nature. The aim was a church unmarked by the world."[12] The earthly remained inferior to spiritual gifts, which was the real concern of the church, just as the body remained inferior to the soul and the world remained inferior to heaven.

This dualism would have as its focus the spiritual life, which depended on the sacraments that nourished it. God's grace moved *only* through the church, especially its hierarchy, and thus the church itself became a proper object of adoration.[13]

> Hence, not only should we cherish exceedingly the Sacraments with which holy Mother Church sustains our life, the solemn ceremonies which she celebrates for our solace and our joy, the sacred chant and the liturgical rites by which she lifts our minds up to heaven, but also the sacramentals and all those exercises of piety by which she consoles the hearts of the faithful and sweetly imbues them with the Spirit of Christ. As her children, it is our duty, not only to make a return to her for her maternal goodness to us, but also to respect the authority which she has received from Christ in virtue of which she brings into captivity our understanding unto the obedience of Christ. Thus we are commanded to obey her laws and her moral precepts, even if at times they are difficult to our fallen nature; to bring our rebellious body into subjection through voluntary mortification; and at times we are warned to abstain even from harmless pleasures. Nor does it suffice to love this Mystical Body for the glory of its divine Head and for its heavenly gifts; we must love it with an

---

[11] José Comblin, *People of God*, ed. and trans. Phillip Berryman (Maryknoll, NY: Orbis Books, 2004), 8.

[12] Ibid., 8–9.

[13] Gustavo Gutierrez, in his landmark article "Toward a Theology of Liberation," implies as much when he states: "The absolute salvation provided by God in the hereafter, which diminishes the present life, has led to a very peculiar outlook: human institutions will considered important if they are oriented to the hereafter. All other institutions have no value because they will pass away." In *Liberation Theology: A Documentary History*, ed. Alfred Hennelly (Maryknoll, NY: Orbis Books, 1990), 67.

effective love as it appears in this our mortal flesh—made up, that is, of weak human elements, even though at times they are little fitted to the place which they occupy in this venerable body.[14]

The People of God

The Second Vatican Council offered a different image of this community called the church. It saw the church both in its human and divine dimensions—and thus first considers it as a mystery. The term "mystery" here indicates that because it is oriented toward God, but in service to the kingdom of God as it breaks in upon the world, it cannot be reduced finally to any concrete and crystal clear understanding. This mystery does not mean we know nothing about it or should be uncritical of its failures. Prior to any distinction between hierarchy and laity, the church understood itself first as a totality. This totality is called the people of God. The order of chapters in *Lumen gentium* supports this interpretation of the document. In the *second* draft released on September 29, 1963, the structure of the document looked like this:

I.   The Mystery of the Church

II. The Hierarchy

III. The People of God and the Laity

IV. Vocation of All to Holiness; Religious

The *final* version of the document, released on November 21, 1964, had a different structure:

I.   The Mystery of the Church

II.   The People of God

III. The Church Is Hierarchical

IV.   The Laity

V.   The Universal Call to Holiness

VI.   Religious

VII. The Pilgrim Church

VIII. Our Lady[15]

---

[14] Pope Pius XII, *Mystici corporis Christi*, no. 92.

[15] Gleeson, "Commemorating *Lumen gentium*: A Short History of a Ground-breaking Charter."

It was no accident that the Council thought it important to consider first the church as a whole. The placement of these chapters offers insight into many important aspects of the document. Yves Congar, the most influential ecclesiologist at Vatican II, had termed former approaches to understanding the church as "hierarchology," a preoccupation with the hierarchy of the church as the only suitable object of ecclesial reflection.[16] Obviously *Lumen gentium* represents a departure from that view, and it does so in three concrete ways.

First, the structure of the document considers the entire church as the people of God. Second, the church is considered primarily a network of people connected and motivated by the love of God exemplified in the life and ministry of Jesus of Nazareth. In this sense, the church manifests Christ to the world by imitating and concretely making real the love he lived, died, and resurrected within. Third, all of those baptized share equally in membership. There is no "two-tiered" system where those ordained are considered holier than laypeople. Thus, there is never justification for clericalism—the practice and attitude of putting ordained functionaries at the center of all decision making and community life.

A new model of leadership emerged that encouraged ordained ministers to draw forth and utilize the gifts and talents of all, in order to improve the communal life and worship of a particular church. Thus *Lumen gentium* states, "The sacred pastors, indeed, know well how much the laity contribute to the well-being of the whole church. For they know that they were not established by Christ to undertake by themselves the entire saving mission of the church to the world. They appreciate, rather, that it is their exalted task to shepherd the faithful and at the same time acknowledge *their ministries and charisms* so that all in their separate ways, but of one mind, may cooperate in the common task" (LG 30; emphasis mine).

Make no mistake though: there is still an irreplaceable need for a hierarchy. Communities need leaders. What now characterized this hierarchy was supposed to be a posture of *servant leadership*. The hierarchy exists in order to serve the people of God and, together with the laity, serve the kingdom of God. Finally, there was a reframing of the relationship of pope to bishop. If the former structure emphasized the pope as singular ruler over the college of bishops, the new understanding would emphasize the pope as first among equals and collegial collaboration as the highest

---

[16] Ibid. This paragraph summarizes Gleeson's section titled, "Abstract."

governing value.[17] All of these new developments in the self-understanding of the church pointed to a significant sea change for ecclesiology. For a more complete understanding of just how different this was, let us look more closely at the new image for church suggested at Vatican II.

Vatican II: The People of God

What is at the root of the "people of God" image and how does this represent a new direction in the church's self-understanding? The term "people of God" emerges at the beginning of the Hebrew Scriptures. The Hebrew people become a people in and through their liberation in the exodus. Recall that prior to the exodus, those in slavery to the pharaoh of Egypt were drawn from various groups of wandering peoples around the Mediterranean. When God broke into human history, it was in response to the suffering of those enslaved peoples. The book of Exodus clearly states: "I have observed the misery of my people who are in Egypt; I have heard their cry on account of their taskmasters. Indeed, I know their sufferings, and I have come down to deliver them" (3:7). The result of this divine compassion is the liberation from slavery of what would become the people of God. This slavery was *not* just physical but political, social, and, of course, spiritual. Politically, the Hebrew people were a part of a large majority serving a small minority (Pharaoh and his family) and had no political rights or representation. Socially, this group was marginalized as slave labor on building projects. Spiritually, Pharaoh was god and everyone did his will.

From this reality a people would emerge who formed a covenant with Yahweh—a covenant they would consistently break and yet always try to fulfill. Various figures guided this people of God. First was Moses, then the Judges followed, and the Israelites were later led by various kings, including Saul, David, and Solomon. When the office of king repeatedly failed both socially and religiously by its turning away from the covenant, various prophets came forth to fill the void of religious leadership until the time of Jesus. These people of God were fickle, constantly trying to live according to the covenant but failing. They were always forgiven by God, even after a traumatic exile to another land (Babylon). Although they never measured up to what they or the prophets had hoped for, they stayed

---

[17] For an excellent study on the relationship between the papacy and episcopacy actually commissioned by Cardinal Joseph Ratzinger when he was head of the Congregation for the Doctrine of the Faith, see Michael J. Buckley, *Papal Primacy and the Episcopate: Towards a Relational Understanding* (New York: Herder and Herder, 1998).

in some relationship with God. Throughout the Hebrew Scriptures this people was always exhorted to treat each other the way God had treated them, with mercy, especially for those most vulnerable. Additionally, they were repeatedly warned by a variety of prophets to never confuse cultic worship in the temple with actually doing God's will. God's will could only be done by helping the widow and orphan—those most vulnerable in the patriarchal society of that day.[18]

> This rooting of the church in Israel makes its concrete and historic nature more manifest. The people of Israel is set in the midst of peoples, with the characteristics of a people. The Bible continually stresses the relations between Israel and the other peoples of the earth. Being people of God does not mean that Israel ceases to be human—with all the values and all the sins of the peoples of the earth. The new people of God will be no less human and no less subject to the challenges of history, with its failures and victories, its virtues and vices, as shown by the prophets of the Old Testament. Indeed, prophets continually emerge within the new people as a reminder of the church's human character.[19]

According to *Lumen gentium*, Christ institutes a new covenant with this people at the Last Supper and thus forms a new people of God from his closest followers, who symbolically represent the new twelve tribes of Israel. The "people of God" is thus a *theological* understanding of a community introduced by Christ and not simply a *sociological* one. This messianic people also have Christ as their head, but it is not simply heaven that is their goal; it is something much more theologically rich: the kingdom of God.

Kingdom of God

The difference in mission set forth in *Lumen gentium* is critically important. *Lumen gentium* clearly states the purpose of the church: "Its destiny is the *kingdom of God* which has been begun by God himself on earth and which must be further extended until it is brought to perfection by him at the end of time when Christ our life (see Col 3:4), will appear and 'creation

---

[18] This message from the prophets is a major theme of the Hebrew Scriptures and is evident in Jeremiah, Amos, Isaiah, and the Psalms, among many others. Recall that in a patriarchal society one's social status depends on one's relationship to the oldest male of the clan. Widows and orphans were cut off from that relationship and thus were the most vulnerable.

[19] José Comblin, *People of God*, 8.

itself also will be delivered from its slavery to corruption into the freedom of the glory of the sons and daughters of God'" (LG 9; emphasis mine). This community, this new people of God, will be the *instrument* through which God brings about the kingdom of God on earth—a kingdom where the will of God and the will of human beings will unite to form a new social and spiritual reality.

In the past, church doctrine on the kingdom of God taught one of two things. First, the kingdom of God was spiritualized as "heaven" and thus the goal of all Christian life. This was realized not in this world but in the next. Second, the church taught that it was the kingdom of God on earth, in line with the thinking of *Mystici corporis Christi*. In *Lumen gentium*, the Church of Christ "subsists in" the Catholic Church, but aspects of it can be found outside the church as well. "This church constituted and organized as a society in the present world, *subsists* in the Catholic Church, which is governed by the successor of Peter and by the bishops in communion with him. Nevertheless, many elements of sanctification and of truth are found outside its visible confines" (LG 8; emphasis mine). The Catholic Church is no longer strictly identified with perfection, and less so strictly with the kingdom of God. Now, it is identified as being in service to the kingdom. Such a small change in language represented a *significant* change in theology.

It is no longer for the glory of the church that one works. Rather, the people of God work for the kingdom of God, as the Lord's Prayer has always reminded us. "Thy kingdom come, thy will be done, on earth." In order for this to happen, the church must be in service to something beyond itself. In fact, it must enter more deeply into the world it formerly viewed itself as being above. This service to the world and for the world is the new work of the church and, according to *Lumen gentium*, especially the work of the laity.

The Role of the Laity

In 1859, Fr. John Henry Newman was repeatedly denounced for suggesting that the faithful, by which he meant especially the laity, ought to be consulted in matters of doctrine. He was forced to resign the editorship of the journal in which he had published an article advancing the idea.[20] The highest ranking English-speaking member of the Roman curia at

---

[20] John Henry Newman, *On Consulting the Faithful in Matters of Doctrine*, ed. John Coulson (Kansas City: Sheed and Ward, 1961). Newman originally published the ar-

the time, Msgr. George Talbot, spoke for many church officials when he dismissed Newman's suggestion as absurd: "What is the province of the laity? To hunt, to shoot, to entertain. These matters they understand, but to meddle with ecclesiastical matters they have no right at all."[21]

Prior to Vatican II, the church was broadly considered under two different aspects: the ordained and "the faithful." The ordained included bishops and priests. The faithful were everyone else who had not received holy orders. *Mystici corporis Christi* (1943) used the term "laity" once: "Indeed, let this be clearly understood, especially in our days, fathers and mothers of families, those who are godparents through Baptism, and in particular those members of the laity who collaborate with the ecclesiastical hierarchy in spreading the kingdom of the Divine Redeemer occupy an honorable, *if often a lowly*, place in the Christian community, and *even they* under the impulse of God and with His help, can reach the heights of supreme holiness, which, Jesus Christ has promised, will never be wanting to the Church."[22]

The care of this "honorable, if lowly" group of people within the church by the ordained class was something Pius XII took very seriously: "Through Holy Orders men are set aside and consecrated to God, to offer the Sacrifice of the Eucharistic Victim, to nourish the flock of the faithful with the Bread of Angels and the food of doctrine, to guide them in the way of God's commandments and counsels and to strengthen them with all other supernatural helps."[23]

On the other hand, the purpose of the laity was fairly narrow: "For the social needs of the Church Christ has provided in a particular way by the institution of two other Sacraments. Through Matrimony, in which the contracting parties are ministers of grace to each other, provision is made for the external and duly regulated increase of Christian society, and, what is of greater importance, for the correct religious education of the children, without which this Mystical Body would be in grave danger."[24] Consistent with Catholic teaching since the time of Thomas Aquinas, Pius XII outlined the role of the laity as discovered in marriage, which existed for the

---

ticle in the July 1859 issue of *The Rambler*. I am indebted to Rev. Michael Himes for material in this section.

[21] Ibid., 41, emphasis mine. See also Michael J. Himes, "Lay Ministers and Ordained Ministers," *Lay Ministry in the Catholic Church*, ed. Richard Miller (Liguori, MO: Liguori Press, 1989), 79–87.

[22] Pope Pius XII, *Mystici corporis Christi*, no. 17, emphasis mine.

[23] Ibid., no. 20.

[24] Ibid.

reproduction and proper education of children. Reproduction was essentially the role of the laity. Finally, the faithful were called to model charity in the world, especially to those most vulnerable. As Pius XII states so clearly, this charity was seen as a pious act that symbolically addressed Jesus himself.

> If the faithful strive to live in a spirit of lively faith, they will not only pay due honor and reverence to *the more exalted members of this Mystical Body, especially those who according to Christ's mandate will have to render an account of our souls*, but they will take to their hearts those members who are the object of our Savior's special love: the weak, We mean, the wounded and the sick who are in need of material or spiritual assistance; children whose innocence is so easily exposed to danger in these days, and whose young hearts can be molded as wax; and finally the poor, in helping whom we recognize as it were, through His supreme mercy, the very person of Jesus Christ.[25]

In terms of engaging the complexity of the world, especially in the midst of the greatest world war (WWII), the church would not encourage engagement. There was no call here for concrete acts to address injustice or overt acts of peacemaking. Rather, it would encourage a flight *away* from conflict and encourage members to turn to prayer. This static view of history, with an elevated sense of the sacredness of the church, did not see human reality as worthy of engagement. This is apparent in the following: "But today that duty is more clear than ever, when a gigantic conflict has set almost the whole world on fire and leaves in its wake so much death, so much misery, so much hardship; in the same way today, in a special manner, it is the duty of all to fly from vice, the attraction of the world, the unrestrained pleasures of the body, and also from worldly frivolity and vanity which contribute nothing to the Christian training of the soul nor to the gaining of Heaven."[26]

Vatican II will see the laity and their role in a very different manner. "Everything that has been said of the people of God is addressed equally to laity, religious and clergy. Certain matters refer especially to the laity, both men and women, however, because of their situation and mission" (LG 30).

Initially *Lumen gentium* defines the laity negatively, by defining them in terms of what they are not: "The term laity is here understood to mean all the faithful *except* those in holy Orders and those who belong to a religious state approved by the church." Only secondarily are they given a positive

---

[25] Ibid., no. 93, emphasis mine.
[26] Ibid., no. 108.

definition, "all the faithful, that is, who by Baptism are incorporated into Christ, are constituted the people of God, who have been made sharers in their own way in the priestly, prophetic and kingly office of Christ and play their part in carrying out the mission of the whole christian people in the church and in the world" (LG 31; emphasis mine).

Undoubtedly, the theological understanding of the vocation of the laity has developed significantly in the last century. The theology of what was called Catholic Action and the groundbreaking work of scholars such as Yves Congar and Henri de Lubac laid the foundation for Vatican II's Decree on the Apostolate of the Laity (*Apostolicam actuositatem*). Vatican II states, "Lay people too, sharing in the priestly, prophetical and kingly office of Christ, play their part in the mission of the whole people of God in the church and in the world" (AA 2). The Decree on the Apostolate of the Laity emphasizes that the focus of the laity's activity is in the world, as contrasted with the clergy's work which is within the ecclesiastical structure. In short, normally the layperson works in the world and the ordained person works in the church. This concept is reinforced in *Lumen gentium*.

> It is the special vocation of the laity to seek the kingdom of God by engaging in temporal affairs and directing them according to God's will. They live in the world, in each and every one of the world's occupations and callings and in the ordinary circumstances of social and family life which, as it were, form the context of their existence. There they are called by God to contribute to the sanctification of the world from within, like leaven, in the spirit to the Gospel, by fulfilling their own particular duties. Thus, especially by the witness of their life, resplendent in faith, hope and charity they manifest Christ to others. It is their special task to illuminate and order all temporal matters in which they are closely involved in such a way that these are always carried out and develop in Christ's way and to the praise of the Creator and Redeemer. (LG 31)

Vatican II teaches that "the common priesthood of the faithful and the ministerial or hierarchical priesthood are none the less interrelated; each in its own way shares in the one priesthood of Christ" (LG 10). Here the document seems to be making the distinction between ordained and lay members in two ways. The first is by function. The ordained work within the church. "Outside" the church and in the world (is the church *not* in the world?), the layperson exercises her or his apostolate.[27] The second

---

[27] This is somewhat odd given that earlier in the document "ministries" of the laity were recognized. Usually this term refers to action for the ecclesial community.

way a distinction between lay and ordained is argued is indicated by the phrase, "they differ essentially and not only in degree" (LG 10). This is an argument from ontology, the study of being. It seems one's "being" is different if one is ordained, though exactly how it is different is never specified. Neither explanation from *Lumen gentium* regarding the distinction between lay and ordained is theologically viable today.

> This theology is completely based on the distinction between sacred and profane as expressed in the texts of Gratian and his followers, though this distinction was the very thing that they were trying to overcome. Indeed, the text has very strange statements, showing that it is not in accord with Christian reality. First, it says that the clergy is expressly devoted to the sacred ministry, but it recognizes that "they may sometimes be engaged in secular activities." Actually, until the current vocation crisis, a large portion of priests, both diocesan and religious, were devoted to teaching in Catholic schools. It did not happen "sometimes": tens of thousands of priests did so. Almost all Jesuits were involved in teaching, and the same was true of many other religious order priests. They were teaching secular subjects, not religion, and they were not exceptional cases at all. So why exclude the profane from the life of priests? It says that the mission of religious is to practice the beatitudes, but Jesus did not reserve the practice of the beatitudes to religious. They are the rule for the entire people of God—including lay people.[28]

Additionally, laypeople work throughout the church, in the church, and for the church in myriad ways. Today there are numerous programs in lay ministry which acknowledge this reality and attempt to properly train laypeople to serve as "ministers." Second, we know that ontologically, or from our very being, all humans are called by God but are capable of sin, regardless of their function in the church.[29] But the most significant change resulting from Vatican II is that now the layperson is encouraged, even required, to work for the kingdom of God here on earth.

---

[28] Comblin, *People of God*, 16.

[29] *Lumen gentium*, no. 32, even supports this understanding, "If therefore in the Church everyone does not proceed by the same path, nevertheless all are called to sanctity and have received an equal privilege of faith through the justice of God."

Universal Call to Holiness

Recall that within the explicitly two-tiered system prior to Vatican II, the most important members of the church were the bishops. To use an ascending analogy, bishops were "higher" and thus closer to the "head" of the church, Christ. According to *Mystici corporis Christi*:

> Consequently, Bishops must be considered as the more illustrious members of the Universal Church, for they are united by a very special bond to the divine Head of the whole Body and so are rightly called "principal parts of the members of the Lord"; moreover, as far as his own diocese is concerned, each one as a true Shepherd feeds the flock entrusted to him and rules it in the name of Christ. Yet in exercising this office they are not altogether independent, but are subordinate to the lawful authority of the Roman Pontiff, although enjoying the ordinary power of jurisdiction which they receive directly from the same Supreme Pontiff. Therefore, Bishops should be revered by the faithful as divinely appointed successors of the Apostles, and to them, even more than to the highest civil authorities should be applied the words: "Touch not my anointed one!" For Bishops have been anointed with the chrism of the Holy Spirit.[30]

This understanding of bishops was consistent with the focus on the hierarchy prior to Vatican II. "The hierarchy has been so sacralized and placed above the church that it has almost lost its human character and become a superhuman mediation—almost on the level of Christ himself."[31] Now, a new proclamation would come forth that called *all* people to holiness. "Therefore, all in the church, whether they belong to the hierarchy or are cared for by it, are called to holiness, according to the Apostle's saying: 'For this is the will of God, your sanctification' (1 Th 4:3; see Eph 1:4)" (LG 39).

This holiness is not some abstract sentiment or quality but is manifest in the "perfection of charity," evident in part when "a more human way of living even in society here on earth" (LG 40). Thus, how we live and interact on a daily basis with those in our community is essential to holiness. This holiness is not only tangible but also imitates Christ and his own movement toward the poor, who "follow Christ, poor and humble in carrying his cross, that they may deserve to be sharers in his glory" (LG 41). Beginning with the bishops and then priests, ministers of lesser rank, and finally laypeople, the document outlines how we should understand this call to holiness.

---

[30] Pope Pius XII, *Mystici corporis Christi*, no. 42.
[31] Comblin, *People of God*, 6.

Interestingly, the model for such holiness adheres to the traditional piety and charity referenced in countless documents throughout church history. The final paragraph of this section even has the ring of pre–Vatican II dualism to it.

> Therefore all the faithful of Christ are invited and obliged to try to achieve holiness and the perfection of their own state of life. Accordingly, all of them must ensure that they keep emotions under proper control, lest they be hindered in their pursuit of perfect love by the use of worldly goods and by an attachment to riches which is contrary to the spirit of evangelical poverty, following the apostle's advice: Let those who use this world not fix their abode in it, for the form of this world is passing away (see 1 Cor 7:31, Greek text). (LG 42)

Contrary to the final sentence of this exhortation to holiness, another document at Vatican II will outline in much greater detail what the actual role of the church is in this world. It will have a different tone, calling for more than charity on the part of the church and her members. This document will come in as the final approved document of the Council— *Gaudium et spes*, The Pastoral Constitution on the Church in the Modern World.

Gaudium et spes

If *Lumen gentium* is the *dogmatic* constitution on the church, *Gaudium et spes* is the *pastoral* constitution on the church in the modern world. What is the difference between a dogmatic constitution and a pastoral constitution? A dogmatic constitution articulates how the church understands itself, whereas a pastoral constitution articulates how the church is to build up the Christian community and serve the world. While both have to do with knowledge and action, a dogmatic constitution looks at the internal workings and self-understanding of the church, while the pastoral constitution looks at the church's interaction with the wider world.

Recall that prior to Vatican II, the church understood its relation to the state officially as *societas perfecta*. These two perfect societies were independent and self-sufficient. This was clearly the intention of Leo XII with the sentence, "even more than to the highest civil authorities should be applied the words: 'Touch not my anointed one!'" referenced above.[32] *Gaudium et spes* embraces a view of the Christian faith which sees

---

[32] Pope Leo XIII, *Immortale dei* (1885), no. 10.

it as actively in service to the world—even when the two perfect societies come into conflict. Because this is a new understanding of the role of the faithful, the document strives diligently to emphasize its importance: "But it is no less mistaken to think that we may immerse ourselves in earthly activities as if these latter were utterly foreign to religion, and religion were nothing more than the fulfillment of acts of worship and the observance of a few moral obligations. One of the gravest errors of our time is the dichotomy between the faith which many profess and their day-to-day conduct" (GS 43).

Because of the recognition that we must work for the kingdom of God here on earth, the church has and will have much to say as it guides and encourages a particular approach to social reality. This is evident from the document's first, famous paragraph:

> The joys and the hopes, the grief and anguish of the people of our time, especially of those who are poor or afflicted, are the joys and hopes, the griefs and anguish of the followers of Christ as well. Nothing that is genuinely human fails to find an echo in their hearts. For theirs is a community of people united in Christ and guided by the holy Spirit in their pilgrimage towards the Father's kingdom, bearers of a message of salvation for all of humanity. That is why they cherish a feeling of deep solidarity with the human race and its history. (GS 1)

In one, clear opening paragraph, the *societas perfectas* approach to church and state has officially been altered. The perception of the church as isolated and separate from the world, a static view of history and the dualism that had only focused on "the above," has been effectively left behind. As the document says in its introduction, "And so humankind substitutes *a dynamic and more evolutionary concept of nature for a static one*, and the result is an immense series of new problems calling for a new endeavor of analysis and synthesis" (GS 5; emphasis mine). Here is a human community, in continuity with its divine founder, which is deeply concerned with the world, "especially those who are poor or in any way afflicted." This statement introduces what has become one of the most difficult aspects of the new church mission to live out—a preferential option for the poor.

Preferential Option for the Poor

The preferential option for the poor is the human attempt to imitate how God interacts with humanity as revealed in Scripture. The measuring stick is the way we treat the most vulnerable beings among us. First, recall that God first revealed God's self to an enslaved people. Second, throughout the Hebrew Scriptures there was always a deep concern by the prophets for those most vulnerable in the communities of their people, be they widows, orphans, or the poor. Finally, a Messiah was born. He was born poor, lived poor, and died poor, and although his ministry was open to everyone, it was directed toward marginalized people in his society and challenged the structures of that society which oppressed them. In all these instances of God's action, God reaches out to those most in need while always loving everyone.

Perhaps an analogy would be helpful here. Imagine that a member of your family is physically and/or mentally challenged. Would that person require more time, energy, and resources than others in the family? Most likely. Does this mean that by giving that person more, you love or value him or her more than other members of the family? Not at all. The person needs more and so is given more. For the church to make this type of commitment from the beginning of this document means two things. First, the church's action in the world is to be defined by its preferential option for the poor. Second, it now has a deeper awareness of the need for social change in pursuit of justice, which ultimately serves the kingdom of God. What is contrary to the kingdom of God is not merely personal sin but the dehumanization of people through poverty and injustice. *Justice*, rather than charity alone, will finally and explicitly define the church's mission to the world.

There are five overriding themes in *Gaudium et spes* which articulate the church's mission to the world in new and bold ways. *First*, when the church looks at the modern world, it affirms quite strongly a new focus on the category of the "person" as the meaning and fulfillment of created reality. This means that of all the ways to analyze and understand the world, the default will always be how any given factor, issue, or system increases or diminishes the dignity of the human person. This is critical to emphasize. When analyzing various systems of economic production and distribution, for example, which one safeguards human dignity? When evaluating particular political systems or social systems, which one safeguards human dignity? The human person exists in the world but is not able to achieve the same level of dignity everywhere. The church's role is to help human beings discover their destiny and dignity. To do this faithfully means to always affirm that God's will is the guarantor of both. "It is the human person that is to be saved, human society which must be renewed. It is the human person, therefore, which is the key to this discussion, each individual person in her or his totality, body and soul, heart and conscience, mind and will" (GS 3). In *Gaudium et spes*, the entire integrated person becomes the center of church concern, not merely the disembodied "soul."

> The human person, though made of body and soul, is a unity. In itself, in its very bodily condition, it synthesizes the elements of the material world, which through it are thus brought to their highest perfection and are enabled to raise their voice in spontaneous praise of the creator. For this reason human beings may not despise their bodily life. They are, rather, to regard their bodies as good and to hold them in honor since God has created them and will raise them up on the last day. Nevertheless humanity has been wounded by sin. People find by experience that their bodies are in revolt. Their very dignity therefore requires that they should glorify God in their bodies, and not allow them to serve the evil inclinations of their hearts. (GS 14)

One sees very clearly in the first fifteen paragraphs of this remarkable document a complete shift from a static view of history to a more dynamic one. What follows is an inductive approach to how we understand the human being as body and soul, created in the image and likeness of God. And what, precisely, does it mean to be created in the image and likeness of God? Augustine and the Catholic tradition have argued that God is best understood as Trinity. The analogy he uses is that God is the one who gives love perfectly (the Father), the one who receives love perfectly (the Son), and the one who shares love perfectly (the Spirit). God is perfect, embodied, relational love—one God in three persons. To say that I am made in this image means that I am made to give, receive, and share love. Human dignity rests in the possibility of realizing the giving, receiving, and sharing of love in life by *first* having adequate material opportunities available for love to flourish. While the human being will always do this imperfectly, it is only through the movements of love in relationships that a person will find any true sense of human fulfillment. This nature of human dignity introduces the *second* major theme in the document: the social nature of human beings.

The document affirms that in their inmost nature, human beings are social and can neither live nor attain their full potential by themselves. Thus, the document moves from a claim concerning the inherent dignity of each individual person to the necessity and goodness of living socially. "But God did not create men and women as solitary beings. From the beginning 'male and female God created them' (Gen 1:27). This partnership of man and woman constitutes the first form of communion between people. For by their innermost nature men and women are social beings; and if they do not enter into relationships with others they can neither live nor develop their gifts" (GS 12). Emerging from the central Christian doctrine that love of God is love of neighbor and love of neighbor is love God, there is an obligation to cultivate interpersonal relations, as the council explains, "this is a matter of the utmost importance to people who are coming to rely more and more on each other and to a world which is becoming more unified every day" (GS 24). This is even truer in a world increasingly characterized by interdependence. Here the document anticipates the globalization that will develop very rapidly in the 1980s and 1990s. And this leads us to the *third* major theme of the encyclical: the criteria for how a truly human society cultivates increasingly complex relationships.

The social nature of human beings should be formed and managed with the *genuine* and *common* good of the human race foremost in mind. A deep concern for the well-being of all is necessary for the goodness and development of the individual. It is not an either/or but a both/and. For many North Americans, this philosophy is counterintuitive. Part of our historical development has included the ethos that by pursuing our individual self-interest, the common good will somehow emerge (invisible hand?).[33] *Gaudium et spes* arrives at quite a different position. By pursuing the common good, our individual good emerges.

From a Catholic perspective, society is not supposed to be a contractual partnership of essentially separate individuals, as it is often viewed and experienced within the United States. It is instead a partnership in the pursuit of goods that are best realized and fulfilled in common. For example, a basic level of health care among all members of a society is necessary for a community to genuinely and truly flourish. Health-care facilities and the treatment they provide are not only commodities for those with substantial financial resources to buy and sell. The church's commitment to the common good as the most basic principle of social, economic, and political relationships challenges the self-interested orientation that is manifest in a radical free-market perspective—a perspective the Catholic Church has been critical of in many of its documents. It is in this free-market style orientation that health care becomes a commodity like other consumer goods whose allocation is solely determined by

---

[33] For an excellent discussion of this, see chapter 6 of Robert Bellah, et al., *Habits of the Heart: Individualism and Commitment in American Life* (Berkely: University of California Press, 2008).

who can afford to pay rather than by right and necessity. These goods are meant to be shared and distributed in an even fashion, working toward the better health for all and contributing to the standard of health for the entire community. One's individual good emerges from a society that cares for its entire people.

Fourth, in order to facilitate the common good, the church deeply commits itself to the pursuit of justice by seeking "more humane and just conditions of life and directing institutions to guaranteeing human dignity." This is remarkably different from a simple commitment to charitable activity. Charity is good but never enough. There will always be the need to provide necessities for those who lack them—water, food, medicine, housing, etc. The church has a long and impressive history of doing charitable work. And yet, working for justice gets at the systemic roots of *why* there is so much need and tries to change the social realities that create the need in the first place. Archbishop Dom Helder Camara of Brazil perhaps said it best when he remarked, "When I give food to the poor, they call me a saint. When I ask why the poor have no food, they call me a Communist." The first part of his statement epitomizes charity—and it is a safe statement because it fails to address the symptoms that result from broken human systems. The second part of his statement represents the initial phase of justice—seeing human reality as it is and asking, why is it so? Here we witness a critical moment when the church understands its own mission in the world. Recall that for many centuries in Latin America the church had given its blessing to the colonial enterprise. Later it resisted calls for independence from within the very countries that had enslaved indigenous peoples. The church, understandably, would alienate many of the poor and marginalized who comprised the majority of Latin America (and still do). But, beginning with *Gaudium et spes*, and especially through later documents such as *Populorum progressio*, as well as documents written by the Latin American bishops, the church would begin to challenge the wealthy. To understand how, we turn now to the *fifth* overall theme of *Gaudium et spes*.

Following the argument outlined above, the fifth and final theme should come as no surprise. All social, economic, and human development ought to be directed to the complete fulfillment of all citizens, with those wealthier individuals and nations opting to help those less developed individuals and nations. The obligation of wealthier individuals and nations to assist those in need has not been embraced by many of the wealthy in either the United States or Latin America (beyond charitable endeavors). Vatican II points out the scandalous imbalance of social and economic resources among countries, nations, and peoples as well as hints at some of the consequences. "In the midst of huge numbers deprived of the bare necessities of life there are some who live in riches and squander their wealth; and this happens in less developed areas as well. Luxury and misery exist side by side. While a few individuals enjoy almost unlimited freedom of choice, the vast majority have no change whatever of exercising personal initiative and responsibility, and quite often have to live and work in conditions unworthy of human beings" (GS 63).

Riches and poverty are relational. As a relational reality, those with riches can no longer understand themselves as unrelated to or not responsible for those in poverty. Unfortunately, this scandal of inequality has both widened and deepened globally since 1965, and while we have seen some progress in development by poor nations, contemporary global economic inequality remains stark.[34] Finally, the pursuit of justice with relation to economic forces goes well beyond the traditional categories of charity. Additionally, the church addresses the reasons for such inequality: "To satisfy the demands of justice and equity, strenuous efforts must be made, without disregarding the rights of persons or the natural qualities of each country, to remove as quickly as possible the immense economic inequalities, which now exist and in many cases are growing and which are connected with individual and social discrimination."[35]

It is clear from *Gaudium et spes* that the tradition of Catholic social teaching, formally initiated in 1891 with *Rerum novarum*, is finally penetrating the ecclesiology that for so long had resisted it. Prior to Vatican II, the social encyclicals seemed to be an unrelated corollary to the true business of the church in the world. This separation, or compartmentalization, is over. *Gaudium et spes* reiterates the core principle of Catholic social teaching and pledges, *as a work of the church*, to articulate this vision more forcefully in the world: "God intended the earth with everything contained in it for the use of all human beings and peoples. Thus, under the leadership of

[34] Economic inequality in the United States has come to mirror global trends. A new analysis from the *Economic Policy Institute* finds that the richest 20 percent of Americans saw their share of all Americans' wealth increase by 2.2 percentage points between 2007 and 2009. The remaining four-fifths of Americans saw their wealth decline by the same amount. The top 20 percent of Americans by wealth controlled 87.2 percent of all wealth as of 2009, according to an analysis by EPI, a liberal-leaning research group. That left the rest of the country with 12.8 percent of all wealth. Referenced on April 5, 2011, http://lifeinc.today.com/_news/2011/04/01/6384619-good-graph-friday-wealth-gap-widened-in-recession.

[35] Ibid., no. 66.

justice and in the company of charity, created goods should be in abundance for all in like manner."[36]

Conclusion

How the Catholic Church understands its role in the world changed at the Second Vatican Council, and this change was nothing less than astonishing. The change includes a transition from a church that perceived itself as above the affairs of the world, and only grudgingly part of it, to a church deeply rooted in mission to the world, as it cooperates with God's grace to build God's kingdom. It moves from a church heavily focused on its hierarchy and holiness to one which validates every member of the church as called to a specific vocation by God. Finally, the church embraces justice, especially for the most vulnerable. It now seeks to address the causes of dehumanization as its main posture toward the world, a posture that will always include charity but never be limited to only charity.

As with any major shift in identity, these changes have been difficult for many members of the church. It could be argued that the majority of North American Catholics have not accepted or internalized the profound changes of Vatican II. There are many reasons for this, but much of the contemporary tension in the church centers on differing interpretations, or outright rejection, of some of these changes. The adjustment has been no easier for the Catholic Church in Latin America.

Shortly after the conclusion of the Second Vatican Council, Paul VI would author an encyclical titled *Populorum progressio*, On the Development of Peoples. This encyclical essentially asks (and partly answers) the question, what does *Gaudium et spes* mean for developing countries throughout the world? Additionally, the Latin American Bishops Conference (CELAM) would meet in Medellín, Colombia, and try to adapt the teachings of both *Gaudium et spes* and *Populorum progressio* to their own situation.

Only after understanding how the Latin American church received Vatican II and accepted its trajectory in its own context, can Rutilio Grande, SJ, and his ministry in El Salvador be understood. Note that thus far, all language of change, all presumption to change, and all action for change has come directly from documents authored by the magisterium of the Catholic Church in a worldwide ecumenical council. This is important to affirm as the effects of this Council become apparent, especially in Latin America.

[36] Ibid., no. 69.

Questions for Discussion:

1. What difference has there been between understanding the church as "the people of God" or as "the Mystical Body of Christ?"

2. How did the role of the laity and its call to holiness change at Vatican II?

3. How did the understanding of the kingdom of God change from pre–Vatican II times in comparison with *Lumen gentium* at Vatican II?

4. How did *Gaudium et spes* challenge the notion of *societas perfecta*?

5. Why is the "preferential option for the poor" such a significant development at Vatican II?

6. What are the five themes of *Gaudium et spes*, and how does it understand the relationship between one individual good and the common good differently than mainstream US culture?

Chapter 4

Medellín: Latin America's Response to the New Mission of the Church

What sermons do I remember? In those times, everything was in Latin . . . the priest with his back to the people. When it came time to speak to us, the priest climbed up into a thing they called a "pulpit." He would begin saying "In-nomine-patri-tefili-tespiritu-santi-deus." And the people would say "Amen."

Who knew what that all meant.

And then he'd begin to speak, and he'd always say the same dumb things: that we should have a lot of respect for the authorities because St. Paul, in one of his letters, says that all authority comes from God; therefore we should never oppose the authorities because to do so would be, according to the priest, to oppose God. And we took it all in with our eyes closed.

He'd give that same talk at meeting after meeting attended by Christians. He said that nobody should rise up against the authorities.[1]

In March 1967, Pope Paul VI released *Populorum progressio* (On the Development of Peoples), an influential document regarding the role of the church in the developing world. One year later the bishops of Latin America would meet at Medellín, Colombia, and issue their own set of documents that would revolutionize the Catholic Church in South America, Central America, Mexico, and the Caribbean. Both the encyclical and the bishops' conference would influence the relationship between theology and mission, the relationship of the church to politics, and the type of evangelization that would come to distinguish the Latin American church.

Paul VI reaffirmed the spirit of *Gaudium et spes* in the opening paragraph of *Populorum progressio*, as well as the centrality of the preferential

---

[1] Maria Lopez Vigil, *Don Lito of El Salvador* (Maryknoll, NY: Orbis Books, 1990), 30.

option for the poor when he firmly stated: "The progressive development of peoples is an object of deep interest and concern to the Church. This is particularly true in the case of those peoples who are trying to escape the ravages of hunger, poverty, endemic disease and ignorance; of those who are seeking a larger share in the benefits of civilization and a more active improvement of their human qualities; of those who are consciously striving for fuller growth."[2]

At the beginning of this document, Paul VI points out what aspects of the tradition he referenced, which were essentially all Catholic social teaching. From *Rerum novarum* in 1891 to *Pacem en Terris* of John XXIII in 1963, he appealed to his predecessors in order to make some very strong arguments advocating for the integral development of marginalized peoples and nations. From this document, theologians and church leaders learned a new approach to ministry, political involvement, and evangelization. Critical to this new approach was the perspective that the quest for human fulfillment required freedom from oppression of any kind—spiritual, economic, political, or social. This embrace of liberation (defined as freedom from oppression of any kind) as essential to human fulfillment effectively put the church on a collision course with many of the most powerful and wealthy individuals and groups throughout Latin America.

In the course of his document, Paul VI affirmed concrete ideas; for example, he argues that riches and poverty are relational, that vast inequality damages relationships between nations and parts of the world, and that "growth" is ambivalent and must be considered to be more than economic growth alone. Additionally, Paul VI asserted that the two dominant economic systems in the world at that time, liberal capitalism and Marxist collectivism, both failed to fundamentally address what human beings needed for fulfillment. Finally, *Populorum progressio* obligated wealthier nations to assist poorer nations, and it asked individuals to search their conscience and be prepared to pay higher taxes and higher prices for goods and to be open to direct service in parts of one's nation and world where there was dire need. By considering how *Populorum progressio* critiqued and encouraged social, economic, and spiritual realities in the modern world, one can see how the council planned to answer the church's call of helping to build the kingdom of God on earth.

[2] Pope Paul VI, *Populorum progressio* (1967), no. 1.

Theology and Mission

If Vatican II redefined how the church understood itself and its mission to the world, *Populorum progressio* tried to apply this redefinition concretely in those areas of the world where wealth, opportunity, and freedom were lacking. Paul VI mentioned how the call for structural reforms was evidenced in how the central administration of the church was altered to accommodate this new vision. "We felt it was necessary to add another pontifical commission to the Church's central administration. The purpose of this commission is 'to awaken in the People of God full awareness of their mission today. In this way they can further the progress of poorer nations and international social justice, as well as help less developed nations to contribute to their own development.'"[3] As a result, the *Justice and Peace Commission* was created. It would try to implement this new mission of the church in the world as defined by Vatican II.

This new emphasis on engaging the world was no accident. The theology of Vatican II now influenced how the church worked concretely in the world, and the consequences were extraordinary. The foundation for this new response to suffering in the world was the example of the early church. In *Populorum progressio*, Paul VI is very specific and uses criteria from this epoch:

> Everyone knows that the Fathers of the Church laid down the duty of the rich toward the poor in no uncertain terms. As St. Ambrose put it: "You are not making a gift of what is yours to the poor man [or woman], but you are giving him [or her] back what is his [or hers]. You have been appropriating things that are meant to be for the common use of everyone. The earth belongs to everyone, not to the rich." These words indicate that the right to private property is not absolute and unconditional.
>
> No one may appropriate surplus goods solely for his own private use when others lack the bare necessities of life. In short, "as the Fathers of the Church and other eminent theologians tell us, the right of private property may never be exercised to the detriment of the common good." When "private gain and basic community needs conflict with one another," it is for the public authorities "to seek a solution to these questions, with the active involvement of individual citizens and social groups."[4]

[3] Ibid., no. 5.
[4] Ibid., no. 23.

What became evident in the document was an integral approach to human development, not only a spiritual or an economic one. In the past, the conditions of this world were generally accepted as part of life that human beings could not change. This idea was reflected in nearly every official teaching of the church, except the more recent Catholic social teaching. What was always most important was one's spiritual health, and this was *not* always understood to be connected to the world in which one lived. Finally, we see in this document an understanding of the human person that takes the material world seriously. What emerged was a humanism which finally treated the human being as an integrated whole containing both body and soul: "The ultimate goal is a full-bodied humanism. And does this not mean the fulfillment of the whole man [and woman] and of every man [and woman]? A narrow humanism, closed in on itself and not open to the values of the spirit and to God who is their source, could achieve apparent success, for man [and woman] can set about organizing terrestrial realities without God. But 'closed off from God, they will end up being directed against man [and woman]. A humanism closed off from other realities becomes inhuman.'"[5]

The obvious targets of this statement were those perspectives on human beings which cut off spiritual needs and only addressed material realities—atheism, communism, liberal capitalism, etc. This statement, properly understood, also functioned as an indictment of a former "spiritualizing" of the human as well—one which cut off the material world as essential to human and spiritual thriving. A very important section of *Populorum progressio* defined development as that which humanizes both poor and rich—where "human" becomes the capacity to freely enter into relationships of love and truth.

> What are less than human conditions? The material poverty of those who lack the bare necessities of life, and the moral poverty of those who are crushed under the weight of their own self-love; oppressive political structures resulting from the abuse of ownership or the improper exercise of power, from the exploitation of the worker or unjust transactions.
>
> What are truly human conditions? The rise from poverty to the acquisition of life's necessities; the elimination of social ills; broadening the horizons of knowledge; acquiring refinement and culture. From there one can go on to acquire a growing awareness of other people's dignity, a taste for the spirit of poverty, an active interest in

[5] Ibid., no. 42.

the common good, and a desire for peace. Then man [and woman] can acknowledge the highest values and God Himself, their author and end. Finally and above all, there is faith—God's gift to men [and women] of good will—and our loving unity in Christ, who calls all men [and women] to share God's life as sons [and daughters] of the living God, the Father of all [humans].[6]

The church did not expect to teach the faith effectively to starving people who lacked even life's basic necessities. Thus, it was necessary to understand development on a larger scale and as a continuum. This revised understanding of development would be enormously influential, especially in Latin America where theologians like Gustavo Gutierrez, the "father" of liberation theology, would take as their starting point *this* definition of development from *Populorum progressio*. He would then ask the question: What relationship existed between the coming kingdom of God and political, social, and economic emancipation today?[7] His answer to this question framed how many came to understand the mission of the church throughout Latin America—especially in El Salvador.

Note how *Populorum progressio*'s definition of development first began in the material world. Do people have the basic necessities that allow for survival, community, social development, and the creation of culture? When those have been addressed, it becomes possible to address other critical areas of human development. Note that material poverty and moral poverty are similarly damaging to the human person. Material poverty does not allow for the development of human potential because of a lack of resources and opportunities. Moral poverty does not allow for the development of human potential because of too much selfishness. This approach to human development corresponded to the ministry of Jesus, as he sought to free the poor, including those suffering from both the economic (the poor widow, the hungry, the naked, the sick) and sociological (Samaritans, tax collectors, prostitutes, lepers, women) poverty of his time.[8]

For those who were materially and/or sociologically poor, Jesus revealed that poverty (in either form) was no barrier to God's love, despite what religious authorities at the time said. He communicated this message by welcoming them into his community of followers, even when it caused

---

[6] Ibid., no. 21.

[7] Gustavo Gutierrez, "Toward a Theology of Liberation" (1968), in *Liberation Theology: A Documentary History*, ed. Alfred T. Hennelly (Maryknoll, NY: Orbis Books, 1994).

[8] This is developed in much more depth by Jon Sobrino in *Jesus the Liberator: A Historical-Theological View*, chap. 2 (Maryknoll, NY: Orbis Books, 1999).

scandal. For those who were economically wealthy, he warned that riches were bad for them and that their riches were accumulated at the expense of others. Thus, riches and poverty were relational. These riches were different from the "abundance" which was blessed by God and should be enjoyed by all.[9] Furthermore, the relationship of the rich to their own material wealth must change before they can follow Jesus. The story of the rich young man, present in all four gospels, speaks to the challenging nature of Jesus' teaching on wealth. The most disturbing aspect of this story, in each gospel, is that Jesus allows the rich young man to walk away.

The theological foundation of this perspective on material wealth is the core of all Catholic social teaching. God created the world for all people, not only for the rich. If we want to cooperate with the will of God—that is, if we want to work for the kingdom—then we need to arrange human affairs to be consistent with the will of God. *Populorum progressio* states this clearly and bluntly, as noted in the following passage:

> In the very first pages of Scripture we read these words: "Fill the earth and subdue it." This teaches us that the whole of creation is for man [and woman], that he [and she have] been charged to give it meaning by his [and her] intelligent activity, to complete and perfect it by his [and her] own efforts and to his [and her] own advantage.
>
> Now if the earth truly was created to provide man [and woman] with the necessities of life and the tools for his [and her] own progress, it follows that every man [and woman] has the right to glean what he [and she] need from the earth. The recent Council reiterated this truth: "God intended the earth and everything in it for the use of all human beings and peoples. Thus, under the leadership of justice and in the company of charity, created goods should flow fairly to all."
>
> All other rights, whatever they may be, including the rights of property and free trade, are to be subordinated to this principle. They should in no way hinder it; in fact, they should actively facilitate its implementation. Redirecting these rights back to their original purpose must be regarded as an important and urgent social duty.[10]

Here we finally have a concrete connection between a theology of creation and how this theology affected the organization of human affairs. We cannot be indifferent to human suffering or the way in which the goods of this world are produced and distributed, as there are spiritual

---

[9] Jon Sobrino addresses this point very well in *Jesus the Liberator*, 171. Sobrino implies that "abundance" is enough to meet one's needs with enough left over to share.

[10] Pope Paul VI, *Populorum progressio*, no. 22.

consequences for both rich and poor. Wealth, and our relationship to it, is a spiritual issue. This topic causes the most deafening *silence* in any parish or classroom in North America.

Because the document is not beholden to any particular economic system, it will be deeply critical of "free competition as the guiding principle of economics," as well as Marxist collectivism or any system which promotes the imperialism of money. When development is defined solely by these values (as if the measurement of a country's GNP really indicates *quality* of life in a given society), the human being suffers. By denouncing these values and criticizing the way economies fail to adequately distribute the goods and services available to developing nations, Paul VI is also creating a new challenge for how the church understands its role in political life. What role will the church play in modern society when it has relinquished its practice of accumulating political power through justifying traditional structures and receiving benefits for it? *Populorum progressio* will try to address this reality, albeit with many contradictions.

The Church and Political Life

For all students of papal encyclicals, it is important to remember that rarely, if ever, are they authored by one person. A close reading of many of the encyclicals will reveal this as self-evident. Although encyclicals may be promulgated under the name of a particular pope, many groups will have had a role in writing and editing various sections of the document. What can pose a challenge to the reader is that often these groups have different perspectives and, as a result, so will the documents. Rather than resolve an issue in favor of one faction over another, many papal documents simply include both perspectives. *Populorum progressio* is no exception to this truism, and its content speaks to this tension very clearly on the topic of the church and its role in political life.

Since Vatican II, it is safe to say that the hierarchical church does not wish to be involved in political life in the form of political power players (i.e., as duly elected or appointed representatives of a nation's people) as members of the government. When a document or articulated church position states that the church desires no political role in a given context, it usually means that it does not want priests running for congress or bishops campaigning for the position of president. It does *not* mean that the church has nothing to say about social or political reality.

Churches in North America and their pastors often make a serious mistake by arguing that homilies can only address spiritual topics, as the church has no overt political role. Commonly, pastors are comfortable weighing in about sexual politics (abortion, contraception, homosexuality, etc.) but not about other social, economic, or political realities—all of which are related to and influence sexual politics. People will often complain if social and political items come up during church services, regardless of the perspective. This is a serious misreading of the principles of Catholic social teaching. It contributes to the compartmentalization of American Catholic faith into the politics of sexuality and away from the world in which it exists. Early in *Populorum progressio*, a similar tension is present.

On the one side, "The Church, which has long experience in human affairs and has no desire to be involved in the political activities of any nation, 'seeks but one goal: to carry forward the work of Christ under the lead of the befriending Spirit. And Christ entered this world to give witness to the truth; to save, not to judge; to serve, not to be served.'"[11] Unlike the *societas perfectas* model of the pre–Vatican II church, *Populorum progressio* argues that church and state are "distinct"—but not unconnected—and yet still supreme each "in its own sphere of competency." This means that the church will never decide whether a particular policy becomes law for a nation. Likewise, the state will never decide what is necessary for salvation. It does not mean that there won't be conversation, conflict, disagreement, or tension as both entities try to fulfill their responsibilities. In fact, this tension is inevitable: "But since the Church does dwell among men [and women], she has the duty 'of scrutinizing the signs of the times and of interpreting them in the light of the Gospel.' Sharing the noblest aspirations of men [and women] and suffering when she sees these aspirations not satisfied, she wishes to help them attain their full realization. So she offers man[kind] her distinctive contribution: a global perspective on man[kind] and human realities."[12]

The church wishes to be of service through its guidance on how to arrange human affairs most consistent with the dignity of human beings. It does not seek the power to make such arrangements; rather, it seeks to guide those who do (the role of the laity put forth by *Lumen gentium*). There is very little chance this service will not conflict, on a variety of issues, with at least some perspectives within the state (i.e., political parties, particular administrations, etc.). This is especially true when vested interests of an oligarchy in any given country become the target of church pronouncements, such as land reform in the following excerpt from the document.

---

[11] Ibid., no. 13.
[12] Ibid.

If certain landed estates impede the general prosperity because they are extensive, unused or poorly used, or because they bring hardship to peoples or are detrimental to the interests of the country, the common good sometimes demands their expropriation.

Vatican II affirms this emphatically. At the same time it clearly teaches that income thus derived is not for man's capricious use, and that the exclusive pursuit of personal gain is prohibited. Consequently, it is not permissible for citizens who have garnered sizeable income from the resources and activities of their own nation to deposit a large portion of their income in foreign countries for the sake of their own private gain alone, taking no account of their country's interests; in doing this, they clearly wrong their country.[13]

The first paragraph cited above could actually serve as a description of most of Latin America between 1560 and 1960. Such a message was particularly difficult to hear in a country like El Salvador, where prior to 1980, fourteen families controlled nearly 90 percent of the land on which the three major agricultural products of coffee, sugarcane, and cotton were grown.[14] There was an immediate outcry from wealthy Catholics that the church was interfering in the political arena in an entirely new manner! That was clearly true; never before had the church been critical of the inequality so dominant in Latin America. Understandably, the oligarchy was confused because the church had previously accepted and benefitted from the status quo of inequality for centuries, with little or no overt opposition.

Archbishop Oscar Romero's four pastoral letters try to explain why this change had occurred. The entry of the church into political life, as a resource and challenge to prevailing trends in socioeconomic and political life, put it in direct conflict with certain states. Most prominently, conflict occurred in Brazil in the 1960s and 1970s, Chile in the 1980s and 1990s, and El Salvador, Guatemala, and Nicaragua in the 1970s and 1980s. Part of the tension came from certain language used in *Gaudium et spes* and *Populorum progressio*. While it is true the church never wished to return to the Christendom arrangement of senior partner to the state, this did not mean that it would remain mute in participatory democracies. Such an arrangement was difficult because while the church had little political power in Latin America after Vatican II, it had substantial authority among

---

[13] Ibid., no. 24.

[14] According to various sources in El Salvador, the agricultural control of those fourteen families has morphed today into eight financial conglomerates, all with overlapping interests.

the people. Contradictory language in *Populorum progressio* does not help the church in its ability to voice an opinion on controversial issues. It is impossible to have "no desire to be involved in the political activities of any nation" while at the same time taking a stance on such concrete issues as land reform, industrialization, human rights, and income disparity. These compromise statements may placate opposing camps in the Vatican, but they led to confusion when the local church tried to articulate its social vision. There is no better example of this tension than how *Populorum Progressio* attempted to outline the criteria for a just revolution: "Everyone knows, however, that revolutionary uprisings—except where there is manifest, longstanding tyranny which would do great damage to fundamental personal rights and dangerous harm to the common good of the country—engender new injustices, introduce new inequities and bring new disasters. The evil situation that exists, and it surely is evil, may not be dealt with in such a way that an even worse situation results."[15]

Let us break down this statement. This section attempts to apply "just war" theory to the situation of revolutions in the developing world. One voice clearly states that revolutionary uprisings "engender new injustices, introduce new inequities and bring new disasters." A second voice argues that revolutionary uprisings are justified when "there is manifest, longstanding tyranny which has done great damage to fundamental personal rights and dangerous harm to the common good of the country." Both are summed up in the final sentence, which declares that there is evil in certain sociopolitical regimes but that greater evil cannot be used to create change. It really is a remarkable sentence. Two opposing perspectives are simply combined in one sentence.

The tension in this document later plays itself out in myriad ways in Nicaragua during the papacy of John Paul II. "At the end of May 1979 the Sandinistas rebels announced a final offensive against the Samoza dictatorship. Within days, the Catholic bishops issued a document listing the traditional conditions for a 'just insurrection,' and in effect endorsed this insurrection."[16] Soon, the conflict and tension would escalate to a level difficult for the Catholic Church in Nicaragua to manage. The Sandinistas would embrace a Cuban-Soviet style of communism, and priests began accepting appointed offices as government ministers. It seemed that all the fears of the wealthy oligarchies throughout Latin America, who had

[15] Pope Paul VI, *Populorum progressio*, no. 31.

[16] Phillip Berryman, *Stubborn Hope: Religion, Politics and Revolution in Central America* (Maryknoll, NY: Orbis Books, 1994), 21.

carefully kept their religious faith compartmentalized from the social, political, and economic world they lived in, were coming to fruition.

Despite difficulties in parts of Central America, the Latin American bishops spoke firmly and clearly in favor of a particular social vision that was highly critical of the stark inequality between the rich and poor that characterized postcolonial nation-states throughout Latin America. As the final documents from the Latin American Episcopal Conference meeting in Medellín (1968) show, the church chose to use its authority to work for the integral development of all peoples in Latin America.

Medellín: The Latin American Church Finds Its Voice

The second general meeting of Latin American bishops, titled, "The Church in the Present-Day Transformation of Latin America in the Light of the Council," was held from August 26 to September 6, 1968. It was an extraordinary meeting of bishops and theologians and drew heavily on regional consultations held by various bishops with people in their dioceses prior to the meeting. In these consultations, bishops explored with fellow believers the challenges and opportunities of what being a church meant to them. Four critical theological, ecclesial, and methodological priorities were decisively confirmed at Medellín. First, the bishops established the relationship between social, political, and economic progress in this world and the kingdom of God for which the church works. Second, there was a call for structural change both in society *and the church* to alleviate suffering and promote understanding. Third, the bishops confirmed their self-understanding of church as the *people of God*, with an explicit option for the poor, affecting all levels of human wealth.[17] Fourth and finally, this conference confirmed that the way in which the church followed its own exhortations would largely determine whether its people would listen to it. Action must accompany new commitments.

The End of Dualism in Mission and Ministry

The bishops began the final documents of Medellín with a tone of humility not seen in many episcopal documents when they said, "We do not have technical solutions or infallible remedies. We wish to feel the problems, perceive the demands, share the agonies, discover the ways,

---

[17] All references from the final documents of Medellín are collected and presented in Alfred T. Hennelly, ed., *Liberation Theology: A Documentary History*, 89–120.

and cooperate in the solutions."[18] This humility took form as they encouraged and promoted new forms of decision making in their communities.
This included a strengthening of professional organizations, especially
for workers and peasants, and the opening of new channels of dialogue
between the church hierarchy and its people. Above all, there was a focus
on the necessity of *action* over ideas. At the outset of the final documents,
the bishops deemed it necessary to answer the following question: What
does this have to do with the real work of the church? They answered
this clearly and decisively by first characterizing the signs of the times in
their own context: "It appears to be a time full of zeal for full emancipation, of liberation from every form of servitude, of personal maturity and
of collective integration. In these signs we perceive the first indications
of the painful birth of a new civilization."[19] These various movements
of liberation (a term first used by the bishops!) must be managed and
directed so the entire human person is reverenced, not just one aspect
or another. This integral liberation, which includes the whole person,
is the connection between temporal progress and the kingdom of God.
The bishops declared this liberation to be both a sign and demand of the
kingdom of God.

> The fact that the transformation affecting our continent had made
> an impact on the whole person appears as a sign and a demand. In
> fact, we Christians cannot but acknowledge the presence of God,
> who desires to save the whole person, body and soul.
>
> For all of us who possess the first fruits of the Spirit, we too groan
> inwardly as we wait for our bodies to be set free. God has raised
> Christ from the dead, and therefore also, all those who believe in
> him. Christ, actively present in our history, foreshadows his escha-
> tological action not only in the impatient human zeal to reach total
> redemption, but also in those conquests which, like prophetic signs,
> are accomplished by humankind through action inspired by love.[20]

This statement is very important theologically. Human zeal for redemption is not enough of a sign of Christ actively present in our history. Prophetic signs present through action inspired by love are also necessary.
They concretely shape human society and give hope that the kingdom
will come. Immediately, the bishops reference the exodus story by stat-

---

[18] Ibid., preface.
[19] Ibid.
[20] Ibid., "Introduction to the Final Documents," no. 5

ing that liberation was liberation because it included delivery from *all* oppression in Egypt.

Recall that the Israelites were enslaved physically, forced to worship Pharaoh religiously, and required to work economically for the royal family along with the other 90 percent of the population. Thus, the delivery of the Israelites signified the passage from "less human conditions" to "more human conditions" in a multitude of ways. Drawing on liberation themes from numerous biblical passages and combining these with the definition of "integral development" from *Populorum progressio*, the bishops will embrace "an eager desire to integrate the scale of temporal values in a global vision of Christian faith."[21]

This was new language for the church. The bishops finally connected and integrated a particular vision of human development with the mission of Christianity. Later in the document, under the doctrinal basis for its reflection on justice, the bishops will affirm, "It is the same God who, in the fullness of time, sends the Son in the flesh, so that he might come to liberate all persons from the slavery to which sin has subjected them: hunger, misery, oppression, and ignorance—in a word, that injustice and hatred which have their origin in human selfishness."[22] Note the connection between sin and concrete social conditions of oppression in the world. The kingdom is prophetically announced when sin, understood as human oppression in every form, is defeated.

At the same time, the bishops were careful to make distinctions between the kingdom of God and historical development, but these distinctions will *not* lead to disconnection. They wrote, "We do not confuse temporal progress and the kingdom of Christ; nevertheless, the former, 'to the extent that it can contribute to the better ordering of human society, is of vital concern to the kingdom of God.'"[23] Reflecting on the doctrinal basis in the "Document on Justice," Medellín sums up the new call to engage the world in the following:

> The Christian quest for justice is a demand arising from biblical teaching. All humans are merely humble stewards of material goods. In the search for salvation we must avoid the dualism which separates temporal tasks from the work of sanctification. Although we are encompassed with imperfections, we are persons of hope. We have

[21] Ibid., no. 7.
[22] Ibid., "Document on Justice," no. 3.
[23] Ibid., no. 5.

faith that our love for Christ and for our brothers and sisters will not only be the great force liberating us from injustice and oppression, but also the inspiration for social justice, understood as a whole of life and as an impulse toward the integral growth of our countries.[24]

This end of dualism, this interest in the development of the world as important for the process of personal and social sanctification, has at its center structural change. Such change was necessary both in society and in the church.

Structural Changes in Society and the Church

Structures are those human institutions and realities that have an impact on every human life but of which we are often scarcely aware. We all participate in structures, yet none of us created them. The education system one has access to (or is denied) is a structure. The banking system one has access to (or is denied) is a structure. The health-care system one has access to (or is denied) is a structure. The level and extent of crime one is exposed to (or not) is a structure. In most cases, individual initiative or free will does not change or significantly affect the structures to which one is subjected. Structures simply exist. To say that structures must change in order for integral development to occur is to recognize the reality of structural sin—when institutions and realities are created and maintained in a manner which dehumanizes people. For example, the bishops saw structural sin in Latin America, mainly through the lack of health, education, and social welfare. To this end, they encouraged numerous social improvements such as equal access to quality education for men and women, intermediary structures between people and governments, stronger organizations for workers and peasants, an approach to business that took Catholic social teaching seriously, and land reform. These structures had an incredible impact on the quality of life in Latin America. For example, if I see a neighbor neglecting his or her children in North America, I have a Department of Children and Family Services I can call to report such behavior. This type of intermediary structure did not exist in Latin America in the late 1960s, nor do they exist in many of the countries even today.

The church saw the greatest deficiency in structural support for the organizing of marginalized peoples. In many countries, workers and peas-

---

[24] Ibid.

ants simply could not organize in a way that was necessary to empower them to negotiate in the workplace. Ever since Pope Leo XIII's social encyclical *Rerum novarum*, the church has always supported strong unions to represent workers' interests in various economic systems. In much of Latin America, the economic situation of the working person in the 1960s was eerily similar to the analysis of working people in 1891: "To this must be added that the hiring of labor and the conduct of trade are concentrated in the hands of comparatively few; so that a small number of very rich men have been able to lay upon the teeming masses of the laboring poor a yoke little better than that of slavery itself."[25] While great strides had been made among the working classes in Europe and the United States from the late 1800s until the 1960s, very little changed in Latin America during the same period. The call to strengthen unions of workers and associations of peasants thus represented a continuation of Catholic social teaching and was consistent with church tradition. What was different was the context into which this teaching would move. Nevertheless, the Latin American bishops were clear in their support of both workers and peasants. In Medellín's final "Document on Justice," the centrality of organized labor and peasants was noted:

> Therefore, in the intermediary professional structure the peasants' and workers' unions, to which the workers have a right, should acquire sufficient strength and power. Their associations will have a unified and responsible strength, to exercise the right of representation and participation on the levels of production and of national, continental, and international trade. They ought to exercise their right of being represented, also, on the social, economic, and political levels, where decisions are made which touch upon the common good. Therefore, the unions ought to use every means at their disposal to train those who are to carry out these responsibilities in moral, economic, and especially in technical matters.[26]

There is no doubt that in many countries of Latin America, workers and peasants usually subsisted on survival wages, often paid in food. *This new call to organize directly threatened the entrenched oligarchy whose economic interests depended on cheap and easily available labor.* Notably, the church mentioned the two competing economic systems of that day: free-market capitalism and Marxist collectivism. In the forms in which they existed, the church

---

[25] Pope Leo XIII, *Rerum novarum* (1891), no. 3.
[26] Hennelly, ed., "Document on Justice," no. 12.

claimed that both "militate against the dignity of the human person."[27] It is important to emphasize here that the church saw serious problems in both systems and canonized neither. But the bishops did not stop there.

> Seeking to live out what they taught, the bishops in Latin America also turned inward and acknowledged their own need for structural change. This change began by emphasizing the importance of ministry to the "base" or "people" who made up the majority of the Catholic community in each country and whom were poor. The bishops sought to do this not through a reliance on paternalistic charity, where the poor continued their dependence on the church or state, but through a process of education which would prove to have explosive consequences. Thus the document on justice asserted: "We wish to affirm that it is indispensable to form a social conscience and a realistic perception of the problems of the community and of social structures. We must awaken the social conscience and communal customs in all strata of society and professional groups regarding such values as dialogue and community living within the same group and relations with wider social groups (workers, peasants, professionals, clergy, religious, administrators, etc.)."[28]

This task of conscientization and social education ought to be integrated into joint pastoral action at various levels.[29] This conscientization, or the social education and response to the situation in which people find themselves, will not occur apart from or separate from the delivery of doctrine and the teaching on faith. It will occur *through* it. Thus, the bishops emphasized how important it was "To be certain that our preaching, liturgy, and catechesis take into account the social and community dimensions of Christianity, forming persons committed to world peace."[30] Integral development demanded an integration of the social and personal, the spiritual and worldly, the eternal and time-bound in the very essence of the church's mission. Integral development demanded integral evangelization.

Structural changes in the church began with the establishment of new diocesan offices, which included a Commission on Justice and Peace, a Caritas program which met the immediate needs of people (food, housing,

---

[27] Ibid., no. 10.

[28] Ibid., no. 17.

[29] Ibid., "Document on Peace," no. 17. It will be through the adoption of this mandate that Rutilio Grande, SJ, will enter into conflict with the oligarchy of El Salvador.

[30] Ibid., no. 24.

education), and various commissions of social action or pastoral service. In all cases, the church was adapting to its new mission in the world by making structural changes to its own organization—changes which ushered in a period of ecumenical dialogue, international collaboration, and unprecedented cooperation between lay and ordained.

The Church and Poverty

Perhaps most shockingly, the Second Conference of Latin American bishops took a long, critical look at itself and the role the church had assumed throughout Latin America and sought to change its relationship to wealth. This is evident in the following: "And complaints that the hierarchy, the clergy, the religious, are rich and allied with the rich also come to us. On this point we must make it clear that appearance is often confused with reality. Many causes have contributed to create this impression of a rich hierarchical church. The great buildings, the rectories and religious houses that are better than those of the neighbors, the often luxurious vehicles, the attire, inherited from other eras, have been some of those causes."[31]

Confronting this perception becomes very important in the document and rightly so, for in order to shift one's mission and pastoral work toward integral development, there must be an honest recognition of one's own privilege and wealth. The bishops acknowledged this reality with a self-critical honesty rarely found in episcopal conference documents.

> Within the context of the poverty and even of the wretchedness in which the great majority of the Latin American people live, we, bishops, priests, and religious, have the necessities of life and a certain security, while the poor lack that which is indispensable and struggle between anguish and uncertainty. And incidents are not lacking in which the poor feel that their bishops, or pastors and religious, do not really identify themselves with them, with their problems and afflictions, that they do not always support those who work with them or plead their cause.[32]

In response to this perception, the document reflected upon different forms of poverty—material, spiritual, and evangelical. The first form of poverty addressed is material poverty, which is "a lack of the goods of this

[31] Ibid., "Document on the Poverty of the Church," no. 2.
[32] Ibid., no. 3.

world necessary to live worthily as human beings, [and] is in itself evil. The prophets denounce this kind of poverty as contrary to the will of the Lord and most of the time as the fruit of human injustice and sin."[33] No person should aspire to this form of poverty. All people ought to respond or struggle to end this type of poverty.

The second type of poverty is spiritual poverty, an attitude that disposes a person to do God's will in the world. We are not our own meaning-givers; God is our meaning-giver. When this is so, while we can "value the goods of this world, we do not become attached to them and we recognize the higher value of the riches of the kingdom."[34] Finally, there is evangelical poverty. Evangelical poverty happens when those with the means to live a comfortable life choose simplicity and austerity in order to be in solidarity with those who suffer from material poverty in the world. Two benefits emerge from embracing evangelical poverty: first, one realizes what is most important by not focusing on material wealth, and second, one's life becomes a testimony which elevates an awareness of the suffering of so many others in the world. Evangelical poverty can take various forms. Among the celibate and ordained it may mean immersion at a level of material discomfort that would be difficult for families with small children. For laypeople, it may mean a way of living which affirms countercultural values such as simplicity, service, and an active engagement with marginalized peoples.

The bishops, inspired by the historical Jesus, encouraged the institutional churches to opt for the second and third types of poverty through choices that include "a distribution of resources and apostolic personnel that effectively gives preference to the poorest and most needy sectors and to those segregated for any cause whatsoever."[35] Additionally, the church must vocally denounce oppression and injustice—it can no longer passively tolerate realities that contradict the kingdom. More specifically, the bishops say of themselves: "We wish our houses and style of life to be modest, our clothing simple, our works and institutions functional, without show or ostentation. We ask priests and faithful to treat us in conformity with our mission as fathers and pastors, for we desire to renounce honorable titles belonging to another era."[36]

---

[33] Ibid., no. 4.
[34] Ibid.
[35] Ibid., no. 9.
[36] Ibid., no. 12.

Priests and religious are called in a special way to witness to this evangelical poverty and be a living testimony to the values the church holds most dear. The final impetus for living a life focused on the preferential option for the poor is that it reflects God's will, which is evident in the ministry of Jesus. Far from being unimportant, the way the church manages its own goods and wealth bespeaks its adherence to its mission in service of the kingdom. "This feeling of love of neighbor is evinced when one studies and works above all with the intention of performing a service for the community; when one organizes power and wealth for the benefit of the community."[37]

Preferential Option for the Poor

In all of the final documents of the conference, there is an emphasis to work for the organization and support the interests of the poor. Both personal and social sanctification, for these are never to be separated, have at their center a preferential option for the poor. "The Latin American church encourages the formation of national communities that reflect a global organization where all of the peoples *but more especially the lower classes have*, by means of territorial and functional structures, an active and receptive, creative and decisive participation in the construction of a new society."[38] There are two important points relative to this call. First, note that the call is not focused on individual acts of charity directed toward poor individuals but rather on participatory changes for entire classes of people. Second, the oligarchies of Latin America continued to thrive by ensuring that the poor or lower classes did not organize or use their collective voice in an effective manner.

The reason why the Catholic Church ultimately supported the political system of democracy was to give the oppressed classes a voice. Repeatedly, the bishops called for greater support in organizing workers and peasants. Those who have been powerless as individuals can assert their collective will when organized. As already noted, "in the intermediary professional structure the peasants' and workers' unions, to which the workers have a right, should acquire sufficient strength and power."[39] This was critical for the kind of development the church wanted to see, a development that required land reform and thus an organized peasant presence in rural

---

[37] Ibid., no. 17.
[38] Ibid., "Document on Justice," no. 7.
[39] Ibid., no. 12.

areas throughout Latin America. Note what is supported here. The peasant population, mainly passive and unorganized, becomes the focus of church pastoral work. This shift in focus will have significant social and political consequences both for the state and the church. Extremely cheap labor was a necessity for expected profit margins in many industries. To organize and empower workers represented an immediate threat to the power of vested interests and thus to profit margins.

> The Second Episcopal Conference wishes to voice its pastoral concern for the extensive peasant class, which, although included in the above remarks, deserves urgent attention because of its special characteristics. If it is true that one ought to consider the diversity of circumstances and resources in the different countries, there is no doubt that there is a common denominator in all of them: the need for the human promotion of the peasants and Amerindians. This uplifting will not be viable without an authentic and urgent reform of agrarian structures and policies. This structural change and its political implications go beyond a simple distribution of land. It is indispensable to make an adjudication of such lands, under detailed conditions which legitimize their occupation and insure their productivity for the benefit of the families and the national economy.[40]

A key aspect of this advocacy for the poor throughout Latin America will include what can be characterized as social and political conscientization. Put simply, the pastoral work of the church sought to engage peasants and the poor in such a way that they began to understand and act against both their poverty and the reasons for their poverty as contrary to God's will. This did *not* happen by teaching them in the traditional sense of depositing knowledge in their minds; it occurred much more dynamically, through an encounter among and within the people of God.

Theologically, the intent of Medellín was best captured later by Archbishop Oscar Romero just before he was killed. It is ironic that while his thought is useful here to summarize Medellín, initially Romero vigorously resisted the application of the final documents in his own diocese. Later, after his slow and steady conversion toward the spirit of Medellín and through a growing contact he enjoyed with the marginalized peoples of El Salvador, he argued forcefully for the ways in which the preferential option for the poor were beneficial to the church.

---

[40] Ibid., no. 14.

In his address to Leuven University, on the occasion of receiving an honorary doctorate shortly before he was assassinated, he stated that the church enjoys three concrete benefits from embracing a preferential option for the poor.[41] The first benefit for the church is a greater awareness of sin. This may seem odd as a benefit, but Romero understood, with the bishops at Medellín, that the greatest deficiency of the Roman Catholic Church in Latin America was its own distance from the vast majority of the people of God (the church) who suffered from the effects of sin through persecution, oppression, and, for many, death. The kingdom cannot be advanced if the anti-kingdom is not confronted and denounced.[42] Just as Jesus entered into the world of the people whom he would save, he also entered into their suffering, persecution, misunderstanding, and, ultimately, death. This awareness of sin, according to Romero, was not an intellectual awareness but an *experiential* awareness. Thus, one can understand the slogan of his episcopacy—S*entir con la Iglesia*—to feel with the church. It is only possible through *accompanimiento*, when the church as the people of God accompanies its most vulnerable members in their lives and with their burdens. Only then can the church begin to understand that sin and death subjugate human beings and this represents a rejection of the kingdom of God. As Phillip Berryman described so poignantly, pastoral ministry in Latin America was emotionally and spiritually brutal: "To baptize a child who is dying of an easily preventable disease is heart-wrenching; to do so repeatedly is radicalizing."[43]

The second benefit for the church through an embrace of the preferential option for the poor was a deeper understanding of the incarnation of Jesus Christ. The incarnation had been understood traditionally as the "descent" of the second person of the Trinity, the Son, into human history. But what does this mean? Why is that important? Its significance lies in the nature of that descent as self-sacrificial love. When persons, in whatever form they are able, leave power, security, contentment, happiness, and relative fulfillment to enter into the pain and suffering of the world's vulnerable in order to love and humanize them, they imitate the action of Christ in the incarnation. It is only through experiencing the effects of sin that one comes to understand the great gift of God in the incarnation of the Son.

---

[41] Oscar Romero, "The Political Dimension of the Faith from the Perspective of the Option for the Poor," Leuven University, February 2, 1980, in Alfred T. Hennelly, ed., *Liberation Theology: A Documentary History*, 292–303.

[42] Kingdom and anti-kingdom language is from Jon Sobrino, SJ, *Jesus the Liberator*.

[43] Berryman, *Stubborn Hope: Religion, Politics, and Revolution in Central America*, 13.

Finally, as a result of the first two benefits, the church enjoyed a deeper faith in God and Christ. Who is God and what does it mean to be faithful to God? God is that person who has moved close to us through the person of Jesus of Nazareth. He descended into our sin and suffering to love and welcome us into the presence of unconditional love, which is both personal and social, a love which characterizes the kingdom of God. This kingdom is the space and time where God's will and human will converge in a common unity, a community. This kingdom begins here in human history but will ultimately find fulfillment in the fullness of the presence of God.

From the Regional to the Local Church

As evidenced in this chapter, a change in the way the church understood itself, its pastoral mission to the world, and its new priorities in light of this new understanding and mission was underway in the 1960s. Beginning with Vatican II and moving forward through *Populorum progressio*, the church articulated this new vision clearly. At a regional level, this vision was accepted and articulated anew by the Latin American bishops at Medellín. Finally, it is possible to see how such a vision articulated by both Rome and the bishops of Latin America was concretely applied in a local context. For such a context, we now turn to the small Central American country of El Salvador.

Perhaps no other person represented the new pastoral strategy of the bishops at Medellín better than a relatively unknown Jesuit priest named Fr. Rutilio Grande, SJ. Rutilio, or Tilo to the people he served, was an intense and compassionate Jesuit who was assassinated by Salvadoran security forces in 1977, *specifically* for the pastoral work he enacted. This work was done in strict obedience to the tradition already outlined in *Gaudium et spes* and especially the final documents from Medellín. In order to understand this priest and the ministry he lived out, we first need to know something about him and the country of El Salvador.

Questions for Discussion:

1. According to *Populorum progressio*, how did Vatican II change the structure of the Catholic Church? Why is this important?

2. What is meant by the term "integral development"? Why is this important?

3. What consequences flow from the central teaching of Catholic social teaching: The recent council reiterated this truth: "God intended the earth and everything in it for the use of all human beings and peoples. Thus, under the leadership of justice and in the company of charity, created goods should flow fairly to all"?

4. How does *Populorum progressio* understand the right to own land as well as the criteria for a just revolution?

5. What were the different kinds of poverty outlined toward the end of this chapter? How were the bishops at Medellín self-critical? Why was this important?

6. How did Oscar Romero link Christology to the mission of the church in his Leuven University address?

Part 3

Ecclesiology in Context:
The New Evangelization

Chapter 5

Rutilio Grande, SJ:
Pastoral Formation and Early Ministry

There was another issue that he was constantly giving us guidance on: resignation. The grandmothers, the old men, the boys and girls, were always going to the priest with their problems, to see what suggestions he could offer: "Padre, my house burned down," "Padre, my cow strangled itself," "Padre, I don't have work," "Padre, my wife is sick and I don't have any money." Then, drawing on what he'd heard in confessions, he would go and give advice. When he got to homilies he gave from that famous pulpit, he always said, "Blessed are the poor, for theirs is the kingdom of heaven," "Blessed are those who weep, for they shall be comforted. . . ."

And so you'd say to yourself: it really is quite important to be poor; it's a privilege to be poor, right? And that's just what we believed. The priest also said: "Blessed are the poor, because while they have suffering and sorrow in this life, they'll have joy in the next life. Because when you suffer in patience, my beloved sons and daughters, God is taking note of all your sufferings, and he doesn't miss anything. And when you reach the house of the Lord, on the day of your death, he's going to send the choirs and angels and the blessed Virgin to bring you, and they're going to lift you up and put you on a throne that's already made and waiting for you. Because every one of you there is already in a special place in the kingdom of heaven."

"On the other hand, my beloved sons and daughters," I remember he would say "never desire what others have, because that is bad. Because, look, covetousness is bad, my beloved sons and daughters. He who covets will not be saved. You must accept what God gives. Because God already knows who he wants to give to, and who he doesn't want to give to. And if he hasn't given us anything, he knows why. Because if now you're a bunch of drunks, if you gamble your money even now, when you're poor, what would you be like, beloved sons and daughters, if you had money? You'd be big drunks, you'd

be spendthrifts. You'd go around ruining lots of people. But God knows that, depriving you of that opportunity, so you'll stay in your homes, calm and peaceful, just as God desires."[1]

Rutilio Grande was born on July 5, 1928, in El Paisnal, El Salvador, the youngest of six children. When he was four years old, his parents separated and later divorced. For financial reasons, his father left El Salvador to look for work in Honduras, and Rutilio was effectively raised by his older brother and grandmother. Due to the separation of his parents, the family went from a position of relative stability in the community to poverty in a short period of time.[2] His oldest brother, Flavio, assumed responsibility for the household, and together the children worked a small plot of land where they planted corn, beans, and rice. The three acres the children farmed was insufficient to meet their needs. Like so many other rural peasant families, they were poor and rented another piece of land to augment their meager production. The typical obligation for the use of land was a bushel of corn per 1.5 acres as well as delivering five hundred sticks of firewood to the landowner's home—the equivalent of one week of work out of a month. According to the only Spanish biography written about Rutilio, this system of payment was one of many exploitation mechanisms used against poor peasants. Says author Rodolfo Cardenal, "Many times what was required by the owner of the land exceeded half the production. This type of arrangement was due to competition between the many landless families who were forced to accept any agreements with the owners of the land available so as to secure a plot to 'get by.'"[3]

Rutilio was a quiet child who stayed in his house the majority of the time, leaving only when his grandmother asked him to run errands but always returning quickly. He didn't play with many children at school and was generally perceived as withdrawn. At four years old, with no mother or father, he rarely received the care or nurturing he needed from those in charge of his well-being. Early in his life, the elderly in El Paisnal recall what they recognized as outward signs of his vocation. His favorite game was to set up altars in the corners of his house and play "church." He would also lead other children in the way of the cross on his patio. Much of his faith was received from and formed by his grandmother, a woman "of the

[1] Maria Lopez Vigil, *Don Lito of El Salvador* (Maryknoll, NY: Orbis Books, 1990), 30–31.
[2] Rodolfo Cardenal, *Historia de una Esperanza: Vida de Rutilio Grande*, Colección Teología Latinoamericana 4 (San Salvador: UCA Editores, 2002), 22–23, translation mine.
[3] Ibid., 24.

people, strong and tough."[4] She was well-known as one who prayed in the community and, similarly, young Rutilio also became pious and devout.

According to Cardenal, the first encounter Rutilio had with the archbishop of San Salvador had important repercussions for him. There was always great excitement when the archbishop came to town to perform confirmations and Rutilio shared in that. When Archbishop Chavez y Gonzalez arrived in El Paisnal, Rutilio went with his grandmother to greet him. After greeting the visiting archbishop, Rutilio was asked if he knew how to pray. "He quickly said yes and stated that he knew the Our Father and the entire Rosary."[5] The archbishop followed up by asking him about Christian doctrine and Rutilio answered satisfactorily to all of his inquiries. Rutilio made quite an impression on Archbishop Chavez, for later he invited Rutilio to accompany him to the next community. Upon their return, he asked the family if he could take Rutilio to seminary in the capital. And because his father was still working in Honduras, his brother Flavio gave familial permission. With that, Rutilio left with the archbishop.

Rutilio left El Paisnal at the age of thirteen and entered the seminary in El Salvador, completely abandoning his complex family situation and the community in which he had been raised. Rutilio became someone very special to the archbishop. He would not only become a seminarian but also serve as a future prefect and professor at the seminary. "This seminary would be the cause of many loves and many great pains over many years."[6] Archbishop Chavez became like another father to him, and Rutilio spoke often of their close and special relationship later in his life.

Rutilio's life in seminary revolved around three basic fundamental realities—piety, studies, and discipline. Piety was understood to be comprised of traditional practices throughout the day, the week, the month, and the year. Rutilio was educated within the minor seminary in this traditional structure, which dovetailed perfectly with what he had learned and practiced with his grandmother.[7] What mattered most in this religiosity was "pious punctuality." "Each seminarian was assigned a fixed location in the chapel from which to recite common prayers with a voice that was slow and devout, neither too high nor too low, that was consistent and natural, and where their attendance and behavior could be monitored."[8]

---

[4] Ibid., 27.
[5] Ibid., 32.
[6] Ibid.
[7] Ibid., 36.
[8] Ibid.

The entire rhythm of daily life was marked by these acts of piety. In addition, each seminarian was expected to make a confession of his sins every week with his spiritual director. One day a month was dedicated to a retreat, and each year, at the beginning of their academic studies, all seminarians would participate in an eight-day retreat with the Exercises of St. Ignatius of Loyola.

Academic study was a serious and complementary obligation to piety. In addition to normal classes, seminarians were required to study at certain times. They were prohibited from reading or using books outside of the assigned texts, and they always entered and left class in a silent line. "The well educated seminarian was distinguished by their silence, their composure, their demonstration of mutual respect and a kind modesty in asking and answering."[9] The curriculum was divided into two areas—inferior and superior, which corresponded with minor seminary and major seminary. The first section was three years of grammar and rhetoric. The second period of studies required three years of philosophy and four years of theology. Rutilio was not an exceptional student but was above average.[10] He seemed to excel later in his academic formation, especially during his studies in Europe and, later, South America.

The third and final dimension of seminarian life was referred to as "discipline." These were actions that regulated seminary life and whose principles were "to protect the children from all outside influences, fill them with piety, motivate them by words and promote the growth of their vocations until their maturity."[11] The purpose of discipline was to help their fragile humanity create habits that would lead to good works. This was accomplished through the repetition of acts. "Therefore, daily life was rigidly demarcated by obligations which could not be ignored without permission from the prefect or his delegate."[12] Discipline was enacted through a long list of prohibitions that framed the life of a seminarian. Seminarians were absolutely dependent on the prefect or his delegate for all issues of internal seminary life and in all of his contact with the outside world.

Consequently, through the practice of isolating vocations in order to preserve them, those in formation were practically locked in the seminary under strict supervision. The only reason most seminarians ever left was

---

[9] Ibid., 37.
[10] Cardenal actually lists his grades from seminary on pp. 38–39 of his biography.
[11] Ibid., 39.
[12] Ibid., 40.

either to visit the bishop or to go to the doctor, and they were always accompanied by someone. The month-long annual vacation could be spent with their families but always under the supervision of their local parish priest, who always reported on how the seminarians comported themselves. While on vacation, they were expected to fulfill all the required acts of piety as if they were in seminary.

During his later years in seminary, Rutilio was chosen as the "watchman" or, in medieval terms, the "beadle" for his dormitory and for the choir. It seems that he was a zealous practitioner of the piety and discipline required in seminary and therefore was chosen to oversee others.[13]

Jesuit Formation and Academic Studies

In 1945, at the age of seventeen, following the conclusion of his last year of minor seminary, Rutilio entered the Jesuit novitiate, beginning a long period of studies outside of El Salvador. Rutilio was a Jesuit who struggled with sickness throughout his formation, where he suffered at least two nervous breakdowns. Cardenal speculates that his sensitive mental health was due to a weak physical constitution that resulted from malnutrition in early infancy—as he himself would attest to in later years. To make matters worse, the diabetes he would develop later imposed serious limitations on his pastoral activity.

According to his diary, Rutilio left El Salvador for Caracas, Venezuela, on September 10, 1945, to enter the novitiate since there was no Jesuit novitiate in Central America. His official entry into the Society of Jesus occurred on September 23, just a few weeks later. Rutilio showed signs of having a serious vocation for the Society of Jesus. Initially, the impressions of the master of novices were very positive; he had no negative comments about Rutilio and his entry to the Society. In the beginning of his time in the Society of Jesus, Rutilio expressed a desire to be a missionary to the East. The spiritual director of the seminary as well as the master of novices recommended, however, that he cultivate a spirit of indifference to these desires. "Indifference" in the lexicon of Jesuit spirituality is best understood as an openness to being called to wherever and however God wishes to use one's gifts for God's purposes. This openness is central to what is known as the "foundation" of the spiritual exercises. Says St. Ignatius of Loyola:

[13] Ibid.

Human beings are created to love God with their whole heart and soul, essentially by loving and serving their neighbors. In this way they participate in God's plan to bring all creation to completion and so arrive at their own ultimate fulfillment (eternal life). The other things on the face of the earth are created for human beings, and to help them to pursue the end for which they are created.

From this it follows that we ought to use these things to the extent that they will help us toward that end, and free ourselves from them to the extent that they hinder us from it.

For this reason it is necessary to make ourselves *indifferent* to all created things, in regard to everything which is left to our free will and is not forbidden, in such a way that, for our part, we not seek health rather than sickness, riches rather than poverty, honor rather than dishonor, a long life rather than a short one, and so on in all other matters, wanting and choosing only that which leads more to the end for which we are created.[14]

Although he accepted the recommendation to practice indifference, Rutilio repeatedly stated he felt called to the Eastern mission of the Society. He even shared this ideal with Archbishop Chavez who wholeheartedly supported him. The master of novices at the time was very satisfied with the Central American novices who, in addition to another Salvadoran besides Rutilio, hailed from Nicaragua and Panama. Rutilio's biographer thought it important to note that this novice director was extremely strict. "His strict and scrupulous personality probably was a critical influence on this young novice."[15]

In September 1947, at the age of nineteen, Rutilio pronounced his vows of poverty, chastity, and obedience to the Society of Jesus. In October 1947, he left Caracas and arrived in Quito, Ecuador, to begin his studies in classical humanities, which he completed in 1950. The following three years were spent as a professor in a minor seminary in El Salvador where he taught sacred history, history of the Americas, the history of El Salvador, and writing.

Shortly after that he was sent to Spain to study philosophy. It was during this time that Rutilio suffered his first nervous breakdown. Various

[14] Dean Brackley, *The Call to Discernment in Troubled Times: New Perspectives on the Transformative Wisdom of Ignatius of Loyola* (New York: Crossroad Publishing, 2004), 10–11. I use Fr. Brackley's translation of the First Principle and Foundation because it fits perfectly with how Rutilio would later come to understand his own spirituality.

[15] Cardenal, *Historia de una Esperanza: Vida de Rutilio Grande*, 50.

reasons and diagnoses were given for his state of mental health—everything from poor early childhood nutrition and anxiety resulting from his isolation as a child to scruples and an overly rigid religious life. Whatever the reason, Rutilio's intensity had both mental and physical consequences, which resulted in a period of convalescence and recovery.

After his studies in philosophy, Rutilio studied theology for four years and finally finished his studies in 1959 at the age of thirty-one. In July 1959, he was ordained a priest in Burgos, Spain. A second period of deep anxiety and mental struggle commenced upon taking final vows with the Jesuits. Rutilio was concerned with whether his internal disposition accurately reflected the promises he would make. "The doubt associated with the existence or non-existence of true and absolute intention in relation to the reception of the three vows stubbornly persisted, provoking renewed anxiety and insecurity."[16] This second breakdown not only affected Rutilio's mental health but made his physical health quite fragile as well—both in the short and long term.

Rutilio's ordination was celebrated in his native country with his first Mass in El Paisnal—a community he last left as the son of a very poor family. He returned with a much higher and more respected social position. For this reason, the community was very proud of "their" priest who had been born and raised among them. His neighbors gave him gifts, such as sweet bread, cornbread, corn, coffee, and mangos, in order to demonstrate their affection. At the Mass he was accompanied by the archbishop who first recognized his vocation, as well as old friends from the seminary.

Following ordination, Rutilio made it clear that he wanted to be considered a part of his community and not above it. "When he visited El Paisnal, he categorically rejected any special treatment because he wanted to be treated and recognized as he had always been."[17] Members of the community recall that "He didn't like to be called 'don Tilo' or 'Padre Tilo,' no; he was always just 'Tilo.'"[18] As for the food, he liked whatever he was given; he wasn't particular about that at all. Furthermore, "He profoundly disliked the huge sacrifices peasants made to feed him special things outside of their normal diet." He became used to saying that he came to share whatever was in the house, that this was fine with him. He expressly stated that "he didn't want to be like 'fat priests who eat

[16] Ibid., 70.
[17] Ibid., 42.
[18] Ibid.

at the cost of the hunger of others. The little hen would be better for the malnourished children of the peasants than for him.'"[19]

The people in El Paisnal soon began to understand over time what kind of priest Rutilio had become. Whenever he visited, the elderly people in the community would fight over who would offer Rutilio hospitality in their houses. He did not sleep or eat in the convent; rather, he sought out the homes of neighbors. "To avoid the dislike of Cupertina Hernandez, who lived in the neighborhood of San Jose, one of the poorest areas of the community, and Virginia Guzman, who lived on the main plaza, he would take turns, religiously, living in one house and then the other."[20] In his later years, diabetes kept him from eating or drinking whatever he wanted when he visited. When this happened the peasants of El Paisnal learned that Rutilio would only eat cooked vegetables and corn coffee. For nearly all his life, Rutilio fought to be of service to his community of El Paisnal. Even though he would travel and study around the world, it was for the people of his own community and for the people of El Salvador that he always struggled.

Following the conclusion of his studies in theology in 1959, Rutilio immediately left for El Salvador where he began two years of teaching in the Archdiocesan Seminary of San Salvador. He was designated as prefect of discipline. As a result of performing this role, change in his exterior life and spiritual life was noted. Unhappy with the previous prefect who was rigid and theoretical, the rector of the community appointed Rutilio to be more practical—and, possibly, more pastoral. Rutilio proceeded in a different way while he served as prefect of discipline, using a style quite different from the usual application of the internal norms associated with seminary life. He confronted all the vices like tobacco, radio, film, and other things in a different way. "He was not afraid of anything and in everything he tried to proceed moderately."[21] According to Cardenal, the case of the cassock was a good example.

Archbishop Belloso had ordained that the cassock, according to canon law, be worn at all times by seminarians. Because of this, seminarians used the cassock all day, both in the cafeteria and in class. For Rutilio and the rector of the seminary, this rule resulted in discomfort, a high cost, and contributed to a lack of personal hygiene. For these reasons, they decided to not require the cassock during "ordinary time" but only for solemn oc-

[19] Ibid.
[20] Ibid.
[21] Ibid., 99.

casions.[22] Contrary to the rigid and authoritarian style of previous prefects of discipline, Rutilio offered friendly, brief, and clear codes of conduct. He delegated authority and autonomy to various levels for ceremonial tasks and, because of this, was quite successful in creating more initiative and responsibility on the part of seminarians.[23]

In 1962, Rutilio returned briefly to Spain to complete his final stage of Jesuit formation, one that had been put off due to his delicate health. Rutilio finished this final stage in 1963 by completing a course of studies at a pastoral institute called *Lumen Vitae* in Brussels, Belgium. Writing home to friends, he stated at the conclusion of his studies there, "Frankly, I am satisfied, very satisfied."[24]

It was at *Lumen Vitae* that Rutilio would acquire the fundamental pastoral orientations that would later help him do his work so effectively in the seminary. Rutilio was influenced at this time in particular by the renewed liturgical biblical spirituality of the Benedictines of San Andres, with whom he spent Holy Week in 1964.[25] This experience caused him great restlessness. Many of Rutilio's friends indicate that his *first* conversion came at this moment: "Very probably in this moment his fundamental lines of pastoral action matured. Certainly a part of this epoch in pastoral theological development was to always look for the greatest participation possible by the base or least empowered part of a community and to never proceed autonomously or without hearing the community."[26]

When Rutilio began teaching at the seminary of San Jose de la Montaña in San Salvador after his studies in Belgium, he served as prefect of theology in 1965 and 1966. There he taught a variety of subjects, including liturgy and catechesis, pastoral theology, and introduction to the mystery of Christ (philosophy).[27] He especially enjoyed the social sciences as well. Priestly ministry was of particular concern to Rutilio. He frequently organized pastoral trips and liturgical functions with the sole objective of maintaining interest in things pastoral for the seminarians.[28] According to Cardenal, it was thanks to Rutilio that the pastoral dimension of seminarian training became such an important part of formation. Rutilio was responsible for renovating the formal retreats as part of his work within

[22] Ibid., 99–100.
[23] Ibid., 100.
[24] Ibid., 73.
[25] Ibid.
[26] Ibid.
[27] Ibid., 101.
[28] Ibid.

the seminary. He began by offering workshops on analyzing one's own reality through the method of "see, judge, act."[29]

Rutilio and Pastoral Formation

The "see, judge, act" method made famous by the bishops of Latin America at Medellín was explicitly introduced by Pope John XXIII in *Mater et magistra* in 1961: "There are three stages which should normally be followed in the reduction of social principles into practice. First, one reviews the concrete situation; secondly, one forms a judgment on it in the light of these same principles; thirdly, one decides what in the circumstances can and should be done to implement these principles. These are the three stages that are usually expressed in the three terms: look, judge, act."[30]

This method would be employed and applied to Latin America by the Latin American bishops at the Medellín conference in 1968. As already demonstrated, the final documents of that conference use the "see, judge, act" method in their treatment of "justice," "peace," and the "poverty of the church." For Rutilio to use this method as early as the mid-1960s indicates that he was aware of new approaches to pastoral theology. This would place him on the cutting edge of the implementation of the Second Vatican Council as it was being worked out by the magisterium in his context. Perhaps his example was prophetic. The bishops' conference at Medellín would state the following goal only a couple of years later: "To achieve in our schools, seminaries, and universities a healthy critical sense of the social situation and foster the vocation of service. We also consider very efficacious the diocesan and national campaigns that mobilize the faithful and social organizations, leading them to a similar reflection."[31]

In addition to emphasizing the pastoral role of the priest as well as the "see, judge, act" method promulgated by Medellín, Rutilio persuaded all the formators of seminaries, especially the Jesuits, to participate actively in the work of pastoral formation. Recall that the formational approach to protecting vocations had essentially been isolation. Rutilio would argue for the opposite approach. This former educational philosophy of the seminary reflected the perception that reality was static and dualistic. Part of the world (the seminary) was "sacred," while the other part (outside the

---

[29] Ibid., 103.

[30] John XXIII, *Mater et magistra*, no. 236.

[31] "Document on Peace," no. 25, in *Liberation Theology: A Documentary History*, ed. Alfred T. Hennelly (Maryknoll, NY: Orbis Books, 1994).

seminary) was "secular" and therefore dangerous to the spiritual development of seminarians. After Vatican II, we know that everyone was called to holiness—both in the church and the world, and especially where the two met in pastoral ministry. The archbishop of San Salvador at the time, Archbishop Chavez, showed great interest in seminarians having direct contact with the pastoral reality of the archdiocese from the beginning of their time in seminary. In fact, the seminary and the pastoral reality of the archdioceses would maintain close contact.[32] Thanks in part to Rutilio's efforts, the model for pastoral formation would shift from isolation to immersion.

An important experiment in pastoral formation was planned and enacted by Rutilio in the mid-1960s. During the allotted vacation time each year, Rutilio gathered mission groups of seminarians from all over the country and immersed them into direct contact with particular communities. The purpose of these immersions was not to prepare children for Communion or to hear confessions, nor to attack Protestant groups working there. These had all been traditional means and motives for pastoral engagement. The purpose was to immerse seminarians into the reality and the peoples they would serve. While this immersion may not seem radical to an observer today, it was radical for seminarian preparation at the time. One major fruit of this experiment was that working in pastoral teams and utilizing teamwork caused a notable transformation for seminarians in the spirituality of living out their vocations. In each of these missions, Jesuits joined the immersions and accompanied the seminarians. In the final immersion, Jesuit novices participated as well.

Prior to leaving on the mission trips, Rutilio prepared seminarians for four days while still at the seminary. He introduced them into an intense atmosphere of personal and communal prayer. The success of the mission would be realized from this commitment to prayer, as it was oriented toward the service of poor communities. "In the Eucharistic celebration, each seminarian participating made an offering of money to the poor."[33] He then organized them into five work groups, with each group covering a particular, predetermined zone of the community. In each group there were theologians, philosophers, and roughly eighteen to twenty seminarians. Each team had a leader, an assistant, and people with a variety of pastoral experiences.

[32] Cardenal, *Historia de una Esperanza: Vida de Rutilio Grande*, 104.
[33] Ibid., 105.

"The essential principle of the village mission was to offer the perspective of service and humility to the community of Quezaltepeque."[34] Rutilio carefully instructed the mission teams that the purpose of their mission was not to teach a system of abstract doctrine or moral theology but first to announce that Christ is present, real, and alive. The purpose was explained this way: "the first contact with the people was to be characterized by a human encounter; to try to enter into their reality in order to leave with a common reality."[35] The principal objective of the catechesis was to bring about an experience of the living God for the people where they lived.

The missions began with a visit to nearly every living space in the community, greeting people, and getting to know the area. At times, the teams played sports with the people, but the purpose was to get to know them and the reality they lived by simply spending time with them. The mission group would meet daily after common prayer to evaluate and plan activities for that day. At each meeting, the group members reviewed the stages of engagement with the community, agreed to the norms of engagement, and discussed various points of view and any difficulties that arose. The group divided up work between subgroups of seminarians responsible for areas such as liturgy, sports, and catechism. On the whole, seminarians carried the weight of the mission, while priests advised and empowered.[36] The general scheme of the mission integrated catechesis in the morning with the children of the parish, prearranged visits to homes of parishioners by pairs of seminarians in the afternoons, and established the formation of youth groups as well as groups of catechists in the evenings. Eucharistic ministry and lectors were also educated in all five zones of the community. And finally, the evening included ministry for adults, offering catechesis appropriate to age and gender.[37]

Rutilio taught the seminarians through these immersion missions that the church and its priestly ministry must meet people in their real lives, where they live, work, and play. God is experienced there in the real lives of parishioners. It is in the real world where the mission of the church is realized, not simply in the church building. Although these mission groups met with great success in the years of 1965 to 1967, the bishops did not like losing contact with their seminarians during the weeks of

---

[34] Ibid. Quezaltepeque is located about fifteen kilometers from San Salvador in the municipality of La Libertad.

[35] Ibid.

[36] Ibid., 106.

[37] Ibid.

vacation. According to Cardenal, the bishops, for whatever reason, wanted the seminarians working on the urgent pastoral needs in their own dioceses. So the immersion missions came to an abrupt end. But through the missions Rutilio learned some very important lessons—lessons that would serve him in his future ministry.

An Experiment in El Paisnal

Throughout his time teaching and forming seminarians during the sixties, Rutilio would often return home to his own community of El Paisnal, when short vacations allowed him to do so. His ministry to people there put him in direct contact with the tremendous problems they faced in all facets of their lives, especially the deep and dehumanizing poverty that characterized their lives. He came to know the struggles in their faith lives. He began to understand the challenges in their self-understanding of their lives. He witnessed them struggle for the basic necessities of living. At the same time, Rutilio worked with groups of people from El Paisnal who lived in the capital of San Salvador. His objective was to do something to help his poor community. Additionally, he began to speak out against political corruption and those elected officials who promised "heaven and earth" and then quickly forgot their promises as soon as the elections were over.[38] During his many visits to El Paisnal, Rutilio began organizing the pastoral outreach of the church. Some of his efforts included organizing men's and women's groups of parishioners, an association of Christian women, youth groups, and catechism classes for First Communion. He also encouraged a devotion to the Sacred Heart of Jesus among the people and tried to improve the central plaza of the town.

At the center of Rutilio's approach to ministry in El Paisnal was a focus on the *adoradores* or worshipers who had a deep commitment to the spirituality of eucharistic adoration. Their principal action of faith was all-night adoration of the Blessed Sacrament. Because of their deep piety, Rutilio thought that this group would be the best people to ground his ministry to the community. A prerequisite for membership in this group was six months of sobriety (no alcohol) and no history of fighting. Rutilio introduced this committed group of parishioners to Bible study and discussion groups where they would converse about hundreds of exemplary stories from the New Testament. These groups spread to other hamlets

[38] Ibid., 109.

around El Paisnal and began to organize with presidents, vice presidents, secretaries, treasurers, etc.

The principal activity of these groups continued to be acts of adoration and traditional piety. Rutilio saw in these committed community leaders the spirit and force he wished to harness for evangelization. His hope was that the intentional celebration of the Eucharist would result in a "mystical community action" that would mirror the early Christian communities where all would sell what they had and put it at the feet of the apostles to be distributed as was necessary.[39] The power of the eucharistic celebration, for Rutilio, was highly explosive. His hope was that devotion to the Eucharist would result in unity, community, and greater fraternity. This momentum would then translate into a life of action with the dynamism to transform a person integrally (economically, sociologically, politically, spiritually) as well as the community in which he or she lived.

This approach that Rutilio promoted tried to blend the integral development championed by Paul VI in *Populorum progressio* with the traditional piety related to sacraments and their power. Approaching exemplars in the community, as indicated by their piety, was a belief that sacraments had the power to transform both people and their reality. However, something was missing. What began as a powerful experiment in pastoral activity and community development seemed to veer off its intended goals. Rutilio began this pastoral work in El Paisnal in 1968, but by 1970 the groups seemed to have lost their effectiveness. Grounding the pastoral outreach in eucharistic piety resulted in a line of narrow moralizing, communal prayer, religious acts, and Scripture discussion. While this centered on what a cooperative society would be, it did not create the desired change. It seemed as though Rutilio's dreams of social and spiritual transformation would not be fulfilled.

The intuition that founded this pastoral approach, while it was not perfect, was an embodiment of the changes introduced by Medellín. "Our pastoral mission is essentially a service of encouraging and educating the conscience of believers, to help them to perceive the responsibilities of their faith in their personal life and in their social life."[40] That intuition was to empower lay leaders in the community to deepen the faith life of all, in collaboration with priests and bishops. The missing element was a way of informing and forming people to respond to their own situation motivated and sustained by their faith commitments. As the social

---

[39] Ibid., 110–11.
[40] "Document on Justice," no. 6, in Hennelly, *Liberation Theology*.

situation deteriorated in El Salvador—especially in poor communities—responding to that reality became ever more important. From personal experience Rutilio understood well the social reality within which he ministered. He manifested this understanding in a short article that illustrated the "see, judge, act" method he taught the seminarians.

"On Violence and the Social Situation"

In 1970, prior to a serious conflict and subsequent disunion with seminary leadership over the type of formation seminarians should have, Rutilio wrote a short piece in *Estudios Centroamericanos* (ECA). The article provided insight into Rutilio's pastoral approach and his effort to integrate social analysis as part of his formation method.[41] "Social analysis" is a way of understanding society through the use of the social sciences such as sociology, anthropology, and economics. While he certainly focused his ministry in El Paisnal on the piety of the community *adoradores*, he was not ignorant of the social situation in which he was working. In fact, his understanding was nuanced, based on a thorough education and informed by the latest in social science research. Additionally, he began to assert, as did *Gaudium et spes*, that the church's competency must extend into social transformation in order for the kingdom of God to embrace the whole person and all people.[42]

Rutilio began his article with a pointed critique of priestly ministry. The social doctrine of the church was not known by "those priests who stay in the sacristy, who speak of love and charity, who teach doctrine to children, who give vouchers for the parish movie and who distribute alms to the needy among their faithful."[43] Obviously there was disagreement among priests about the best model for ministry. Rutilio made the distinction between those who tried to implement Catholic social teaching and those who perceived charity on the model of paternalism as the

---

[41] Rutilio Grande, "Violencia y Situación Social," in *Estudios Centro Americas* 262 (1970): 369–75.

[42] *Gaudium et spes*, no. 40: "In pursuing its own salvific purpose not only does the church communicate divine life to humanity but in a certain sense it casts the reflected light of that divine life over all the earth, notably in the way it heals and elevates the dignity of the human person, in the way it consolidates society, and endows people's daily activity with a deeper sense and meaning. The church, then, believes that through each of its members and its community as a whole it can help to make the human family and its history still more human."

[43] Grande, "Violence and the Social Situation," 369, translation mine.

best way to minister. This critique was made even clearer when different interpretations of priestly ministry were put forth.

> Some say that a priest should be a good man who does not go where he is not called. And they are right; this is how a priest ought to be, among other things.
>
> But it happens that they do get called about very serious things and they become involved in things not mentioned above, and because of this, there are those who criticize and accuse these priests of meddling, of being revolutionaries, and so on.
>
> It is often said by some that the priest should not get involved in economic or social matters. If he does, he will be called a communist. They will give the following reasons: if you are an engineer you shouldn't get involved with morality, in the same way a priest should not involve himself in economic or social matters. But the comparison is not valid, for while technical things pertain to the engineer and the economist, etc., social and economic realities are necessary to be human, they pertain to all people, and are thus a part of morality.[44]

Rutilio proceeded by arguing from tradition to support his approach to pastoral engagement with social and economic reality. He began with Leo XIII (1878–1903) who insisted that social issues are more than simply economic as they have a human dimension that cannot be ignored: "Some say, and this error is fairly widespread, that the social question is a purely economic one, conversely, we are certain that the social question is principally moral and religious. For this reason, it should be settled in accordance with the laws of morality and religion."[45] Even when issues were overwhelmingly about topics related to work, wages, and labor strikes, Pius X (1903–1914) argued that there is a moral dimension that must be addressed by the church. "The social question and the controversies surrounding it are derived from the nature and duration of labor, the level of wages, and workers strikes, and these are not only of an economic nature. For this reason, they cannot be resolved outside the authority of the Church."[46] For those who wanted to separate the economic and moral dimensions of human being, he cited Pius XI (1922–1929): "It is an error to affirm that the economic order and the moral order are so distant from

---

[44] Ibid., 369.

[45] Leo XIII, *Graves de communi* (1901), no. 10, as quoted in Grande, "Violence and the Social Situation."

[46] Pius X, *Singulari quadam* (1912), no. 3, as quoted in Grande, "Violence and the Social Situation."

each other that the former has nothing to do with the latter."[47] Finally, he cited Paul VI (1963–1978), who argued emphatically that economic life and technology must serve human beings and not vice versa.: "Economics and technology have no meaning except in relation to the human person, whom they should serve."[48] This was so because "Development cannot be reduced simply to economic growth. To be authentic it should be integral, that is, it must benefit all people and the whole person."[49]

What Rutilio had done in the first part of this article was to argue persuasively against those who wished to compartmentalize life so that faith was purely private and focused largely on personal moral sanctity. Complementary to this personal moral focus was the social doctrine of the church radicalized at Vatican II. This shift was most obvious in *Gaudium et spes*:

> This council exhorts Christians, as citizens of both cities, to perform their duties faithfully in the spirit of the Gospel. It is a mistake to think that, because we have here no lasting city, but seek the city which is to come, we are entitled to evade our earthly responsibilities; this is to forget that because of our faith we are all the more bound to fulfill these responsibilities according to each one's vocation. But it is no less mistaken to think that we may immerse ourselves in earthly activities as if these latter were utterly foreign to religion, and religion were nothing more than the fulfillment of acts of worship and the observance of a few moral obligations. One of the gravest errors of our time is the dichotomy between the faith which many profess and their day-to-day conduct. As far back as the Old Testament the prophets vehemently denounced this scandal, and in the New Testament Christ himself even more forcibly threatened it with severe punishment. Let there, then, be no such pernicious opposition between professional and social activity on the one hand and religious life on the other. Christians who shirk their temporal duties shirk their duties towards his neighbor, neglect God himself, and endanger their eternal salvation.[50]

In response to those critical of the role of a priest who involved himself in the social, economic, or political realities of his people, Rutilio convincingly demonstrated the contrast with the tradition of Catholic

---

[47] Pius XI, *Quadragesimo anno* (1931), no. 42, as quoted in Grande, "Violence and the Social Situation."

[48] Paul VI, *Populorum progressio* (1967), no. 34, as quoted in Grande, "Violence and the Social Situation."

[49] Ibid., no. 14.

[50] *Gaudium et spes*, no. 43.

social teaching. As we will find out later, it was the conservative side of the church, within the laity, religious, and the episcopate of El Salvador, who promoted this compartmentalization. Refusing to compartmentalize the faith was a challenge to the oligarchy and the root of their power. This power was possible due to the concentration of wealth in the hands of a small minority within the country, a concentration that dated back to the Spanish conquest.

As Rutilio began his social analysis of El Salvador, he made it clear from the beginning that it would take much more than simple structural change to reverse the injustice against so many. While Marxists may have thought that structural change was all that was necessary, Rutilio's vision was much broader. "We need people convinced of the necessity of modifying the existing structures and who will do so despite the greatest enemy— human selfishness. To change the structures, alone, would only promote a harmful revolution. People with preparation and disinterest have the capacity to change the necessary structures, but this must be a struggle for justice and development as well."[51] Justice and development, in the sense that Rutilio advocated, involved conversion and spiritual growth. Faithful to the sources he had so carefully cited, Rutilio never separated the social and economic dimensions from one's lived faith.

Rutilio based his social analysis on census data relating to literacy, income, housing, and land distribution. Just as the bishops at Medellín instituted and modeled a "see, judge, act" model for addressing injustice in Latin America, this part of Rutilio's article, in observing the circumstances of the majority of the Salvadoran people, would epitomize his "see" moment. According to the 1961 census of El Salvador, 51 percent of its population ten years and older were literate. Per capita income was 281 dollars a year on average, but half the income actually went to 8 percent of the population. As a result, "when the other half is distributed equally among the rest of the population, this corresponds to 153 dollars annually. With this income, the maximum amount that a person can earn monthly is 13 dollars."[52] The availability of housing was another difficulty facing the people of El Salvador. "The urban housing deficit was calculated in 1969 at 178,400 while the rural housing deficit was at 275,000 units. If we assume an average of five people for each unit of housing, we have 1,377,000 people in the country living in homes that

---

[51] Grande, "Violence and the Social Situation," 370, translation mine.

[52] Ibid., 372. Rutilio mentions the exchange rate at the time in his article; I adjusted all monetary amounts to the same scale.

do not deserve that name."[53] In terms of land distribution, the inequality was even more pronounced. According to Rutilio, less than one percent of large farms over 250 acres took up nearly half the available land in the country. As a result, "The holdings of the .05 percent cover more land than the holdings of the 85.19 percent of the population." To emphasize this point further, he reminded his readers "that sometimes large estates are owned by the same person."[54] What this data suggested to Rutilio, and the message he wanted to convey to the reader, was the urgent need for a comprehensive land reform that not only redistributed land but tailored agricultural production to meet the needs of all, especially rural peasants who depended on it for their livelihood. Thus he stated: "This reform should include the use of uncultivated land, sanitation and better cultivation of existing holdings, the selection of crops, the overcoming of monoculture, the industrialization of agricultural products, the increase of national and international markets, the assistance of communication, money and credit for the agricultural industry and above all, the education of the peasant and their professional formation."[55]

Knowing that a call for land reform would occasion a heated response, especially from the oligarchy of El Salvador whose wealth largely resided in large land holdings at that time, Rutilio again argued from the tradition of Catholic social teaching. He began with Pius XII, who in 1944 stated, "the Church has frowned upon, as contrary to natural justice, the assumption that private property is an unlimited right without any subordination to the common good." He continued in this line of argument by citing Paul VI again in *Populorum progressio*, "Private property does not constitute for anyone an absolute and unconditioned right. No one is justified in keeping for their exclusive use what they do not need when others lack necessities."[56] What Rutilio did *not* reference, but something surely known by landowners, was another statement from the same document: "If certain landed estates impede the general prosperity because they are extensive, unused, or poorly used, or because they bring hardship to peoples or are detrimental to the interests of the country, the common good sometimes demands their expropriation."[57] The fact that Rutilio did

---

[53] Ibid.

[54] Ibid.

[55] Ibid., 373.

[56] Paul VI, *Populorum Progressio*, no. 23, as quoted in Grande, "Violence and the Social Situation."

[57] Ibid., no. 24.

not cite this particular passage shows he understood the delicacy and the difficulty that land reform would involve. He completed his argument from tradition with a quote from *Gaudium et spes* which advocated the social nature of all property. "By its nature private property has a social dimension which is based on the law of the common destination of earthly goods."[58] This evidence all pointed to the foundation of Catholic social teaching—the earth and all its goods were created for the enjoyment of all people, not just the wealthy.

The social and economic analysis stated thus far in Rutilio's article prepared the way for a discussion on the topic of violence. It is important to note that for Rutilio, the root of violence was inequality, poverty, and injustice stemming from the social and economic inequality in El Salvador. His first word on violence was a flat rejection of it as a means to an end. "We repeat what Pope Paul VI stated, 'Violence is neither Christian nor evangelical.'"[59] This rejection also included "social injustice" which he defined as a form of *structural* violence. Rutilio quoted from the final "Document on Peace" put forth by the Latin American bishops at Medellín: "It is obvious that actual violence is the 'situation of injustice that can be called institutionalized violence when, because of a structural deficiency in the quantity of industry and agriculture, of national and international economy, cultural and political life, 'entire populations lack necessities, live in such dependence that hinders all initiative and responsibility, as well as every possibility for cultural promotion and participation in social and political life, thus violating fundamental human rights.'"[60]

Rutilio witnessed two levels of violence in El Salvador. The first was "institutional violence" and the second was "armed violence." Institutional violence seemed to have two aspects. The first aspect was the historical situation itself which did violence to people through oppressive economic, social, and cultural forces. The second aspect of institutional violence was the use of the national military to enforce the will of social and economic elites by keeping in place structures that oppressed the impoverished majority. Armed violence also appeared to have two aspects. The first was violence among and between people as a result of oppressive structures; the second was violence against the government as people yielded to the temptation of violence in response to their oppression. Rutilio made it clear that all violence was unacceptable. "Conscious of the complexity of

---

[58] *Gaudium et spes*, no. 71.
[59] Grande, "Violence and the Social Situation," 374.
[60] Ibid.

this issue, of the danger of demagoguery and of being susceptible to multiple interpretations, we want to say that in El Salvador there is no place for any type of violence."[61] His response to the reality of violence was to analyze and reveal the inequality of economic resource distribution, which he argued was its cause: "We recognize the necessity of capital that can strengthen work and of wealth, and never advocate a 'joyful sharing of assets' [as communism does]. We would like it if in El Salvador there was no armed or institutional violence. But we also recognize that according to the data given, there exists an 'excessive' disproportion in the distribution of goods that could give occasion and explain, without defending, the armed violence as it does in other countries."[62]

What Rutilio modeled in this short article from 1970 was a sophisticated social analysis of the situation in which he was doing ministry. In order for this ministry to make any sense to the people, there must be a moment of seeing, which was followed by a judging in line with Gospel and church teaching. The fact that Rutilio used census data to understand the overall structure of the reality within which his ministry occurred pointed to an engagement with his context that was a departure from traditional approaches to pastoral ministry. It was this departure from traditional methods of ministry that made him effective. Unfortunately, it also alienated him from ecclesial leadership in the seminary and throughout the country.

Conflict over Priestly Formation

At roughly the same time that his pastoral experiment in El Paisnal was taking place, Rutilio had a falling-out with diocesan seminary leadership over the philosophy that determined how seminarians pursued their education. Eventually this disagreement led to a break with the seminary where he had taught and directed pastoral formation. According to Cardenal, traditional categories of seminary education ultimately caused the split between Rutilio and the leaders responsible for the formation of seminarians. He explains it this way:

> In the seminary there is a long tradition of isolation from the world and a safeguarding of the priestly vocation for the candidate. The world was contaminated and contaminating, putting into danger

---

[61] Ibid.

[62] Ibid., 375. My inclusion of "as communism does" is my interpretation of the phrase "joyful sharing of assets."

the strength of vocations. The first, fundamental force stipulated is the necessity to isolate the candidate in order to fortify the vocation and later he could encounter the world with success. Because of this, the preferred areas of focus were piety and studies. Pastoral work was marginal or reduced to a minimal expression because it implied in one manner or another that you were in contact with the world outside the seminary. The long years of reclusion during the candidate's early years (minor seminary, philosophy and theology) were an opportunity to know and be known by the seminary educators. Or better, this was the adequate time to weigh the vocation.[63]

Rutilio disagreed with this fundamental orientation of the seminary because he believed it was dangerous to separate one's intellectual life and spiritual development from the apostolic work of the church. Without this integration, it was more difficult for priests to leave seminary, relate to the people they were serving and use their common language (versus academic language) to express the pastoral activity of the church. He seemed to notice and critique the fact that priests were formed in the tradition of monasticism but then were thrown out into the world to live out their priesthood completely unprepared to meet the integral needs of their people. Rutilio wanted an equilibrium between prayer, study, and apostolic activity—only the three activities *together* would ground a healthy priestly ministry.

This tension, evident in the church of El Salvador, was probably felt in many places in Latin America and throughout the world. The Second Vatican Council's reorientation of the mission of the church in the world challenged older models of seminary education and formation, where spirituality and intellectual pursuits were largely divorced from the people whom the church served. In Rutilio's view (as well as the opinion expressed at Vatican II), the kingdom of God would begin here on earth, and the priest was the prophet of this new way of being together.[64] For this reason, priests were called to live and minister in the poverty and material misery of their people in order to announce the integral liberation of all human beings.[65] According to Medellín, the priests had to be

---

[63] Cardenal, *Historia de una Esperanza: Vida de Rutilio Grande*, 114.

[64] Ibid., 117.

[65] This is explicitly stated in the Medellín final documents, and reinforced later in 1975 in *Evangelii nuntiandi*, no. 40, by Paul VI when he states that it "is therefore primarily by her conduct and by her life that the Church will evangelize the world, in other words, by her living witness of fidelity to the Lord Jesus—the witness of

in the middle of the reality of their people: "We exhort priests also to give testimony of poverty and detachment from material goods, as so many do, particularly in rural areas and poor neighborhoods."[66] Where there was injustice, there must be a prophet who would proclaim that justice be restored. Ultimately, the tension and friction between the new method of forming seminarians preferred by Rutilio—that of immersion and engagement—and the resistance to this method by authority figures within the seminary would lead him to resign his position at the seminary.

After a period of conflict with authorities in the church on this issue and, finally, a kind of reconciliation over his criticism of the seminary system, Rutilio travelled to Quito, Ecuador, in February 1972. There he enrolled for five months in the Latin American Pastoral Institute (IPLA) where he learned how to apply the pastoral paradigm emerging from the Medellín conference. Upon his return to El Salvador, this method would have spectacular success and explosive consequences for Rutilio as well as the people of El Salvador.

Questions for Discussion:

1. What was important in Rutilio's early life in El Paisnal as well as the kind of piety that formed him?

2. How was the formation of seminarians structured during Rutilio's time in seminary?

3. How did Rutilio try to change the traditional formation of priests in El Salvador? What was the reaction to his proposals and why?

4. What were the main problems outlined by Rutilio in his article "On Violence and the Social Situation"?

5. How did Rutilio achieve his understanding of El Salvador? What did he use?

---

poverty and detachment, of freedom in the face of the powers of this world, in short, the witness of sanctity."

[66] "Document on the Poverty of the Church," no. 15, in Hennelly, ed., *Liberation Theology*.

Chapter 6

A Turning Point for Rutilio:
Pastoral Formation at the IPLA

The priest we had used some methods which really were appropriate. And he made it very clear that women had just as much value as men, and had exactly the same rights. Then he motivated the men not to leave their wives in the house, but that they go together to Mass and to meetings, that they participate in catechism classes and the other activities of the church.

He said to the men, 'if you don't do this, because you want to leave your wife at home to watch over the house, why not have one of you come to Mass on Saturday and then the other one can come later with the children. The important thing is that everyone participate. . . .'

That was important. First we applied it to religious issues. Later, in exactly the same way, we applied it to our political work. The woman equal to the man. I'm not saying there weren't problems at the beginning. To be sure, there were. . . . Little by little, as we guided people this way, they all began to understand and accept what we were saying. And women and men were growing equally. And so were the children. I would say there were even times when the women and children were ahead of the men.[1]

The Pastoral Institute for Latin America (IPLA) based in Quito, Ecuador, was an outgrowth of Medellín which combined training in pastoral theology with service to the lived ministry of the church. Even after years of working in seminaries in El Salvador, it was at this institute where Rutilio finally discovered "the reality of Latin America and the Church of Latin America."[2] Initially, IPLA was conceived as a travelling team of pastoral

---

[1] Maria Lopez Vigil, *Don Lito of El Salvador* (Maryknoll, NY: Orbis Books, 1990), 55–56.
[2] Rodolfo Cardenal, *Historia de una Esperanza: Vida de Rutilio Grande*, Colección Teología Latinoamericana 4 (San Salvador: UCA Editores, 2002), 193. See http://www.celam

teachers who would move throughout Latin America giving workshops on pastoral leadership. In 1968, it was transformed into an institute based in Quito, Ecuador, in association with the Latin American Conference of Bishops (CELAM). Two bishops were instrumental in the formation and identity of this institute: Manuel Larraín (bishop of Talca, Chile) and Leónidas Proaño (bishop of Riobamba, Ecuador).

At the inaugural ceremony of IPLA in 1968, Bishop Proaño named the objective of IPLA as the capacity to determine a pastoral strategy for Latin America adequate to its circumstances and necessities. Thus, the primary focus of IPLA was to discover and know the Latin American reality with clarity and objectivity.[3] After coming to know the reality one was working with and in, theological reflection could then lead to pastoral planning and implementation. The goal was to transmit a spirit "that would lead with the audacity and creativity of the Holy Spirit."[4]

Candidates for IPLA, both lay and ordained, had studied theology and had at least five years of pastoral experience in Latin America. The program opened with a course on the reality of Latin America with a focus on its socioeconomic and cultural dimensions. Later, candidates studied theology with an eye toward the "signs of the times," the secularization of faith, and other ideologies. Following the path set forth by Vatican II, participants studied with special interest the relationship between the church and society, with a concentration on the Christian perspective on change, revolutions, violence, liberation theology, and the sociopolitical implication of pastoral work. This is certainly what the council's document *Gaudium et spes* had in mind when it taught, "In pastoral care sufficient use should be made, not only of theological principles, but also of the findings of the secular sciences, especially psychology and sociology: in this way the faithful will be brought to a purer and more mature living of the faith."[5]

.org/itepal/index.php. Today, IPLA is part of a larger entity. "The ITEPAL, in its present name *Theological Pastoral Institute for Latin America,* was founded in 1972 and opened in 1974 with the merger of four Institutes of expertise, founded and promoted by various departments of CELAM Catechetical Institute Latinoamericano (ICLA) created in 1960 and based in Chile, the Institute for Pastoral Liturgy (ILP), founded in 1965 and based in Medellín, a second catechesis Institute, based in Manizales (ICLA north) and the Latin American Pastoral Institute (IPLA), created in 1968 with headquarters in Quito, Ecuador."

   [3] Summarized from my translation of Cardenal, *Historia de una Esperanza: Vida de Rutilio Grande,* 193.

   [4] Ibid.

   [5] Cardenal, *Historia de una Esperanza: Vida de Rutilio Grande,* 193, citing *Gaudium et spes,* no. 62.

The vision of the church emerging from IPLA stressed the following themes: the church and the kingdom of God, salvation and the visible church, the church as sacrament, communion and context, theological and pastoral sense of ministers, the laity, pastoral ministers and consecrated life, and base Christian communities. All of these themes come directly from the documents of Vatican II as well as the Medellín conference. According to Cardenal, Rutilio attended IPLA from March through July 1972. Without a doubt the most important time for him was the three days he spent in Riobamba with Bishop Proaño. Rutilio's time at IPLA was not simply an academic exercise, for it also included the important contributions of pastoral experiences of the participants, intense community life, teamwork, and liturgical celebrations, all of which gave an experience of the Latin American church. To fulfill the first level of work, the participants completed research on a small community directed by professors of anthropology and sociology. Additionally, students assumed responsibility for the direction of the course by organizing workshops and seminars. To conclude this section of the course, students, either individually or as a team, created a pastoral booklet.[6]

Rutilio made many friends during his time at the institute. He was remembered in particular for his "firm determination to work with the poor," and many recognized his great pastoral sensibility. Others from El Salvador also attended this institute, but upon their return, Rutilio lost touch with them due to his time-consuming duties in the parish and for the archdiocese. For Rutilio, the opportunity to attend the institute was a providential experience. During his time in Quito he discovered a second vocation specifically within his general vocation to religious life. During these months he formulated what he called "my primary and fundamental option."[7] More important to him than the experience of IPLA was "the great luck to meet the content of IPLA, incarnated in a man, in Bishop Proaño, who has the same experience as Paulo Freire and his method who is . . . the Incarnation of Evangelical values in a philosophically prophetic method."[8]

Bishop Proaño: Understanding Latin American Reality

What was Bishop Proaño's vision for the Latin American church that so impressed Rutilio Grande? Fortunately, there is an excellent source for de-

---

[6] Cardenal, *Historia de una Esperanza: Vida de Rutilio Grande*, 194.
[7] Ibid.
[8] Ibid.

termining this. In December 1975, Proaño published an article in *Búsqueda*, the journal of the Pastoral Commission for the archdiocese of San Salvador, titled "The Role of Christianity in the Process of Development."[9] The article is divided into three sections, respectively titled "The Reality of the People of Latin America," "The Christian Message of Liberation," and "Christian Engagement and Development." Because the pastoral institute directed by Proaño would share a significant portion of his understanding of Latin America, it is worthwhile to analyze this contribution closely.

This overview of the social situation in Latin America, and the Catholic Church's perspective on it, is important for understanding how Rutilio Grande and, later, Archbishop Oscar Romero, would come to understand the role of the church in their context. Not coincidentally, it was a five-month course in Ecuador in 1972 at IPLA, founded by Bishop Proaño, that energized and educated Rutilio by helping him to formulate a pastoral plan for Aguilares and El Paisnal. A close consideration of Proaño's analysis of the social reality in Latin America and the role of the church within it will lead to a better understanding of Rutilio's journey to Ecuador and back to El Salvador. The following is a commentary on my translation of Bishop Proaño's article.

Proaño developed each theme outlined above: (1) the reality of people in Latin America, (2) the Christian message of liberation, and (3) Christian engagement and development. He did this from four different perspectives, the first being in relation to God, the second in relation to the world, the third in relation to people, and the fourth in relation to history. By reframing and re-presenting the Christian understanding of reality in this context, Proaño demonstrated how one's faith can be present to God, the world, other people, and even to how we understand history.

Reality of People in Latin America

Proaño first recognized there were two types of believers in Latin America, and therefore two churches. The first were the elites or the oligarchy described as the following: "traditional conservatives [who] have made a **separation between their faith and social responsibility**. The faith, for them, is adhesion to a creed and clear, determinate moral principles. This type of traditional faith is especially conscious of one's

[9] Bishop Leónidas de Proaño, "El Papel Del Christianismo En El Proceso De Desarrollo," translated as "The Role of Christianity in the Process of Development," *Búsqueda* 3, no. 2 (December 1975): 7–15, translation mine.

status in the church, and they want to serve their own social, economic, and political interests."[10] On the other side of this is what Proaño terms "revolutionary faith": "Revolutionary faith is more than a personal relationship with God, it is a social responsibility. For this group, actions of service to one's neighbor substitutes for prayer and liturgy. Their crisis of faith emerged when they do not see the hierarchical Church seriously committed to social problems and the poor."[11] The danger for this group was the temptation to abandon the church and, out of frustration, embrace Marxist movements. There was a small group between these two oppositional movements whom Proaño named "developmentalists." Their problem was a growing religious indifferentism.

For the vast majority of Latin Americans—the poor common people—Proaño saw a type of popular religiosity which understood the Christian faith as "deformed and mixed with native religious practices where the Christian faith becomes almost tyrannical; there is the danger of being influenced by superstition and magic which reveal something utilitarian but also a fear of the divine."[12] When pagan influences, especially from nature religions, became mixed with Christianity, faith became hostile to human existence. At the same time it was recognized that these popular manifestations "emerge from authentic religiosity, and can be expressed through culturally appropriate elements which are available."[13] The questions of enculturation and syncretism were, and continue to be, extremely difficult cultural challenges to evangelization in Latin America. This brief overview of the peoples of Latin America and their religious orientation illustrated an awareness of the great variety and complexity of religious identity in this region.

Because of the diversity of religious perspectives, the world and how the people of Latin America related to it differed as well. Said Proaño, "The Latin American person views the universe with religious awe. The sun, the moon, the stars, the ocean, the mountains, the storm, the lightening all have something of the divine; they are considered powerful instruments of divinity, if they are not considered gods. Latin American people look upon all reality with religious respect, even religious fear."[14]

---

[10] Ibid., 7. The bold is Proaño's emphasis from the original document. For this understanding of traditional conservatives, he is referencing a document from the Medellín Conference titled Pastoral Theology of the Elites.

[11] Proaño, "The Role of Christianity in the Process of Development," 8.

[12] Ibid.

[13] Ibid.

[14] Ibid.

This was especially true of indigenous peasants who existed very close to the land and for whom the earth itself was like a mother: "she gives them food, she feeds the animals, provides the material for their clothing and she lovingly covers them when they die."[15] As Proaño explains, these same people, peasants throughout Latin America, had not yet discovered their productive capacities for a variety of reasons. First, they used antiquated technology to farm. They also lacked the capacity or initiative for innovation in producing the items they sold. They could mimic outsiders who came in and innovated, but for some reason the capacity to innovate rarely came from them.[16] According to Proaño, what was lacking in their quest for simple survival was a vision for understanding the world "as God's instrument for human beings to realize their integral growth."[17] Or, to put it another way, oppressed peoples will imitate but not initiate, because that requires freedom and safety.

In terms of relationships between and among peoples, there was great injustice. The most fundamental human relationship, the family, was deeply affected by various social indicators. These social indicators revealed the quality of life for many people in Latin America as the following: "At the beginning of the Medellín documents about 'Family and Demography' we read the following: '. . . the family suffers in a special way from the serious consequences of underdevelopment: bad conditions of life and formal education, a poor level of health, a low capacity for change, conditions from which transformation cannot be realized adequately.'"[18]

Additionally, there were specific cultural factors that applied in a unique way to Latin Americans, including *machismo*, realized through male infidelity. This, of course, resulted in a high number of illegitimate children.[19] Infidelity was a key factor in what Proaño termed the "demographic explosion" that resulted in a number of social disorders, exacerbating other

[15] Ibid.

[16] This is well-attested historically: "In spite of the Indian's instrumental and choral skill, no Indian, not even a master in the Reduction schools of music, was ever found who could compose a single line of music. None could be taught to produce a song, even in his own language; the instrumentalists never departed from their score, whatever instrument they played, nor added or altered anything by harmonies or trilling; they usually held the score in front of them, but they played equally well whether they looked at it or not." Philip Caraman, *The Lost Paradise of the Jesuit Republic of South America* (New York: The Seabury Press, 1976), 222.

[17] Proaño, "The Role of Christianity in the Process of Development," 9.

[18] Ibid.

[19] This is one of the few references to *machismo* and the damage it does I have ever seen in understanding of social reality put forth by the church of Latin America.

social problems. As a result, the family was not as it was intended to be, which is "the social nucleus that promotes love and understanding, help, respect, freedom and personal growth, and a common spirit." Instead, it often became "the place of domination, exploitation, oppression, deceit, neglect—a reflection of the social system in which we live."[20] Because the family failed to educate children in an integral way, it was left to the educational structures of the state to assume that duty. Proaño had deep criticisms of this structure and the "education" it promoted. Quoting from the "Document on Education" written at Medellín, he stated:

> Without forgetting the differences that exist with respect to education systems among different countries of Latin America, it appears to us that the programmatic content within these systems, in general, is far too abstract and formal. The teaching methods are more preoccupied with the transmission of knowledge than with critical thinking. According to this social point of view, the education systems are oriented toward maintaining the prevailing social and economic structures, rather than their transformation. It is a uniform education, when the Latin American community has a richness of human pluralism; it is passive, when it is time for our people to hear who they are really meant to be, full of originality; it is oriented to sustaining an economy based on the desire to "have more," when Latin American youth need to "be more" in the joy of self-realization through service and love.
>
> In a special way, the professional formation at the middle and higher levels sacrifices the profundity of humanity in place of the pragmatic and the immediate, in order to meet the needs of the job market.[21]

This method of education, which was uncritical of economic systems, continued and exacerbated the deep inequality that already existed in many countries of Latin America. The root of this, according to Proaño, was avarice or greed, especially by the upper social classes. "The dominant social sectors have not hesitated to use all the means at their disposal to exploit humanity. Not only are they made wealthy by the cost of work, of hunger, of the suffering of the great majority but they have also maltreated and oppressed through their words and actions. They have taken

---

[20] Proaño, "The Role of Christianity in the Process of Development," 9.

[21] "Document on Education," no. 4, in *Liberation Theology: A Documentary History*, ed. Alfred T. Hennelly (Maryknoll, NY: Orbis Books, 1994).

away the benefits of culture, they have oppressed, they have repressed, and they have dehumanized."[22]

In addition to the upper social classes oppressing, there was also what he referred to as "outside domination," when "Multinational businesses are taking the wealth of Latin American countries and, as a result, the gap between economically developed countries and economically underdeveloped countries is widening."[23] What resulted from all of this structural oppression—familial, educational, economic and international—was the "temptation to retaliation, to struggle, and to violence."[24] This, in general, characterized human relations among and between people and peoples of Latin America.

Finally, in relationship to history, the peoples of Latin America needed to reimagine the purpose and end of human history. This process of reimagining was particularly difficult to implement because of the long history of oppression and repression that resulted in a "special psychology of the oppressed."[25] As Proaño stated, these marginalized peoples were a special focus of the Medellín document: "The Medellín document on education speaks of this in relation to people marginalized from their own culture, the illiterate and especially the indigenous illiterate, saying: 'Their ignorance is inhuman bondage. Their liberation is a responsibility of all Latin American people. They ought to be liberated from prejudice and superstition, from their complexes and inhibitions, from their fanaticism, from their fatalism, from their fearful incomprehension of the world in which they live, from their lack of confidence and from their passivity.'"[26]

What deeply concerned Proaño was the fatalism resulting from a "psychology of oppression." Events were attributed to the will of God because there was no hope or sense of effective human agency in the world. Without these two components, there was no vision for how the world could be transformed. "They begin to believe that it is the will of God that established the existence of rich and poor, and for this reason, nothing can be done to change unjust structures. It is fatalism."[27]

Proaño then made an interesting analogy using what he called "the road of time." Time is the highway of history; that highway is part of

---

[22] Proaño, "The Role of Christianity in the Process of Development," 10.
[23] Ibid.
[24] Ibid., 11.
[25] Ibid.
[26] Ibid.
[27] Ibid. It was also the theological justification for societal structures that oppressed for centuries.

God and it led to God. The tragedy of the oppressed is that their servitude "impedes their ability to walk on that highway."[28] This servitude and this oppression manifest themselves in four ways on the highway. First, the oppressed cannot walk on the highway because they cannot see it; they are blind. Second, they are blind because they are marginalized. Third, they cannot see the highway because they are sitting on it, not walking or moving. Fourth, they cannot see it because they have become beggars. When servitude, exclusion, passive fatalism, and immediate needs become the purpose of life, one thing becomes quite clear: "This person is not the author of their own history. This person is not the subject of their own development."[29]

Those who promoted "development" instead of "liberation" didn't really change the situation of the poor—in fact, they may have even made it worse.[30] Proaño likened development to "offering an arm to a blind person."[31] Development would meet some of their immediate needs, similar to giving alms to a beggar or leftover clothing to a naked person. Finally, many people perceived these victims of oppression as responsible for their own situation. "For these people, the oppressed person is a waste of humanity, a useless drag which impedes progress."[32] Without liberation from the structures of oppression which kept the oppressed literally out of "time" or "history," the development of the oppressed was not possible. Written in the same year (1975), this concept was remarkably similar to the following message of Paul VI.

> It is well known in what terms numerous bishops from all the con- tinents spoke of this at the last Synod, especially the bishops from the Third World, with a pastoral accent resonant with the voice of the millions of sons and daughters of the Church who make up those peoples. Peoples, as we know, engaged with all their energy in the effort and struggle to overcome everything which condemns them to remain on the margin of life: famine, chronic disease, illiteracy, pov- erty, injustices in international relations and especially in commer- cial exchanges, situations of economic and cultural neo-colonialism sometimes as cruel as the old political colonialism. The Church, as

---

[28] Ibid.

[29] Ibid., 11–12.

[30] I would posit here that Proaño means "charity" when he states "development." Today developmental economics is a highly sophisticated field, certainly advocating that people become agents of their own history.

[31] Ibid., 12.

[32] Ibid.

the bishops repeated, has the duty to proclaim the *liberation* of millions of human beings, many of whom are her own children—the duty of assisting the birth of this *liberation*, of giving witness to it, of ensuring that it is complete. This is not foreign to evangelization.[33]

This proclamation was in tension with the teaching on integral development put forth by the church, a subject that Proaño treated thoroughly.

The Christian Message of Liberation

In the second section of his article, Proaño argued that human relationships become broken when human beings replaced God's meaning and vision for reality with their own meaning and vision. When human beings rejected God's meaning and put their own selves as the center of created reality, suffering and sin ensued. "You will be like gods" was the original temptation. Humanity is continually saying "yes" to this temptation. For centuries, those in power have tried to control reality, people, homes, and jobs, as well as exploit them accordingly: "In various ways and through various routes, human beings have aspired to become idols—their own gods: idols through the power of money; idols through the power of might; idols through the power of prestige; idols through the power of politics; idols through the power of physical beauty; idols through physical force. These are what St. Paul called the powers of the world. They are the powers of sin."[34] The basis of both humanity's break with God and humanity's break with itself has its source in sin defined as wanting to be like gods. This sin first manifested itself in how humanity had misconstrued its relationship to the world.

According to the tradition of Catholic social teaching, the basis for the fulfillment of all human needs was the following: "The earth, with all its riches, has been created by God for the use of all people."[35] The problem has been that people have hoarded more than they need and thus have perverted God's will. "The LORD God took the man and put him in the garden of Eden to till it and keep it" (Gen 2:15). This meant that human beings were originally created to be collaborators with God in the care of this world (recall, this passage in Genesis is *prior* to the Fall). This collaboration was theologically significant. "In this way, human beings become

---

[33] Paul VI, *Evangelii nuntiandi*, no. 30, emphasis mine.

[34] Proaño, "The Role of Christianity in the Process of Development," 12–13.

[35] Ibid., 13. This is recognized as the foundation and first principle of Catholic social teaching.

collaborators with God, or as some authors have affirmed, co-creators with God."[36] Thus, while amazing discoveries and inventions in technology have been created and utilized, they have also been exploited for the personal gain of some while others suffer.

Because of our broken relationship with God and our fractured relationship with our fellow human beings, people sought domination rather than love in their social and individual relationships. This domination affected many people and made it more difficult to develop integrally as human beings. As long as the self was the basis and motive of our being, we failed to progress in the way we should have. "People are called to work together, to conquer together, to unite their efforts, to complete the use of all their diverse abilities. People are called to build community, to become the family of God."[37]

This love and the capacity to work and grow together was what we were created for—not the domination that has come to characterize the human race and the way it orders its social relations. "It is a profound necessity that each person love and be loved, to communicate this love, to surrender to this love, to search for this communion far and wide and to deepen its personalization, to mature in this love, in a word to grow."[38] In this way we participate in God's encounter with human history, what is known as salvation history, the only history that actually existed and exists.

> God is the principle and foundation of all things. God is the end of all things. He created everything. He created everything for the human person and for all people. "All that exists belongs to you." To make all things theirs, humanity received from God the capacity to form history. To the extent that they form reality, human beings develop and make history in a permanent return to God, the beginning and end of all things.[39]

What made this return to God possible? How could human beings see the integral development of people in their journey to bring history to be according to God's will? According to Proaño, this happened through "the Christian message of liberation, or, better, the announcement of Christ as the Liberator of humanity."[40]

---

[36] Ibid.
[37] Ibid., 13–14.
[38] Ibid., 14.
[39] Ibid.
[40] Ibid., 15.

The primary work of Christ was "to restore the kingdom of God, or, better, to reestablish the proper relationship between humanity and God, to reestablish relationships between people, to reestablish God as the final end for the world, to reestablish a sense of History."[41] This kingdom came against its opposite, the kingdom of wickedness, and the ministry of Jesus forced people to make a choice, as the two worlds were irreconcilable. To choose the kingdom of God, in the end, was to choose voluntary poverty over its alternative.

> While the mission of Christ is the restoration of the kingdom of God over the world and, similarly, the salvation offered to all people, the Son of God made human beings to choose to be poor. This option is directly in line with the restoration of the kingdom of God over the earth, because, as we have seen the perversion of the designs of God have occurred through the pride of the heart, through selfishness, through ego-centrism, through the ambition to dominate others, through injustice and all its consequences.[42]

How do we know this is true? We simply look at what Christ embodied as the perfect human being. Christ chose poverty in the most simple and profound meaning of the word. He was born poor, lived in a poor family, was subject to Joseph (poor in power), chose disciples who were poor or willing to become poor, and exalted the poor through his Beatitudes. His condemnations were solely reserved for those who abused their religious or economic power or attempted to accumulate excessive and unjust wealth.

> The preaching of Christ was an extension of this poverty and its liberating message. When he came to Nazareth, where he had been brought up, he went to the synagogue on the Sabbath day, as was his custom. He stood up to read and the scroll of the prophet Isaiah was given to him. He unrolled the scroll and found the place where it was written: "The Spirit of the Lord is upon me, because he has anointed me to bring good news to the poor. He has sent me to proclaim release to captives and recovery of sight to the blind, to let the oppressed go free, to proclaim the year of the Lord's favor" (Lk. 4:16-19).[43]

This humility of the kingdom of God was opposed to the arrogance and power of the kingdom of wickedness. Not only did this humility fight

---

[41] Ibid.
[42] Ibid.
[43] Ibid.

personal sin but also social sin and the structures supporting it. "Jesus fought in a practical and devastating way the social structures of sin, works of legalism and appearances, oppressive structures and slavery. He said, for example, that the Sabbath is made for man; man is not made for the Sabbath."[44] This battle to confront not only personal sin but social and structural sin as well was the intention of the term "Christian liberation."[45]

The church has always known that liberation was never *only* economic, educational, social, or political. For liberation to be integral, it had to include the whole person and all people. No individual could do all of the work for liberation; rather, human beings must collaborate with others and contribute what they can. Ultimately, Christian liberation responded to evil in the world, replaced it with love, and emerged from an acceptance of God's grace. Says Proaño, "Liberation, for the Christian, consists not only in the destruction of chains that later are replaced with other chains, for example in the destruction of tyranny another worse tyranny can take its place. It is a permanent endeavor to build up what has been destroyed, or, better, that the displaced chains are conquered by love and freedom and, in liberating, make real the process of the integral development of people."[46]

What made such liberation possible was our encounter with Christ. "For this to happen, it is necessary to first have an encounter with Him, it could be casual, as in the case of the Samaritan woman; it could be wanted or expected, as in the case of the two disciples of John the Baptist who was heard to have said 'This is the Lamb of God,' and immediately followed Jesus. To discover Christ is to encounter Him in the everyday bustle of life, in the hearing of the Good News, in contact with people, in big and small events. . . . This is the first step toward a knowledge of Christ."[47] Following this initial encounter or engagement with Christ was the acceptance of him, which meant *imitating* the mission he embodied in this world. This includes working for the kingdom of God: "And just as the mission of Christ is the salvation of all people, and his option is for the poor, and the completion of his mission will occur by destroying

---

[44] Ibid., 16.

[45] *Personal sin* is the breaking of a good relationship with self, others, and God through personal actions or attitudes. *Social sins* are sinful realities that everyone participates in but no one individual is responsible for (e.g., racism). *Structural sin* is committed when institutions embody and promote social sin (racist governments which exclude indigenous people from voting, for example).

[46] Ibid., 17.

[47] Ibid.

the world of sin in order to establish the kingdom of God on earth, the disciple of Christ must be engaged in doing the same, at the risk of being hated by the world, suffering persecutions and losing his life, because the disciple cannot be in a better condition than his teacher."[48]

Faith as knowledge, though, was not enough. When faith as knowledge moved toward faith as praxis, the disciple of Christ imitated the ministry, and sometimes passion, of Christ. Discipleship was (and is) engagement with the work of Christ; it was through this engagement that liberation began. From this integral commitment to Christ (in knowledge *and* action) all forms of idolatry were rejected. All forms of injustice were battled, including oppression, servitude, and the violation of fundamental human rights. With this commitment to Christ came the end of hunger, suffering, vice, anxiety, and insecurity. Our participation in this building of the kingdom mirrored Jesus' own ministry insofar as it included more than simply an individual effort. "Nobody is liberated alone. No person is the liberator of another person. We are all liberated together, united in Christ with our brothers and sisters."[49] For all the above reasons, integral liberation preceded integral development: "economically developed peoples may well be suffering underdevelopment in other, possibly more important aspects. Conversely, economically underdeveloped peoples can have more noble human values than those with material riches. Both are called to bring what they can to the achievement of authentic human development."[50] Because of this, the poor not only needed the rich but the rich also needed the poor. The whole person and *all* people are necessary for integral liberation.

The evangelizing work of the church must always be liberating and lead people to integral development.[51] The key to this type of evangelization, according to Proaño, was the conscientization of both poor and rich which would educate people "to discover the concrete situation of [the] sin in which we live, in order to incarnate the Gospel into human problems as their answer."[52]

In summary, Bishop Proaño offered a new Christian cosmology set in the Latin American context of oppression. He was faithful to the core

---

[48] Ibid.

[49] Ibid., 18.

[50] Ibid. John Paul II expanded and emphasized this theme in both *Sollicitudo rei socialis* (1987) and later social encyclicals.

[51] Cf. Paul VI, *Evangelii nuntiandi* (1975), no. 9.

[52] Proaño, "The Role of Christianity in the Process of Development," 18.

doctrines of Christianity (such as creation, original sin, incarnation, redemption, and sanctification) and yet he applied these creatively and constructively to his own social, political, and economic situation. Far from the distant universalizing of abstract theology, he proposed a Christianity of particularity, faithful to the tradition received and responsive to the world it served. Proaño's call for conscientization over traditional methods of education was vitally important to understanding how the church in Latin America initially responded to the call to evangelize for integral development. It is toward a deeper understanding of conscientization, and specifically how Rutilio came to learn about it, that we now turn.

Christian Engagement and Development: Paulo Freire and Conscientization

According to Paulo Freire, "Freedom is acquired by conquest, not by gift. It must be pursued constantly and responsibly. Freedom is not an ideal located outside of [humanity]; nor is it an idea which becomes myth. It is rather the indispensable condition for the quest of human completion."[53]

Following his formation at IPLA, Rutilio and a friend traveled to Riobamba, Ecuador, where Proaño was bishop, and for two weeks they worked to implement the method developed by Brazilian educator Paulo Freire. This method, known as conscientization, was utilized in that diocese in its ministry with Christian base communities.

In 1968 Freire published a book titled *Pedagogy of the Oppressed*. This book argued for a philosophy of education that combined classical approaches with anticolonial and neo-Marxist overtones. Explicitly Christian, both Freire and his work became instrumental in overturning and unmasking the dynamic between "oppressor" and "oppressed" throughout Latin America.[54] Of particular interest to Freire was responding to what Proaño had termed the "psychology of oppression," so characteristic among the poor common people of Latin America. Thus, Freire was focused on the capacity for the oppressed to separate from their oppressors. This was only possible through conscientization which fundamentally rejected charity, or what Freire called "false generosity," as a model for human development.

---

[53] Paulo Freire, *Pedagogy of the Oppressed*, trans. Myra Bergman Ramos (New York: Continuum Press, 2006), 47, gender inclusion mine.

[54] There is a long history of using non-Christian sources to better educate believers in the faith, from Augustine's use of Greek philosophy and Thomas Aquinas's use of Aristotle to various liberation theologians utilizing themes put forth by Marx and others.

This, then is the great humanistic and historical task of the oppressed: to liberate themselves and their oppressors as well. The
oppressors, who oppress, exploit, and rape by virtue of their power
cannot find in this power the strength to liberate either the oppressed or themselves. Only power that springs from weakness of
the oppressed will be sufficiently strong to free both. Any attempt
to "soften" the power of the oppressor in deference to the weakness
of the oppressed almost always manifests itself in the form of false
generosity; indeed, the attempt never goes beyond this. In order to
have the continued opportunity to express their "generosity," the
oppressors must perpetuate injustice as well. An unjust social order
is the permanent fount of this "generosity," which is nourished by
death, despair, and poverty. That is why the dispensers of false generosity become desperate at the slightest threat to its source.[55]

The dynamic between oppressed and oppressor is a complex one. For
hundreds of years in Latin America, the social situation of the poor had
three general explanations. First, it was understood to be the will of God,
later perhaps bad luck, and, according to others, the fault of the poor
themselves. Freire would unflinchingly name the cause of poverty and
suffering as *injustice*—caused by some who had much by oppressing others
who had little. Here, poverty was *caused* and it was always *relational*. The
question then became, how could one educate people for liberation? For
Freire, this struggle had to be "an act of love" opposing the lack of love by
the oppressor.[56] Power through the weakness of love was also the essence
of the mystery of the incarnation and, thus, was thoroughly Christian.

According to Freire, the first step to overcome the situation of oppression was for people to "critically recognize its causes, so that through
transforming action they can create a new situation, one which makes
possible the pursuit of a fuller humanity."[57] One can immediately see how
close this method would be to the "see, judge, act" method of Catholic
social teaching explicitly adopted by the bishops' conference in 1968,
wherein they write:

We wish to affirm that it is indispensable to form a social conscience
and a realistic perception of the problems of the community and of

---

[55] Paulo Freire, *Pedagogy of the Oppressed*, 44. One can anticipate that the idea of
"power from weakness," which Freire will later name "love," is explicitly Christologi-
cal in reference.

[56] Ibid., 45.

[57] Ibid., 47.

social structures. We must awaken the social conscience and communal customs in all strata of society and professional groups regarding such values as dialogue and community living within the same group and relations with wider social groups (workers, peasants, professionals, clergy, religious, administrators, etc.) This task of *conscientization* and social education ought to be integrated into joint pastoral action at various levels.[58]

According to the method of conscientization, the struggle "to be more fully human, has already begun in the authentic struggle to transform the situation."[59] The barrier to such transformation was a fear of freedom, which the oppressed possessed because "they prefer the security of conformity with their state of unfreedom to the creative communion produced by freedom and even the very pursuit of freedom."[60] Not until the oppressed understood themselves as separated from their oppressor (as opposed to wanting to be like them) could they truly participate in their own liberation. Simple awareness was not sufficient for transformation. When the oppressed understood their oppression and its reasons, something else was still necessary: they must *act* upon their understanding. Awareness without critical intervention in the reality of the situation did not liberate. According to Freire, *Pedagogy of the Oppressed* was supposed to be "an instrument for their critical discovery that both they and their oppressors are manifestations of dehumanization."[61]

There were two general stages to the process of conscientization. The first was that the oppressed, as well as those in solidarity with them, unveiled the world of oppression and through praxis committed themselves to its transformation. Only then could the oppressed begin to believe in themselves as agents of their own development.[62] Second, when reality was in the process of transformation, this form of teaching and learning (pedagogy) belonged to all people in the process of permanent liberation, not just some elite. Freire explains, "The insistence that the oppressed engage in reflection on their concrete situation is not a call to armchair revolution. On the contrary, reflection—true reflection—leads to action. On the other hand, when the situation calls for action, that action will

---

[58] "Document on Justice," no. 17, in Hennelly, ed., *Liberation Theology*, italics mine.
[59] Ibid.
[60] Ibid.
[61] Freire, *Pedagogy of the Oppressed*, 48.
[62] Ibid., 65.

constitute an authentic praxis only if its consequences become the object of critical reflection."[63]

Members of the oppressor class, those privileged and open to change, could try to help or accompany the oppressed in their liberation, but often these people did not trust the oppressed. What became necessary, then, was a communion with the oppressed based on solidarity and mutual respect with and for them. In that sense, "teachers" did not teach liberation while their "students" learned it; rather, real leadership was "co-intentional education."[64] A common reflection and action in light of that reflection, according to Freire, would deepen our common humanity and, thus, our liberation. "In this way, the presence of the oppressed in the struggle for their liberation will be what it should be: not pseudo-participation, but committed involvement."[65] A careful analysis of the teacher-student relationship would reveal precisely how this was possible.

The traditional teacher-student relationship included a "narrating Subject [the teacher] and patient, listening objects [the students]."[66] Teachers traditionally gave students information—usually disconnected from their lived reality—and expected the students to memorize and repeat back what they had learned. "Narration [with the teacher as narrator] leads the students to memorize mechanically the narrated content. Worse yet, it turns them into 'containers,' into 'receptacles' to be 'filled' by the teacher."[67] Insofar as students were receptors for teachers' knowledge, Freire named this the "banking" model of education. Teachers made deposits into a student's mind until they made a withdrawal. This method of educating was stultifying at best and harmful at worst, as it made the learning process one of drudgery disconnected from the world one inhabited.

Conscientization embraced a different approach, described by Freire in the following: "Knowledge emerges only through invention and re-invention, through the restless, impatient, continuing, hopeful inquiry human beings pursue in the world, with the world, and with each other."[68] Thus, the more students were educated according to the banking model,

[63] Ibid., 66.

[64] Ibid., 69.

[65] Ibid.

[66] Ibid., 71.

[67] Ibid., 71–72. Elementary school education in many parts of Latin America, including places I have lived, such as the Dominican Republic, Haiti, El Salvador, and Bolivia, all use board work and copying as the main pedagogical technique in both public and private schools.

[68] Ibid., 72.

the less critical consciousness was developed and the more improbable it was that oppression would be identified and resisted.

This new model of education, this conscientization, would also alter the relationship between student and teacher. Replacing the former hierarchy would be a communicative solidarity where a teacher brought a knowledge of theory and the student brought a knowledge of their reality. The teacher and student then worked out how and where they might inform each other. This partnership would actually mean equality and a mutual learning, easier in some disciplines than others. For example, a kind of mutual mentoring could result where knowledge was shared. Both agents are open to how it changed them and both could grow in their relation to the world. Thus, "Authentic thinking, thinking that is concerned about reality, does not take place in ivory tower isolation, but only in communication."[69]

Applied to pastoral interaction, this model of conscientization would totally transform the role of the priest in relation to the community within which he ministered. In the past, priests were holy members of the sacred who brought in disconnected grace or universal knowledge to people in the secular. Now, the priest was someone who dialogued with the community and tried to make connections between the tradition of faith and the reality within which people lived. This would bring the texts and doctrines of the past into dialogue and eventual acceptance in the present—through mutual communication and sharing. Conscientization, of course, would transform pastoral ministry from simple delivery of sacraments or narrow moralizing (the banking model of ministry) into real engagement. Freire explains, "Education as the practice of freedom—as opposed to education as the practice of domination—denies that man[kind] is abstract, isolated, independent, and unattached from the world; it also denies that the world exists as a reality apart from people. Authentic reflection considers neither abstract man[kind] nor the world without people, but people in relations with the world. In these relations consciousness and the world are simultaneous: consciousness neither precedes the world nor follows it."[70]

---

[69] Ibid., 77. For a very helpful example of conscientization and its application, see Joseph Nangle, OFM, *Birth of a Church* (Maryknoll, NY: Orbis Books, 2004), 64–66. While Nangle's context is Peru, his experience with a parish in Lima in the years during and after Medellín contain some excellent examples of how communities tried to implement new ways of ministry.

[70] Freire, *Pedagogy of the Oppressed*, 81.

Of particular importance here was that "A deepened consciousness of their situation leads people to apprehend that situation as an historical reality susceptible of transformation."[71] This "education for liberation" unmasked the banking model as not only ineffective but actually harmful. How, then, could this liberation model of education actually be applied to pastoral work so it worked toward transformation of an oppressive reality?

Many times education had been (and continues to be) oppressive because educators made their personal views of reality the basis of their pedagogy. Another approach could change that. It was vital that the educator, or in Rutilio's case the pastor, considered the people and their situation as the starting point, which may require time in a community simply *listening*. In this sense, a pastor is not trying to persuade a community to support one social or political solution over another. Rather, a pastor began in the reality of the community with whom he was in dialogue and tried to "fight alongside the people for recovery of the people's stolen humanity."[72] Therefore, a priest did not begin his ministry where people ought to be (an ideal) but where they were (actual reality).

Applied to pastoral theology, this meant that Rutilio's original immersion education with mission teams in El Paisnal and Aguilares was incredibly insightful. *First, go and learn the situation of the community, their aspirations and their reality—then respond to it with the resources of the tradition and the church with the people.* For Freire this was critical: "The starting point for organizing the program content of education or political action must be the present, existential, concrete situation, reflecting the aspirations of people."[73] Without this basis as a starting point, any outside intervention in a community would simply be a "cultural invasion," regardless of one's intention.[74]

What was the best method for beginning in the reality of an oppressed community? For Freire, it was dialogue. The first step was to enter into a community as an investigator, someone who was trying to understand the realities of a particular context. It was only in this interchange with human beings that an educator could begin to understand the reality within which he or she was working. "It is not our role to speak to the

---

[71] Ibid., 85.

[72] Ibid., 95.

[73] Ibid.

[74] Many short-term missions fail in this manner, whatever their type (medical, construction, etc.). Very rarely are people from the outside, especially North America, able or willing to listen to the needs of a community and then engage them in mutual service and liberation.

people about our own view of the world, or to attempt to impose that view on them, but rather to dialogue with the people about their view and ours. We must realize that their view of the world, manifested variously in their action, reflects their *situation* in the world."[75]

According to Freire, the best method for helping people understand and change their situation is to ask evocative questions about what he called "generative themes." Generative themes are issues which moved or provoked recognition of contradiction: "In its original Portuguese and later in Spanish 'to conscientize' was a reflexive verb. That is, one did the process for oneself—no one 'conscientized' another. Each person came to his or her own conclusions in learning and understanding these 'generative words.' For that reason, a guiding principle in Freire's method was absolute respect of teacher for student. No imposition of thought or analysis or conclusion was tolerated. Those who followed this rule helped produce independent-thinking and often self-starting communities of oppressed people."[76]

Generative themes emerged from "limit situations" or real problems in a particular situation. Such themes could lead to change if engaged. For example, "why is there no running water in this community?" This limit situation evoked a contradiction—some communities had running water while others did not. Why? Once the question had been asked, the role of the educator was to encourage a "process of search, of knowledge, and thus of creation, it requires investigators to discover the interpenetration of problems, in the linking of meaningful themes."[77] Once knowledge of reality emerged from a grasp of contradictions, even provisionally, the community could then act upon that knowledge and intervene in reality. This was the realization of conscientization. While this process seemed simple on paper, the skills and methods for its effective use required extensive training and reflection. It is clear that Rutilio received this training at IPLA, and with it he would confront the reality of El Salvador upon his return from Ecuador.

How would Rutilio Grande utilize this method of conscientization to serve the communities he worked with and pastored in El Salvador? What would the process look like? And why did this threaten so many people and ultimately lead to his assassination? Fortunately, Rutilio wrote about this experience in depth. In an article titled "Aguilares: An Experience of

---

[75] Freire, *Pedagogy of the Oppressed*, 96.
[76] Joseph Nangle, *Birth of a Church*, 64.
[77] Freire, *Pedagogy of the Oppressed*, 108.

Rural Parish Evangelization," Rutilio takes the reader through a step-by-step process containing two stages.[78] The first stage was from September 1972 until Pentecost 1973. The second stage was from Pentecost 1973 to the Festival of Corn in August 1974. With Proaño's context in mind and Freire's method understood, it is now possible to examine Rutilio's ministry in Aguilares, El Salvador.

Questions for Discussion:

1. How were various sectors of people understood to be "religious" according to Proaño?

2. What did Proaño and the Latin American bishops find lacking in the education systems in their countries?

3. What is "fatalism" and the "psychology of the oppressed" that Proaño seeks to address?

4. How is Christ, and thus the church, a "liberator" according to Proaño?

5. How is Paulo Freire's book *Pedagogy of the Oppressed* explicitly Christian?

6. What is conscientization and the role of generative themes within it?

[78] Rutilio Grande, "Aguilares: Una Experiencia de Evangelización Rural Parroquial," translated as "Aguilares: An Experience of Rural Parish Evangelization," *Búsqueda* 3, no. 8 (El Salvador, March 1975): 21–45, translation mine.

Chapter 7

Rutilio Grande:
The Gospel Grows Feet in Aguilares
(Part 1)

> *I was a catechist. I think it was because I always liked working with people. Whether we were doing something good or something bad, what I liked was being with people. I was like that. For that reason I was there working alongside the priest when he was giving those talks. And he liked me a lot. When they gave him a piece of chicken, he gave me a leg. And that was love, right? And when people gave him money, he'd give me a bit too. And I felt he was being very good to me. And he'd take me by the shoulder and say, "My son, behave well; my son, this, my son, that. . . ." And I would seize upon his words as if they were the most important thing in life.*
>
> *And it wasn't just that. During the electoral campaigns he'd call me aside and say, just to me, "My son, I want to give you a piece of advice. Never vote for any party but the government party, because the government is the authority which God has put here to guarantee our happiness and watch over things to be sure that we are all well. Therefore we should be grateful to our government. And there's also no need to be causing the government problems, right? Because it's got lots of work and to cause problems would be an injustice."*
>
> *Believe me, he had us so domesticated that, truly, we put ourselves unconditionally at the service of the three people who governed our town: the major, the judge, and the comandante.*[1]

Upon his return to El Salvador from Ecuador in March 1972, Rutilio considered a number of different possibilities. His vice provincial at the time suggested he form a team and travel throughout Central America

---

[1] Maria Lopez Vigil, *Don Lito of El Salvador* (Maryknoll, NY: Orbis Books, 1990), 33.

146

engaging Jesuits who were active in pastoral work and helping them update their ministry.[2] Rutilio's response to this suggestion was negative. He agreed with the vice provincial on the nature of the problem—a lack of Jesuit integration into the pastoral projects of various dioceses, as well as the marginalization of the "option for liberation" made in 1970 to implement the decrees of Jesuit General Congregation 31.[3] Rutilio's response to this challenge, though, was quite different from his vice provincial. "In effect, Rutilio thought the correct solution should be to address the roots of the problem."[4] Until that point in time, the office of the vice provincial had not planned pastoral activity for the Jesuits under his supervision. The various Jesuit residences had little to no group dynamics or team goals. In fact, they really didn't have a common objective. For this reason, Rutilio decided to form a team of Jesuits to begin an experiment in rural evangelization that would change the face of pastoral work in El Salvador. What he embarked on could aptly be termed "immersion pastoral activity." This activity was conducted through a team of priests and lay associates. Rutilio brought the Jesuits along and into the diocesan pastoral activity of San Salvador—an activity that had begun with a new model implemented four years earlier in the town of Suchitoto.

> In December 1968 Father Jose Inocencio Alas, a young diocesan priest, was sent by his bishop, Monseñor Luís Chávez y González, to the parish of Suchitoto thirty miles north of San Salvador. Alas had just spent several months in Ecuador studying how to develop a pastoral program that would directly involve his parishioners in the daily life of the church. The technique that Alas focused on was the creation of *Comunidades Eclesiales de Base* (Christian Base Communities—CEB's). CEB's are small, closely knit groups within parishes that meet regularly for Bible study and often develop other goals according to the interests of the group. When Alas arrived in Suchitoto, he lost no time putting his newly acquired knowledge into practice.[5]

---

[2] Rodolfo Cardenal, *Historia de una Esperanza: Vida de Rutilio Grande*, Colección Teología Latinoamericana (San Salvador: UCA Editores, 2002), 4:195, translation mine.

[3] A general congregation of the Jesuits is called when the superior general either dies or resigns and a new one must be chosen. Representatives from around the world are invited to attend, and new directions are often charted or officially affirmed at such meetings for the worldwide Society of Jesus.

[4] Cardenal, *Historia de una Esperanza: Vida de Rutilio Grande*, 196.

[5] Tommie Sue Montgomery, "The Church in the Salvadoran Revolution," *Latin American Perspectives* 10, no. 1 (Winter 1983): 62.

Three years prior to Rutilio's enrollment, Alas attended IPLA where he learned the same methodology for engaging the reality of Latin America. Of particular interest to successful pastoral activity was the formation of new small-scale faith communities which read the Bible and began to interpret its message in their own context. "Within a few months thirty-two CEB's were functioning."[6] Local leaders began to emerge through a pastoral activity that encouraged them to become agents of their own development. Within this emergence of local leaders, conflict over land took center stage.

Suchitoto, a small farming community on the shore of Lake Suchitlan, suffered from the same situation of grossly unequal land distribution as did much of Central America. According to Montgomery, at the time Alas began his ministry there, wealthy landowners in the Suchitoto area were making loans to other wealthy landowners "to purchase large farms at low prices, then subdivide them and sell the small parcels at exorbitant prices."[7] This scheme rightly outraged the townspeople, resulting not only in a large demonstration in Suchitoto but also in "the first non-government sponsored campesino demonstration since the 1932 peasant uprising" in the capital of San Salvador.[8] Coincidentally, at the same time, the priests of the archdiocese of San Salvador had their monthly meeting and Fr. Alas asked Archbishop Chavez to support the peasant's cause. The response to his request was telling:

> Alas recalls that Chavez, not having been confronted with such a request previously, "did not know exactly what to do. Yet he did not oppose the idea." The result, according to Alas, was a "very violent meeting because, for that era, it was very difficult for the clergy to accept such a task. It was believed that the work one must do in the countryside was evangelization, defined as administering sacraments." In the end Chavez and two other priests, Rutilio Sanchez and Alfonso Navarro, supported Alas and the peasants' demand for a price of $200 per manzana.[9]

While the peasants ultimately failed to push their pricing proposal through the National Assembly and into law, they did emerge from this

---

[6] Ibid.

[7] Ibid. Montgomery states this case as an example: "In Suchitoto Roberto Hill purchased the Hacienda La Asunción for $97 per manzana (one manzana = 1.73 acres), subdivided it and put it back on the market for $280 to $680 per manzana."

[8] Ibid., 63.

[9] Ibid. Fr. Alfonso Navarro was assassinated in May of 1977. He is buried in the Cathedral in Suchitoto.

struggle energized and determined to continue to exercise their rights. Perhaps for the first time, the church had begun to take the side of the poor in El Salvador. Alas continued to form CEB's in the Suchitoto area by empowering Delegates of the Word through classes on the bishops' conference at Medellín relating to the final documents on justice and peace. Delegates of the Word were the Salvadoran version of lay ministers chosen by the people to facilitate a reading of the Bible and its integration into community life.[10] For his part, Alas deepened his commitment to agrarian reform—a commitment that "almost cost José Alas his life."[11]

The reason for this danger was his participation in a National Agrarian Reform Congress, which invited various sectors of society to participate—including the Roman Catholic Church. "Archbishop Chávez handpicked a progressive group of priests and lay persons to represent the Church. Alas was chosen to speak for the Church on this issue."[12] Shortly after presenting his views to the congress, he was abducted by men in civilian clothes and disappeared. Because of the strength and bravery of an auxiliary bishop (Rivera y Damas) and a monsignor (Urioste) who refused the explanations of the government as to his whereabouts, Alas was later found beaten, drugged, and left naked on the edge of a cliff south of San Salvador. This was the price paid for church involvement in the social and political world of El Salvador as early as the 1970s.

---

[10] "Delegates of the Word" was the unique form that lay ministry took in El Salvador. Other countries in Latin America had different, very robust lay ministry formation and designations. For example, in the Dominican Republic, the Catholic Church depends on *Presidentes de Asamblea*, *Animadores de Asamblea*, and others who are trained with priests over the course of three years and include both men and women. See Thomas Kelly, *Lay Ministers of the Future: Lessons in Trust and Collaboration from Latin America*, proceedings of the L.E.S.T. V Conference, in the *Bibliotheca Ephemeridum Theologicarum Lovaniensium* (BETL) (Leuven: Peeters Press, 2009).

[11] Montgomery, "The Church in the Salvadoran Revolution," 63.

[12] Ibid., 64. The archbishop of San Salvador was supportive of the progressive element of the Salvadoran church in the line of Vatican II and Medellín. "It is true that the archbishopric was the only Salvadoran diocese, among five nationally, in which progressive Catholicism received official support. The bishops who controlled the other four dioceses (centered in the departments of Santa Ana, Usulután, San Miguel, and La Union) were conservative supporters of the religious status quo and discouraged pastoral agents—many of whom grew up in impoverished rural areas and until 1972 trained in the Jesuit-run San José de la Montaña seminary—from implementing programs that challenged elite ideologies." *Landscapes of Struggle: Politics, Society and Community in El Salvador*, ed. Aldo Lauria-Santiago and Leigh Binford (Pittsburgh, PA: University of Pittsburgh Press, 2004), 106.

Alas returned to his parish work in 1972, roughly the same time that Rutilio returned to El Salvador from his own formation and work in Quito at the IPLA Institute. The work of Alas began to bear even greater fruit with the integration of peasants into an organization of campesinos responding to government plans to build the Cerron Grande Dam on a river south of Suchitoto. The plan required the flooding of thousands of acres of farmable land, resulting in the displacement of hundreds of poor families. The Christian Federation of Salvadoran Peasants (FECCAS) had been founded in the 1960s. They were invited to Suchitoto where, along with two student organizations, they formed a national organization called the United Popular Action Front (FAPU) in 1974. Alas was an important player in that meeting and in organizing the collaboration of these groups. Recall that according to the bishops at Medellín, this activity was a legitimate, even necessary, pastoral ministry of the church.

It is important to understand that when organizations like FECCAS and FAPU looked for local leaders, they invariably chose those already in positions in CEB's who had been trained by the church.[13] Even though Rutilio Grande's work was purely pastoral, as opposed to José Alas's more political organizing, both of their ministries fed into the popular political organizing that was ongoing at the time. This organizing was seen as an extension of one's faith in the context in which one lived.

This type of faith-in-action resulting in social and political involvement was called for by *Lumen gentium* and *Gaudium et spes* at Vatican II, later in the encyclical *Populorum progressio* (1967), and finally in the final documents at the Medellín conference (1968). Far from being merely activists, these leaders were faithful and orthodox Catholics. It is also important to note that the work of both priests was fully supported by the Latin American bishops. Creating peasant organizations, building faith communities relevant to their context, and advocating for land reform were all *specific* topics advocated in the practical sections of the conference's concluding documents.[14] Jose Alas and Rutilio Grande each pursued the pastoral work of the church, albeit in different ways.

---

[13] Dean Brackley, SJ, makes this exact point in "Liberation According to the Gospel," *Jesuit Journeys*, produced by Don Doll, SJ (Wisconsin Province of the Society of Jesus, 2001), DVD, minute 40 in the part titled "El Salvador."

[14] Hennelly, "The Church in the Present-Day Transformation of Latin America in the Light of the Council" (August 26–September 6, 1968). For example, in the introduction to the final documents under a section titled "Commitments," it reads, "To encourage the professional organizations of workers, which are decisive elements in socio-economic transformation" as well as again explicitly in paragraph 9: "The Second

The story of Jose Alas and the parish of Suchitoto is an essential preamble for understanding the context in which Rutilio began his experiment in Jesuit pastoral engagement in a rural environment. It is also instrumental for understanding "the means by which the Catholic Church in El Salvador became involved in the increasingly rapid process of political radicalization that occurred in the country after 1968."[15] The debate over agrarian reform, as well as the public position taken by the church on it, were both momentous "firsts." Unfortunately, so was the first direct attack on the church in the form of the abduction and beating of José Alas. According to Montgomery, this signaled the beginning of "a history of persecution against the Church that could be characterized by both random and systematic violence that would be directed at both clergy and laity."[16] The events of 1968 to 1974 in the area in and around Suchitoto, as well as the national conversation about agrarian reform, initiated a distinct period that was new for the Catholic Church, previously supportive of the oligarchy in El Salvador for centuries.

> In short, the Agrarian Reform Congress marked a turning point not only in Church-state relations but even more significantly in the Church as a political actor. At the same time, the more sweeping impact of the Church's new-found activism was represented by what was going on in Suchitoto and in dozens of other parishes around the country and after Medellín.[17]

It is not that the church suddenly became political with the Agrarian Reform Congress of 1970—the church had *always* been political. Now, it

---

Latin American Episcopal Conference addresses itself to all those who, with daily effort, create the goods and services which favor the existence and development of human life. We refer especially to the millions of Latin American men and women who make up the peasant and working class. They, for the most part, suffer, long for and struggle for a change that will humanize and dignify their work. Without ignoring the totality of the significance of human work, here we refer to it as an intermediary structure, inasmuch as it constitutes the function which gives rise to professional organization in the field of production."

[15] Montgomery, "The Church in the Salvadoran Revolution," 65.

[16] Ibid.

[17] Ibid. Some argued this commitment emerged in theory with Medellín. "In 1968, however, the second Latin American Episcopal Conference, meeting in Medellín, Colombia, signaled the Catholic Church's recognition that the existing status quo in the continent was intolerable, and the bishops committed themselves to the 'option for the poor.'" Claribel Alegría, "The Two Cultures of El Salvador," *The Massachusetts Review* 27, no. 3 / 4 (Fall–Winter 1986): 496–97.

finally began to side with the poor and oppressed at this congress—and this is the real shift. It is during these same years (1972–1974) that Rutilio took a team of Jesuits into a community located only twelve miles from Suchitoto named Aguilares, where he immersed, formed, and solidified a pastoral model that had explosive consequences.

Rutilio Grande and the Evangelization of Aguilares

Unlike the pastoral activity of José Alas in Suchitoto, there is a direct moment-by-moment account of how Rutilio Grande and his team of Jesuits entered, engaged, and evangelized the community of Aguilares, El Salvador. Fortunately, he wrote a twenty-three-page article detailing this experience in the archdiocesan journal *Búsqueda*.[18] In this article, Rutilio lays out an approach to evangelization which expressly promotes what he termed "the religious" option. Alas and his work in Suchitoto most likely promoted what was termed "the secular" or "political" option. This is an important distinction to make because within the Salvadoran church at this time, there was serious division about *how* the church's mission to the world should be conducted.

As discussed earlier, the majority of bishops in El Salvador and a minority of priests at this time preferred "an institutional, sacramentalist view of the Church's role, with a corresponding respect for established political authority and its ecclesiastical partners in the church hierarchy."[19] Bishop Rivera y Damas and Bishop Romero as well as Monsignor Urioste became leading proponents of what has been termed the "pastoral" variation of liberation theology.[20] The term "liberation," notably, comes from papal encyclicals and episcopal documents relating to the social mission of the church. One of the greatest misunderstandings of the use of the terms "liberation" and "liberation theology" is how some have characterized them as coming from outside the Catholic tradition.[21] While Rutilio and

---

[18] Rutilio Grande, "Aguilares: Una Experiencia de Evangelización Rural Parroquial" (Aguilares: An Experience of Rural Parish Evangelization), *Búsqueda* 3, no. 8 (March 1975): 21–45. All page numbers indicated in future references to this work refer to my translation. See appendix of this book for the full translation.

[19] Montgomery, "The Church in the Salvadoran Revolution," 68.

[20] Monsignor Urioste served as Archbishop Oscar Romero's vicar general in the archdiocese of San Salvador.

[21] Cf. Pope Paul VI, *Evangelii nuntiandi* (1975), no. 9: "liberation from everything that oppresses man but which is above all liberation from sin and the Evil One." Even the Congregation for the Doctrine of the Faith (1984) uses the term: "The powerful

Romero reflect the pastoral strain of liberation theology, "about one-third of the younger priests had adopted a more Marxist-influenced variation which emphasized beginning with social analysis focused on transforming reality. In the words of one young priest, we 'use the analysis of Marxism because it is objective and scientific. But we are not Marxists. We are not able to understand Marx as a religion because we are Christians.'"[22]

The major difference between the pastoral and the Marxist versions is their starting points. The pastoral version of liberation begins in evangelization called for by the church, which has significant social and political consequences. The Marxist or "political" version of liberation begins from an analysis of societal structures and a call for their transformation in light of the faith. Both approaches have been used throughout Latin America in the pastoral work of the church, though we will see that for very concrete contextual reasons, Rutilio preferred to begin in the explicitly "religious" or "pastoral" version.

The rest of this chapter will detail the first phase of Rutilio's work in Aguilares, which took place from September 1972 until June 1973. Rutilio is very clear about the motive, means, attitudes, and goals of this "Grand Missionary Tour" as he named it. By carefully going through the steps he outlined, we can understand better the uniquely pastoral strain of liberation theology actualized in Aguilares. We will also clearly see some of the social and political responses that emerged from an evangelization for liberation.

Missionary Team Orientation

From the very beginning of his article, Rutilio makes it clear that the Jesuit mission team will first have to choose which sector of the population to focus its evangelization upon. "At the foundation of this experience there is a fundamental option by all the members of the team for a pastoral ministry focused on the marginalized majorities. Such majorities are crystallized in the suburban and rural masses."[23] According

---

and almost irresistible aspiration that people have for liberation constitutes one of the principle signs of the times which the church has to examine and interpret in light of the gospel."

[22] Montgomery, "The Church in the Salvadoran Revolution," 69. The question becomes, can we accept a method or parts of a method without becoming a full-fledged believer in the philosophy? Can one accept parts of Freudian psychology but not be a Freudian, or aspects of Plato's philosophy without being a Platonist?

[23] Grande, "Aguilares: An Experience of Rural Parish Evangelization," 1, translation mine.

to the article, this option formed while Rutilio attended IPLA, and upon his return from Ecuador he saw the opportunity to realize this option in El Salvador. The motivation of the team is clear: most clergy at the time served the wealthy minority. For this reason, "it seemed urgent to insert us into the marginalized majorities, the poor peasants, who are the great reservoir of religious people in the country."[24]

The pastoral goals of this Jesuit team were strictly in line with church teaching and were stated as the following: "Evangelization in order to re-create a Church of living communities of new people, pastoral agents conscious of their human vocation who become promoters of their own destiny and who bring change to their reality along the lines of Vatican II and Medellín." The attitude of the team was one of humility. They realized, from the beginning, they must first learn *from* the people they will serve if they are going to impart the faith effectively. "First we have to be conscientized by their reality through a sensitization and aware-ness of their world which brings us to incarnate and identify with their problems." The method they used to interact was consistent with their attitude. Such an approach does not speak the truth from above in order to be received below; rather, the team wanted their ministry to be "per-sonalizing, dialogical, creative and critical, based on the pattern of action-reflection-action, that theologized their reality starting from the solidarity of love, faith, and hope in this person, here and now."[25] To "theologize reality" was to view one's context through the lens of the Gospel. True evangelization with people in oppressive contexts moves away from the paternalistic imparting of knowledge (sacred or secular) or charity (do-nation for immediate needs) and into dialogical creativity that results in action responding to the roots of oppression. In order to do this effectively, the role of the church shifts with "priority given to evangelization and conversion before the sacramental and cultic."[26]

This new model for the church was vastly different from former static models which focused on participation as the proper observance of rituals. Most importantly in this new method, the community became the center for evangelizing activity since it was also the community, not only the priest, responding to the oppression. "We want a mobile church, not a church that waits for people to come to it, or brings the church to the

---

[24] Ibid., 2.

[25] Note the influence here not only of Medellín but also of Paulo Freire's method learned by Rutilio at IPLA.

[26] Grande, "Aguilares: An Experience of Rural Parish Evangelization," 2.

people, but to be the church of the people." This is how *Lumen gentium's* "people of God" is appropriated and lived out on the ground in El Salvador. Finally, and most critically, the evangelical goal is to remove the mindset of fatalistic surrender to poverty and the situation of sharp inequality shared by the vast majority of people. The goal is now "Awareness: to realize the surrounding problematic through reflection and structural analysis."[27]

While these motives, goals, attitudes, methods, and criteria were different from former approaches to pastoral engagement, what was the first step in order to accomplish it? Interestingly, the first move was very concrete: "First, we separate money from the sacraments and worship. Give priority to the marginalized and to the community over the individual. In conflicts, be with the oppressed. Avoid the traps and compliments of the powerful who want to monopolize clergy."[28] It is quite telling that the pastoral team thought the role of money and power in a community often preferred the *status quo*. By separating money from sacraments and avoiding the powerful who want to co-opt those ordained, the team had cleared the way for a new way of faith organizing. In this way, the powerful were always welcome, but they no longer dictated the content or method of ecclesial pastoral engagement. The relationship of the clergy to wealthy members of the community was well known in El Salvador. The following describes this relationship during the early 1960s in a northern area of the country:

> Like many priests, [Fr.] Argueta benefited materially from a rural class system that kept most people subordinate to a few rural merchant and agrarian capitalist families. In Jocoaitique he ate without cost at the homes of the local elite, who increased their cultural capital by associating with him. And when he visited poor, outlying areas, he was often met at the entrance of the community by officials and welcomed with fireworks and music from a local band. For most people a visit from the region's only priest was a rare and important occasion. After Mass Argueta ate alone in a local home or the church sacristy, for no one would dare break bread with a literate man of God—nor did the priest ever invite them to do so. The community served him its richest fare: chicken, eggs, cream, and milk that most peasants rarely consumed. People who required the priest's council, or wished to request a favor, usually sought out the assistance of an

---

[27] Ibid.
[28] Ibid., 3.

intermediary, whether judge, church official, the mayor, or another person of status. The priest's relationships with his "flock" were marked by paternalism exercised by large rural landowners and merchants toward peasants and rural workers. Surely Argueta was aware of the relationship between his practice and the dominant order, for on the occasion of elections he sometimes used the pulpit to urge people to vote for the National Conciliation Party (PCN), formed by the military government in 1961.[29]

What Rutilio proposed directly undermined this dynamic of domination by local clergy. It would be replaced with a servant-leader model that was very effective.

This approach and the encounter with oppressed communities could not be a short-term mission where teams swooped in and swooped out. Rather, it needed to comprise a period of years and be conducted in such a way that the chosen and formed lay leaders could sustain the mission long after the missionary team had departed. Finally, it was the participation of the layperson that became the center and focus of missionary efforts. Clericalism had no place in a pastoral ministry aimed at liberation. "One of the objectives is that laypersons take their responsibility and place in the church and that the priest, only by substitution, does what can and should be done by the layperson."[30]

The actual execution of the mission revealed a formidable effort in planning and community engagement. Prior to the mission, opinion polls targeting the general population were circulated that asked where the mission was most necessary or desired and why. Requests were formalized, needs were put forward, and details were specified. When the mission arrived, it began by moving into a designated zone to first *listen*.

> A general description of a day of mission: family visits in homes. The priest and their associates spend some time in each home. This is the way to approach the community and particular problems within it. With the data collected in these visits and other data more systematically obtained in the continual dialogue with qualified elements there, the team will begin to create an anthropological record of the

[29] Lauria-Santiago and Binford, *Landscapes of Struggle: Politics, Society and Community in El Salvador*, 108–9.

[30] Ibid. I define "clericalism" as centering the pastoral work in a community around the needs and desires of the cleric over those of the people, in an authoritarian manner. This approach to ministry is almost exactly the opposite of mainstream parish ministry in North America today.

place: fiscal, economic, social, political, cultural, and religious reality. These will be the basic themes generated that can be treated in corresponding decoding of selected bits of the New Testament. With the associates reviewing activities, data is compared, contrasted, and codified, and evening sessions are planned.[31]

Note what was happening from the earliest visits to people—there was an effort to understand their complex reality and bring it into dialogue with Scripture and the tradition. This process could take as long as fifteen days of visiting and compiling data on the various aspects of life in a particular zone. Following a period of data gathering, a large community meeting commenced with a threefold objective. First, the team wanted the community to begin the process of self-evangelization. Second, the team wanted the community to begin to become a new kind of faith community. Third, the team encouraged the community to begin self-selecting Delegates of the Word. These were lay leaders who, after intense training, began the process of faith formation at the base ecclesial level.

The large community session began with a variety of songs that reinforced the goals of the mission. Next, a copy of the New Testament was given to those who wished to receive it, even if they could barely read. The team searched the New Testament and highlighted texts that were directly relevant to the problems and challenges in the community, gleaned from the anthropological data gathered. Certain texts were read out loud—sometimes two or three times—by both women and men. The large group then divided into smaller groups of eight to ten people and they named three people for very specific jobs. The first job assigned was the *reader*, who reads the text verse by verse. The second job given was the *animator* who encouraged and moderated participation in the small group. The third job designated was the *reporter* who wrote down a list the group compiled. The goal in the small-group activity was maximum participation from everyone.

Following these small-group meetings, "plenary sessions" of sixty to seventy people were held. These sessions were managed by the missionary team. The purpose of these sessions was to gather the summaries of the reporters and try to gather themes that were common among the small groups. At the end of the plenary sessions, the priest summarized the main themes that emerged from the small groups. After the session, the team met to discuss who participated in their small groups the most. These participants were then targeted and invited back for more sessions

---

[31] Grande, "Aguilares: An Experience of Rural Parish Evangelization," 4.

with the team. After these people had been identified, the same dialogical method was explained to them since they were emerging as natural animators of the community. At each successive night of meetings, they were further evaluated to correct any problems and improve their dialogical method. Ultimately, these emerging leaders were the key to the progress of the mission. At the end of the mission, the leaders were elected by the community according to the criteria of "responsibility, dynamism, and animation."[32] The hope was that the two weeks of mission activity "will help men and women of initiative, mobility and influence come forth from the community."[33] The ultimate criteria for leadership in the community, a virtue emphasized by the team, was the exercise of "service, and not as domination." This approach intended "to avoid all elitism and paternalistic power players who wish to 'grow the others.'"[34]

The purpose of this method, of course, was for the community to self-select leaders. This was very important. Outsiders who came into a community and appointed their own leaders left the community dependent on the judgment of others who did not share or live their experience. A community began its transformation by putting forth those it recognized as leaders. The missionary team simply affirmed the community recognition and helped train the leaders to be more effective. The team was constantly on the lookout for signs of leadership. Rutilio indicated that before the mission began, a list should be kept of those who were interested or helped in the mission, such as those who mobilized their parish to make formal preparations, those who had responsibilities in the communities, and those who provided ideas, initiatives, and even practical things like decorations or lights. Anyone involved in self-giving service to the community was identified and scrutinized by the team.[35] During the mission this scrutiny continued with a list of people identified as repeatedly participating in public. This was important because they felt comfortable speaking in front of others—an essential leadership skill. After their first evaluation, these emerging leaders were constantly encouraged not to be preachers but to encourage others and to seek truth, unity, action, and organization in the community.[36] In the final days of the mission, the list

---

[32] Ibid., 5–6.

[33] Ibid.

[34] Ibid., 6.

[35] Ibid., see chap. 5. Note how different this approach is from his first effort in Aguilares which targeted those who were most pious.

[36] Ibid.

of potential leaders was reduced to those who had attended and actively participated in activities, interventions, and any other events. The next to the last night, the community election was held.[37]

The community election was a central part of the conclusion of the direct mission period and the criteria for the election were clearly put forth: "service, commitment, initiative, responsibility, sacrifice for others, and availability." After the community suggested leaders, those named indicated their willingness to serve and, finally, were chosen by a majority of those present. Following their election, they were designated as "Delegates of the Word of God in service to the community."[38] This call by the community is essential to understanding this service as a ministry. "Ministry begins with the Christian community, flows out of the Christian community, and nourishes and expands the community."[39]

According to Rutilio, this process of communal selection of leaders "resulted in one delegate for every four or five people," comprised of both men and women depending on the location, with the position and number of delegates open to revision. Initially, it was important to have numerous delegates "in order to place the engine of the community within the community." The means and motives for transformation came from within the community. Numerous delegates also allowed for a diversification of their roles and the ability to purge or self-eliminate someone if they didn't finish the work the community had entrusted to them.[40]

On the last night of the mission, the elected delegates accepted publicly and individually their unique call from the community. "From this moment on, they will be in charge of leading and caring for their community." Of course, they did not do this alone. They were mentored by an older delegation, foreign missionaries, or another community who helped ensure their growth. In the final liturgy, the sacraments of baptism, marriage, and First Communion were oriented toward community commitment. Rutilio suggested the following symbolic way to articulate this: "The Delegates elected by the community make a commitment, light a candle and pass it to the community that makes a commitment, who then takes the light and passes the light to the parents and godparents who are

---

[37] Ibid., 7.

[38] Ibid.

[39] Thomas O'Meara, OP, *Theology of Ministry* (Mahwah, NJ: Paulist Press, 1999), 146–48. O'Meara argues, convincingly, that being called by a community is one critical aspect of what is termed "ministry."

[40] Grande, "Aguilares: An Experience of Rural Parish Evangelization," 7.

having children baptized, as well as those getting married, and finally the candles are passed to parents of children receiving First Communion."[41] In this way "commitment" to the community was the overriding theme of sacramental reception, not merely the elevation of personal holiness. Or rather, personal holiness came to be defined as being in service to the common good and not merely one's individual salvation.

Following the departure of the mission team, a priest stayed behind who embarked upon an "essential and delicate work requiring patience in accompanying the community in its growth without ever abandoning it."[42] The priest "directly assumes responsibility for the village and accompanies the peasants while visiting the communities, attending its meetings, dispelling doubts and confusion and evaluating with the community on the one hand and with the Delegates on the other the progress of the community and of the Delegation." To instruct a priest to "accompany the peasants" was an important statement to make in the culturally polarized society of El Salvador as a result of the reasons outlined in the following paragraphs.

Following the indigenous peasant uprising of 1932 where "thirty thousand peasants were methodically massacred in cold blood," the ruling class in El Salvador promoted what was known as the "black legend." This was a justification for the killing of so many at this time. It presented poor rural villagers as "peasant hordes, rampaging with machetes, commit[ing] innumerable atrocities, cutting off heads and raping virgins during the three days the uprising lasted."[43] So, to be a peasant was not only to be uneducated and poor but also to be less than human in the eyes of the Salvadoran elite. When Rutilio called upon priests "to accompany peasants," he was really calling for a full and complete immersion into the social marginalization experienced by the peasant class. This was truly servant leadership.

Such priests could be foreign missionaries who wanted to assist in the ministry of the archdiocese or other native clergy.[44] They often partnered with the two Jesuit houses in Aguilares, some of whom were studying at the UCA in San Salvador. The priest who stayed behind continued to

---

[41] Ibid.

[42] Ibid., 8.

[43] Alegría, "The Two Cultures of El Salvador," 496.

[44] An excellent example of a foreign missionary who assisted before and during the Salvador civil war was Fr. Paul Schindler from the archdiocese of Cleveland, Ohio. He was based in La Libertad, El Salvador. You can see him and some of his work in the documentary *Roses in December*, Ana Carrigan (1982).

develop and guide the lay leadership in the community by helping form "preparers," as well as "envoys of the zone." Preparers were Delegates of the Word who prepared two celebrations of the Word every fifteen days with a priest in the community chapel. It is important to note that the preparer was in charge of the celebrations, while the priest accompanied and guided but did not control. A celebration of the Word focused on a reading of a scriptural text followed by an application of that text through conversation about the challenges facing the community. Envoys of the zone were sent to various centers throughout the pastoral zone from each delegation (of Delegates of the Word) to help communicate and unify the various groups of delegates and compare the work being done. In this way, work in one community became connected to the work of delegates in other communities, and zones began to organize very effectively.

Results of the First Stage of Evangelization

Noting feedback from delegates and their communities, Rutilio acknowledged a number of palpable results from the first stage of the missionary tour. Among them were the following:

- "Great discovery of the Gospel by themselves: 'we are now removing ignorance . . .' 'We were in the dark. . . .' An appetite for the Word has been opened and they comment and make it applicable in their own way."
- "The Gospel and the situation in which they live come together quickly: 'we are bringing the Gospel from the spiritual to the material.'"
- "They begin to rise out of their magical consciousness: 'what can the poor actually do . . . ?' 'to be conformed to the will of God,' and they have begun to realize there is no will of God that things have been the way they are."
- "They have confidence in themselves: they lose the widespread complexes, the shame, the disability, and discover they can express themselves."
- "They begin to realize that many ills come from not 'being united' and they are acquiring a sense of community."
- "They start to distinguish what is primary in their religiosity and what is more secondary."
- "They are experiencing the possibility of change and betterment from their religiosity."

- "The reception of sacraments as repetition and sacramentalism decreases, but the sense of the same as change, commitment and vital signs increases."[45]

What became evident from a preliminary consideration of these palpable results was a significant shift in knowledge, faith, and perception of reality, self-image, and the capacity for change.

With acknowledgment that ignorance was the former state of existence, through the Gospel a new way of understanding their reality has emerged. This new view was understood in terms of the kingdom of God, and the basis of the kingdom was Jesus' ministry, life, death, and resurrection. This knowledge was not static or abstract, nor was it merely conceptual. Rather, this knowledge was an applicable dynamism that changed how people understood their reality and their very selves. The movement from spiritualizing everything (abstracting reality) to applying faith to their material world (theologizing reality) signified this change. Faith was not only oriented toward the next life but also to the transformation of this world through cooperation with God's grace in the welcoming of the kingdom. This, of course, was perfectly consistent with the ecclesial vision of Vatican II.

When the Gospel worldview replaced superstition and fatalism, the "magical consciousness" of the people evaporated in favor of a view of reality with explanations, including causes and effects. With this little bit of knowledge and control of their own context, the people grew in confidence. Now they perceived themselves as more than simply victims of unknown external forces. No longer was the "will of God" allowed to justify pain, suffering, or unjust social or political structures. From this came the realization that perhaps things can change! This change does not come from individual effort alone but from a strong community of faith united in pursuit of the common good. All religious action was now oriented not toward repetition or the fulfillment of personal cultic obligation but rather toward humanizing change, commitment to others, and a dynamism toward the kingdom.

To consolidate the first stage of missionary activity, the team called for a huge multi-community celebration on the feast of Pentecost. This was no accident, as Pentecost celebrates the gift of the Holy Spirit to the followers of Jesus who were then inspired to preach and teach fearlessly what the Lord had done for them. At the same time, Rutilio was aware

---

[45] Grande, "Aguilares: An Experience of Rural Parish Evangelization," 9.

of the criticism that was leveled at the communities as they progressed along the new path of pastoral engagement as proscribed by Vatican II and later by *Evangelii nuntiandi* (1974). The homily he gave on this occasion was a greeting to the people of God and it first encouraged them, gave them confidence, and tried to dissipate difficulties. Among those difficulties were accusations along the following lines: "The first accusations against them will be of 'Protestantism,' of moving to the material and not the spiritual, of communism, of politics, of illegal meetings that are bad and the National Guard who will come and tie their hands and take them away, and what will happen with internal conflicts of power, threats, and fear? The same accusations were made against Jesus and will be made against all true Christians."[46]

By way of response to these critiques, the missionary team confirmed the following points in this article, in order to be absolutely clear about its motives and commitments:

- Before everything else, we are MISSIONARIES for the entire community; it is said we are SENT to proclaim the Gospel cleanly and simply, without pretense or other personal interests, according to the mandate of Jesus to his apostles: "Go and proclaim the Gospel to all peoples."

- According to this, under no pretext will we administer any sacrament to those not adequately evangelized, for we gravely betray the Gospel and our conscience if we do.

- We have nothing to do with political groups of any class or party. We owe everything to the community.

- Our only POLITICS are to be faithful proclaimers of the Gospel which has to do with all human activities aligned with God in order to transform the world.

- We will denounce with energy and without pretense all sorts of injustice and abuses against the human person, wherever they come from, whether they be private individuals or groups.

- Our goal is to build together with you, A COMMUNITY OF BROTHERS AND SISTERS, COMMITTED TO BUILD A NEW WORLD, WITHOUT OPPRESSORS OR OPPRESSED, ACCORDING TO THE PLAN OF GOD.[47]

---

[46] Ibid.
[47] Ibid., 10, emphasis from original.

What became clear through this final message preached at the conclusion of the first stage was that Rutilio and his team promoted a pastoral version of liberation that began with the proclamation of the Word of God to all people. Such a proclamation had significant social and political consequences, but the social and the political were secondary in terms of means and motive. What mattered most was the faith formation and preparation necessary for people to understand, partake in, and live out the sacraments they received in a new and integral way.

While some of the positions emerging from this faith stance aligned themselves with one party or policy over another, doing so was not the primary intention of the team. The goal was to focus all human activity and orient it in line with God's will—i.e., to humanize and lead people into integral development. Part of integral development was denouncing the "anti-kingdom," or those parties, policies, and people who dehumanize others. Finally, the overall intent and goal of the mission team was a new faith community which imaged the kind of covenantal relationships in the plan of God.[48]

Conclusion

What began in 1968 with José Alas and the political option in Suchitoto would take a different form with Rutilio in Aguilares. The religious option exercised by Rutilio and his missionary team of Jesuits began in Scripture and an explicit faith commitment by a community, as it turned the lenses of the Gospel upon the reality within which they lived. This pastoral liberation ministry took place in the midst of a polarized church hierarchy divided between the four bishops who rejected Vatican II and the conclusions of Medellín and two bishops who accepted them. Additionally, there was a deep cultural polarity between rural peasants and affluent city dwellers. Due to cultural and political stereotypes, rural peasants were systematically denied a humane life. All of these factors created a mix for what would become an explosive reaction to communities of the poor living out their faith in deep transformational terms.

Rutilio brought with him from IPLA a similar approach to that of Alas, however, his approach was configured in different ways. Rutilio's approach began from humility, empowerment, listening, and an ecclesiology in-

---

[48] A covenantal relationship "is a mutual commitment of self-donation between free beings capable of self-conscious reflection and self-possession." John F. Kavanaugh, SJ, *Following Christ in a Consumer Society* (Maryknoll, NY: Orbis Books, 2006), 75.

tended to awaken the base of the church to its own humanity and God's love for them in light of the Gospel. The method by which he approached this work was systematic, thoroughly planned, cleanly executed, and open to revision and adaptation. In addition, he employed the social sciences of sociology and anthropology in service to his ministry. Understanding whom he ministered to was the most important step and impacted the way he worked with the people.

Also critical to this first phase of the mission was the development of a community that began to self-evangelize and self-select leaders who brought forth the gifts of their fellow peasants. This differed radically from methods that arrogated or dominated. The result of such effort was the creation of a servant-leader team of Delegates of the Word who were chosen for their commitment to others by their own community. Through a gentle nurturing of this group and a careful mentoring of their development, the team implemented a more sustainable pastoral model that empowered people to take responsibility for a faith that did justice in very practical ways in their community.

In the next segment of Rutilio's article, he provides a description of the consolidation of this first phase through a careful analysis of the geographic, social, political, cultural, and religious realities that comprised the targeted communities. With a deeper and more detailed knowledge of the areas of ministry, this second stage sought to deepen, in every sense, what was initiated in the first stage.

Questions for Discussion

1. What was the purpose of Christian base communities? Did it matter how leaders were chosen?

2. How is Rutilio's long-term engagement in Aguilares different from a short-term mission model?

3. Why was it important for the mission team to listen and learn from those they were serving?

4. What is fundamentally different between the starting points of Rutilio Grande and José Alas?

5. Why was the relationship between money, sacraments, and community life important according to Rutilio?

Chapter 8

Rutilio Grande:
The Gospel Grows Feet in Aguilares
(Part 2)

And then one day he said to us: "Wouldn't you like to talk about the Bible some day? You've already told me that you met with the other priest. So you could do it for me. Who's interested?"

"I am! I am!" said a few of us.

Inspired by the first ones who said yes, more and more said they were interested, too. And he began to go over the Bible with us. He read from the fifth chapter of the letter of James, the criticism of the rich and all that.

"Oh, is that in the Bible?" we asked, without really believing it.

"Sure. Look, you can understand this if you see that you're children of God and that Christ came as the son of a poor woman and . . ."

And he began to put this question of "the poor" into our heads.

I remember it well. It was then we began to realize that it wasn't sinful to speak badly of the rich, since God was condemning them right there in the Bible. And if God was condemning them, how is it that God has made them and blessed them with money, and yet in the Bible he was condemning them? So we began to feel a great inner contradiction. And also we had disagreements among ourselves because we still hadn't quite caught on to this thing. Some of us began to lean in one direction, and some in another. We were taking positions.[1]

Following the implementation and stage 1 of the "Grand Missionary Tour," Rutilio called for a period of reflection where the knowledge gained from that first stage could be processed and better understood. The reflective moment that marked the beginning of the second stage had

---

[1] Maria Lopez Vigil, *Don Lito of El Salvador* (Maryknoll, NY: Orbis Books, 1990), 38–39.

three parts—evaluation, maintenance, and planning. Evaluation brought together "disparate data to be examined critically. An interpretation and systematization of the same data is made and deficiencies are seen which will be acted upon consequently."[2] Maintenance occurred when "the accompaniment, the animation and the deepening of the Gospel is studied in every missionary community as well as the quality of the preparation of Delegates of the Word and community animators." Basically this was where "best practices" were learned and implemented. Finally, the planning stage indicated "new frontiers of work, correction of errors, and growth in programs to meet the work that needed to be diversified in the same communities: with children, young people, adults, marriages and Delegates of the Word."[3] Thus, the reflective phase was really a diagnosis of the state of the mission, its challenges, and its future direction.

Three main concerns framed the team's entry into the second stage of the mission. Rutilio defined these concerns as sustenance, growth of living communities, and opening new frontiers. The first concern centered on the nature of sacramental life in the rural parishes of El Salvador. He thought that the traditional pastoral work of sacraments needed to be "purified and transformed." At the same time, he wished to preserve the values through which the sacraments were promoted. He wanted to see the community "take responsibility for and participate in sacramental life."[4] In Rutilio's own words, "The base needs to be involved as co-creator so the community will not fall into clericalism or paternalism." Doing this required the community to "Untie the economic maintenance of the church from the sacramental and cultic." The fear of clericalism and paternalism was very real for Rutilio, largely because it would undo everything the missionary team had worked toward.

Communities that were not empowered from within (e.g., self-selection of leadership) could not know or act upon their own situation in order to change it. They could never take ownership for themselves and their faith commitments if an outside leader imposed his or her own. In a similar manner, a community of faith would not take ownership for its beliefs and the living out of those beliefs if an authority figure, such as a priest, made himself the center and focus of worship life. Just as the community

---

[2] Rutilio Grande, "Aguilares: Una Experiencia de Evangelización Rural Parroquial" ("Aguilares: An Experience of Rural Parish Evangelization"), *Búsqueda* 3, no. 8 (March 1975): 10, translation mine. See appendix 1 of this book for the full translation.

[3] Ibid.

[4] Ibid., 11.

should not look outside of itself for a savior to solve its problems, neither should a faith community totally depend on a priest for the practice of its faith. This was much more than simply a preference for a leadership style—what was at stake here was the true sense of Christian liberation.

Notable in this section on sustenance was the second reference to money (church maintenance) and how it was connected to the delivery of sacraments. It was obvious that Rutilio thought something debilitating was happening to communities because of the way in which the sacramental practice of the church was tied to the wealthy and powerful members in the community. His response to this, though vague, was to "pursue a greater autonomy of the Communities and of the support of the priests." In this way, money and sacraments could be disconnected, and the community could actualize its sacramental life in ways that were more life-giving and dynamic. Paternalism and clericalism were the opposite. Paternalism sought "help" from outside; it was a dependence on charity, on handouts, rather than a focus on justice that began with an understanding of the roots of one's situation of injustice followed by action to change it. Clericalism undermined pastoral liberation; it occurred when the pastoral work in a community, in an authoritarian manner, centered on the needs and desires of the cleric over those of the community. There was and continues to be an indispensable role for priests in the pastoral ministry of the church, but a priest should never displace community initiative or the role of laypeople in that initiative.

The second concern for Rutilio involved the qualitative growth of what he called "living communities." Distinct from quantitative growth, quality points to the critical role of Delegates of the Word and whether they were truly bringing forth the gifts of the community to integrate the gospels with their lived experience. A "nonliving community" was a community that practiced a faith disconnected from its lived reality. The focus was piety without reference to the real moments of sin and grace lived out daily. This particular set of concerns related to the diversity of functions taken on by the delegates and "how they can be formed without falling into elitism or distancing themselves from the base."[5] Again, leadership of the community was vital, but it must be a *servant* leadership in practice, not in name only. Its model was the ministry of Jesus. Anything less would undo the conscientization needed for the community to discover its own challenges and act to address them.

---

[5] Ibid.

Finally, Rutilio was concerned with new frontiers in city ministry (i.e., in the urban slums) that could lead to two undesirable results. The first was what he termed a "desperate activism," by which he meant an activism not based on the Gospel but rather on political and social ideologies external to Christianity. The second was a dependence on activists "from outside the community." In both cases, Rutilio was concerned about outside groups using desperate communities to manipulate their own political agenda. In response, he wanted to find a way to form people that left communities able to depend on internal leadership. "The ideal pursued is to create conditions and form people in a way that in the remote future they can be responsible for pastoral duties with one or two diocesan priests."[6]

Evaluation of Parish Reality

Rutilio indicated that the first part of the reflection brought together various forms of data to be analyzed critically. By this he meant that various forms of sociological and anthropological data needed to be collected, analyzed, and acted upon in order to better understand both the macro and micro reality of the people being served. This was consistent with the recommendation of Vatican II in *Gaudium et spes* when it stated, "In pastoral care, sufficient use must be made, not only of theological principles, but also of the findings of the secular sciences, especially of psychology and sociology: in this way the faithful will be brought to a purer and more mature living of the faith."[7] The analysis embarked on by Rutilio utilized the University of Central America and its Institute of Public Opinion and included an analysis of the following realities: the geophysical, population issues, socioeconomic reality, the rural village, social stratification, worker-boss relationships, family situations, cultural and religious reality, and pastoral reality. Through a careful consideration of each, the team arrived at enough knowledge of the situation to adequately shape its pastoral ministry.

The Lord of Mercy parish in Aguilares was founded in 1952 and covered 170 square kilometers.[8] It inhabited the northern part of the department of San Salvador and was located on the Troncal Norte, the only paved road "crossing the plain from the South to the North." Aguilares was joined to Suchitoto through an unpaved road served by various buses. The parish

---

[6] Ibid.

[7] *Gaudium et spes*, no. 62.

[8] Grande, "Aguilares: An Experience of Rural Parish Evangelization," 11.

had thirty-three thousand inhabitants spread the throughout the city (pop. ten thousand) as well as villages nearby including El Paisnal (pop. two thousand).

The socioeconomic reality of the area reflected Aguilares and its location as a transportation crossroads within the country. According to Rutilio, the population consisted of "small commercial businesspeople, simple skilled professions, and peasants who are piling up in the peripheral areas leading to the new neighborhoods and settlements that lack the most basic urban services (like water, sewer, electricity, etc.)." Market days transformed Aguilares from Thursday to Monday "into a motley confluence of diverse occupations and backgrounds."[9]

The area in and around Aguilares, the area the parish served, was dominated by landowners who inhabited more than thirty-five large estates. Sugarcane occupied most of the flat land that remained. The land not owned by the large estates, or used for sugarcane, was rocky terrain rented by peasants in order to grow subsistence corn. Ranches raising livestock were beginning to claim about half of that rocky land. Finally, "The three great mills of La Cabana, San Francisco, and Colima, with some other sub-centers of less importance, temporarily absorb the peasant labor of the region which increases during harvest with workers and truckers from other areas."[10]

Social stratification was clear and socially significant. The highest level of the social strata was a group of property owners who lived in the capital city, San Salvador. Their intentions were paternalistic (they wanted to help in a way that wasn't sustainable), but in general they colluded with other landowners to "fatten" themselves at the cost of the peasant worker. Among the landlords who managed the actual farms in the area for the landowners, there were those engaged in sugarcane farming and those "for whom the mill is the single most significant business interest within the agricultural-industrial, trade and banking activities that manage the country."[11] The medium and small landlords taxed the profits on the mills and most were dedicated exclusively to agriculture. Many also supplemented their income through businesses in the city. Peasants, those on the bottom of the social ladder, had their huts and small pieces of land in order to "cover their sustenance." Some took on temporary work in the mills and those who owned small shops were taxed from their trading

[9] Ibid., 12.
[10] Ibid.
[11] Ibid.

with city merchants. Because their tiny pieces of land often did not provide sustenance, they rented "the rocky ground that cannot grow sugarcane for their own small farms." The goal was to harvest enough to pay off the debts incurred by renting land, buying seed, and using fertilizer.[12] Many peasants settled in the area who could not buy land for sustenance, and according to Rutilio, "they are basically slaves" because sugarcane was seasonal work and land laws only covered full-time employees. Because of this, "evictions are becoming endemic because nobody wants to have unwanted people on their farms who could cause conflict."

The relationship between bosses and workers in the area around Aguilares was one of "domination and exploitation." This was so because the Salvadoran job code did not correspond to the reality on the ground. "Nearly all of it refers to the permanent worker, and jobs, outside of the rare case of the employers, are considered temporary."[13] Measures such as minimum wage and other rights were laughed at "because their interpretation always aligns with the interests of the employer." While there was the appearance of a law, there were various ways to get around it, and employers did. Inspections by the Ministry of Labor, for example, "easily filter into the offices of the employers" so that changes could quickly be made, allowing them to protect themselves. Those who came to speak to workers were met by workers who didn't want to talk because they feared reprisals such as being fired or other abuse that would worsen their situation. Even if the peasant's place of work was fined as punishment, in the end this money "will come from their own sweat." Rutilio painted a grim portrait of the worker in El Salvador—a laborer with few rights in a system rigged to benefit owners.

In terms of family life, the mission team characterized it as "unstable, with high fertility and mortality rates and broken homes." The basic necessities were absent—nutrition, health, electricity, water, sewer, and dignified housing—and unknown or not understood by those who lived outside of these communities. Over 50 percent of the population was under twenty-five years old, and the level of illiteracy was very high. On the whole, the people from around Aguilares were "enslaved by all these personal and environmental ills, marginalized progress, and historical actions done in the country." For all of these reasons, they became easy victims of "sexism, alcoholism, prostitution, and a high level of criminality." Finally, the life of women was even more difficult: "If this could

---

[12] Ibid., 13.
[13] Ibid.

be said of human beings in general, it is the female peasant who suffers most when the men project their actions and frustrations upon them."[14]

Socioculturally, the mission team saw oppression as well. The people of the area had neither voice nor the ability to express it; "they do not know how to 'say their word.'" The expressions they did emulate were those imposed by the popular media in the city through radio and other propaganda. Because Aguilares was a crossroads of commerce in the country, the reality there "relegates all the cultural and religious traditions of their place of origin to second place." Consequently, people could only rely on tradition which "weighs little in Aguilares." This resulted in "ambivalence for the pastoral process."[15] Because people left their own cultural and religious traditions when they came to Aguilares, they lacked "the matrix that can feed and sustain their popular religiosity." The result was that many became absorbed in what Rutilio called the "semi-pagan environment."

Politically, people in the area of Aguilares understood the system to be a sideshow that they observed—it did not represent "an expression of their will or aspirations to achieve a better situation for everyone." They feared the local police, obeyed even an oppressive local strongman, and could "barely emerge from paternalistic or populist motivations."

Religiously, according to the mission team, the church incorporated people into the scheme of oppression even if it did so unintentionally through an exploited-exploiter dualism. Rutilio articulated the situation in this way:

> The priest has some knowledge and magical powers with which he is able to manipulate everyone. God is a capricious king with whom we must be content. His will is blamed for all that exists and happens and is something with which "we must still comply in all things." To Him they go for certain needs and at certain times, like a pharmacy or a benefactor.
>
> Religiously predominant in the rural areas is traditionalism, magic, individualism, the rites of passage, and fatalism. One lives the religious sphere through alienating traditions. Their Christianity is nothing more than semi-magical devotions, without content, with some peripheral and confused notions highlighted by a great pastoral abandonment and the absence of almost any evangelization.[16]

---

[14] Ibid.
[15] Ibid., 14.
[16] Ibid., 14–15.

This description of the religious state of peoples is interesting, and it was consistent with Bishop Proaños's description discussed in chapter 6. Rutilio seemed to imply that the church kept its people ignorant with traditional explanations regarding the evil they experienced from the structural and social sin within which they were immersed. Of course, the new evangelization of Vatican II was totally different from the traditional approach, but the religious state of peoples in and around Aguilares reflected a traditional form of ministry and ecclesiology.

The pastoral reality was complex as well. While nearly everyone claimed membership in Christianity through baptism, nearly all lacked evangelization. Evangelization is the ongoing education and integration of faith into daily life in a meaningful way. After the first stage of the mission, Rutilio estimated that a group of between twenty and twenty-five thousand were without evangelical impact. Around five thousand people had questions, while two thousand considered the Gospel "something." In the end, he identified about only four hundred as "committed" in some way. Immediately following this overview of the numbers, Rutilio summarized his own pastoral-evangelical vision.

> As our people are in the center of the coordinates between God and world, time and history, we can affirm with the language conscious of Paulo Freire, that the great majority have an immersed or quasi-immersed consciousness, magical and intransitive of their reality, from which they cannot distance themselves in order to objectify and criticize that reality. This reality dominates and crushes the human being who becomes an object rather than a subject and ruler. This person does not make history and without being this maker of history, they can hardly be liberated. Only a small number of people have an emerging consciousness or are in transition to one, even if it is naïve; they are being evicted of their oppressors—king, priest, God—there is a widening of the horizon of perception and awareness that the problems of the world raise, but their consciousness is not easily manipulated nor does it have the capacity to respond. They will be the subject of their own liberation and begin to make history. It is the man in Exodus who is very appropriate to receive the Easter message from the New Man, brother of human beings and Lord of history and the universe. These will be those who are able to build a new, open society in which there is room for the word and for criticism, for dialogue and responsibility, to be the managers of their own destiny and creators of history.[17]

---

[17] Ibid., 15.

The goal for Rutilio and the mission team was to translate this vision into the context of El Salvador. They did so by making what they called, "an option for Christ and his message." The problem was not that there was *no* Christianity among the people they served; rather, what was problematic was the *kind* of Christianity that was present. Baptismal commitments were only "something general." Even those advanced in the faith had "no global vision or even a minimum scheme within which to anchor their faith." Christ and Christianity were "reduced to a series of topics or recipes with a general commitment to the better; the expressions of Christian life are nothing more than moralizing or a tangential encounter with Christ and the Gospel."[18] What was necessary and urgent was a different approach grounded in Scripture and the tradition.

The mission to evangelize was transposed as "going to all the peoples of the parish to make present the reign of God." This began with the *kerygma*: "to opt for Jesus, this is the evangelization to re-Christianize." There were three "moments" in that kerygmatic option. The first was the moment of "*metanoia* or change of personal attitude toward the kingdom." The second moment was "*koinonia*: to make a community of faith; this is catechetical-liturgical evangelization." The third moment was "*diakonia*: a commitment to change the world, this is the evangelization of actual experience."[19]

How Rutilio and the mission team understood the relationship between these three moments was *very* important. They thought that in both the community of faith moment (*koinonia*) and in the commitment to change moment (*diakonia*), "we should put an emphasis on the beginning of all evangelization: the *metanoia* or change of personal attitude toward the kingdom."[20] Rutilio's reasons were important as well, especially given the highly politicized environment at this time, just prior to the civil war in El Salvador. "If the insistence was solely on community or toward promoting change, it could become politicized, and that Christianity ran the risk of being weak because of a weak base." There would always be a political dimension of the faith, that was a given, but when it became "politicized," faith was merely used for political ends by external forces who may not be sympathetic to any personal faith dimension.

---

[18] Ibid., 16.

[19] Ibid., emphasis mine. Often these terms are translated in the tradition as "conversion" for *metanoia*, "community of faith" for *koinonia*, and "service to and for the community" for *diakonia*. All of these terms are self-descriptive of early church communities both within the New Testament and afterward.

[20] Ibid.

In this emphasis it was possible to see the difference between José Alas and Rutilio Grande—at least in terms of their pastoral emphasis or approach. Rutilio continued by seeing all three aspects of evangelization as integrated, but in a specific order: "We think that to preach the Word without reductionism will involve the other dimensions and will be the touchstone which will purify the truth of the prophetic."[21] The fear of reductionism here was a warning to not reduce the Catholic faith to specific and concrete political action of a particular kind—a simplistic mistake made by both the far right and far left wings of the political spectrum. The far right made the fight against communism a direct translation of the Catholic faith while the far left did the same with its condemnation of the oligarchy and capitalist oppression. In *both* cases the faith was reduced and enslaved by external political forces in favor of very specific actions.

Rutilio's response to this reductionism was to put Christ and the Gospel back in the center of evangelizing—even when there were concrete political dimensions for doing so. Thus he stated, "The prophetic ministry will be that which proclaims, provokes, accompanies, confirms, presides, celebrates, and verifies faith in Christ and his Gospel as bearers of a dynamism of values able to lead to a new heaven and a new earth, through a different society of human communities, new and free people. This is the horizon for which we want to create the conditions of possibility under the constant goals and objectives mentioned above."[22] One of the first aspects of this proclamation of the Gospel and Christ to understand was how the mission team understood and lived out its own priestly ministry.

Priestly Identity

As with everything else in the church following Vatican II, priests and their roles shifted, and some adapted to a new reality, a new ecclesial vision, and a new engagement with the world. Rutilio and his team of priests were no different, and their particular challenge of priestly identity was contextual as well. What they wanted, and needed, was a priestly identity somewhere between the two extremes that seemed to represent the polarization of the church over its new role. On the one side were priests who only performed sacraments and who kept what was considered the

---

[21] Reductionism is "any method or theory of reducing data, processes, or statements to seeming equivalents that are less complex or developed: usually a disparaging term." *Webster's New Year Dictionary*, 2nd ed. (New York: Simon & Schuster, 1984), 1191.

[22] Grande, "Aguilares: An Experience of Rural Parish Evangelization," 16–17.

"faith" removed from social, economic, and cultural challenges facing their people. On the other side were priests committed almost exclusively to political work with little or no emphasis on evangelization, catechesis, or sacramental integration. As Rutilio put it, "Between the priest who only performs sacraments and the priest who only works in politics, there is a spectrum of priests for everyone. Between these two extremes we tried to find our position."[23]

What followed was a fairly nuanced theological argument about the role of priests and their relationship to their communities in light of Vatican II. "Derived from the prophetic-priestly-kingly character of the people of God, the presbyterate (priesthood) is ordained to serve with ministers of the Word, through worship and animation, charisms instituted by God for the community and mediated by it. Just as with both Jesus and the Apostles, these ministers highlight the prophetic service of evangelization. If anything, we should be 'professionals' in the manner of Christ, Paul, etc. in the ministry of the Word."[24]

This summary of priestly identity is interesting for a number of reasons. First, the identity of a priest did not exist as a separate reality from a community; a priest was always a priest of a community and in a community. The values at the basis of ordination emerged from the *people of God*, in their role as prophet, priest, and king. The charisms of worship and animation, or critical roles of leadership within the community were given by God to the community (not solely the priest) and mediated by the community (not solely the priest). The model for this was from the New Testament, especially in the roles of Jesus and Paul, to proclaim the Good News and its significance in a prophetic manner, for a particular people in a particular place and time. This ministry of the Word thus required a priest who both evangelized in terms of content and applied this content *prophetically* in his context. In this way, both pure sacramentalism and pure political activism were avoided.

"Woe to me if I do not preach the Gospel!" Rutilio exhorted in his article and asks, "What do we understand by evangelization?" Evangelization, for Rutilio and the team, was measured by the kind of people who emerged from it. They wanted to proclaim a "new person, our Paschal person, the whole person found in all situations and circumstances." Indicative of this type of person were the following values: "austerity, poverty, generosity in what they have socioeconomically." They were "profoundly religious

---

[23] Ibid., 17.
[24] Ibid.

in their culture." They exhibited "dedication, endurance, and sacrifice in their political potential." The hope was that the "beatitudes become vital and concrete in the person, though they don't know it." Evangelization was thus the creation of a new person marked by generosity, deep faith, commitment to his or her community, and an embodiment of core Christian values. Rutilio and the team knew they had failed to evangelize a person if he or she remained "dependent, alienated, and oppressed." This included trying to conform to "what should be" or what "must be" in the culture. Finally, they knew they had failed if people failed "to make explicit those radically evangelical values which are dynamic and able to conscienticize the new person who is paschal, liberated and liberator, always in Exodus to a new land."[25]

This "to be more" that the team sought for the people they evangelized was not only material or economic. To mistake it as such was both dangerous and non-evangelical. "Therefore, this 'to be more' is not primarily based in ownership, knowledge, or power which are not liberating and even less salvific but rather in those realities attendant to true liberation."[26] At the same time, there were concrete social and political implications to letting the Gospel lead one's life: "This is how we are going to meet people today in the here and now as alienated but requiring the Good News—evangelization—to be consciousness-raising and politicizing as necessary dimensions, but only insofar as they are related to full evangelization. We must always have evangelization include and transcend consciousness-raising and this, in turn, include and transcend political consciousness-raising. This leads us to study the ways of evangelization and to choose one."[27] This section of the article was very important for understanding the method and intentions of Rutilio Grande and the mission team in Aguilares. The benchmark for any and all consciousness-raising and politics was the Gospel—*not* vice versa.

There was a primacy here to evangelization which proclaimed what Jesus proclaimed—the kingdom of God. But the kingdom of God was not simply a spiritual reality in the next life; rather, it was initiated by Jesus and embodied by his actions in relation to the poor and marginal peoples of his day—i.e., the kingdom of God had social and political consequences at the time of Jesus and continues to have them now. By beginning with the proclamation of the kingdom, Rutilio was in a position to say with absolute certainty that God did not want the oppression of any people

---

[25] Ibid
[26] Ibid., 17–18. This is a thoroughly Ignatian emphasis on MAGIS—the "more."
[27] Ibid., 18.

to continue. This is why the message of God and God's will must have a primacy over the other dimensions mentioned.

Rutilio seemed to anticipate magisterial teaching here, for his approach was entirely consistent with *Evangelii nuntiandi* (On Proclaiming the Gospel), Pope Paul VI's encyclical on evangelization that came out only two years later (1975). According to Paul VI, "As an evangelizer, Christ first of all proclaims a kingdom, the kingdom of God; and this is so important that, by comparison, everything else becomes 'the rest,' which is 'given in addition.' Only the kingdom therefore is absolute and it makes everything else relative." The concreteness of the kingdom is further reinforced in Paul VI's definition of salvation as "liberation from everything that oppresses man[kind] but which is above all liberation from sin and the Evil One."[28] Perhaps most importantly, the definition of evangelization that Paul VI offers in *Evangelii nuntiandi* resonated perfectly with Rutilio's experience. The document offered the following definition of evangelization: "the Church evangelizes when she seeks to convert, solely through the divine power of the message she proclaims, both the personal and collective consciences of people, the activities in which they engage, and the lives and concrete milieu which are theirs."[29] Evangelization goes far beyond catechism.

The self-critical tone set by Rutilio and the team, both in terms of ecclesial contributions to social oppression in El Salvador and the open discussion of priestly identity, was exactly in line with what was percolating in Rome at the time. "The Second Vatican Council recalled and the 1974 Synod vigorously took up again this theme of the Church which evangelized by constant conversion and renewal, in order to evangelize the world with credibility."[30] What became critical for Rutilio and his team now was whether to choose a secular way to evangelize or a religious way to evangelize. These terms, their careful consideration, and an explanation of which one the team finally chose now becomes the focus of our attention.

Ways of Evangelization: Secular and Religious

While the team did not weigh in as to which approach was more Christian, it did have a choice to make. The members realized that beginning with the oppressive conditions of the world and the effects of those con-

---

[28] Pope Paul VI, *Evangelii nuntiandi* (1975), nos. 6 and 9.
[29] Ibid., no. 18.
[30] Ibid., no. 15.

ditions first (the secular) required a response from the perspective of the kingdom of God (the religious). Both aspects must be in either approach; the question becomes which ought to be primary, and thus most beneficial, in their particular context. As Rutilio put it, "They are not mutually exclusive concepts; on the contrary, both need to be included so that the goal is truly Christian. If the religious is included in the cultural, the religious way will break open a dimension in nothing alien to the secular. In other words as we can divide one method from the other, we will always end up covering the other side if it is true evangelism, for our goal we can have no dichotomies: either be evangelized or be deceived."[31]

Rutilio and the team chose the religious way for the following reasons. First, the religious weighed heavily in the "popular mind"; that is, because the Salvadoran people were deeply religious, this was a solid starting point. Second, because of the religiosity they displayed, "radically Christian values" were not alien. Finally, for "the efficacy and practical viability in our environment, we tactically choose the religious way, even though strategically we agree with the objective of the secular way."[32] Arguments against the secular way included the fact that all activity "with overtones of consciousness-raising, politicization, and even the mere gathering of people" was immediately suspicious to the authorities. Conversely, "the religious way of evangelization cannot be dismissed as ineffective or already exhausted. We believe that what has failed in our popular Catholicism is precisely the evangelization which has tried to Christianize it. The experience begun in these two years, rather than contradict, supports our option in the majority of cases."[33]

So the way to transform the superstition, the fatalism, and the oppression associated with popular Catholicism was to first evangelize with the religious option, which then led to consciousness-raising and political action. Perhaps the most important argument Rutilio put forth as to finally choosing this way over the more secular way was that those in the "traditional church" supported this option, even if the Jesuits favored the secular option. This was important to Rutilio—being in line with Rome, the Second Vatican Council, and even traditional priests within his own country. He summarized his perspective on the dangers of beginning ministry from the secular way in the following:

---

[31] Grande, "Aguilares: An Experience of Rural Parish Evangelization," 18.
[32] Ibid.
[33] Ibid.

Christ is mutilated when he is reduced to an object of devotion such as when a guerilla sound bite refers to Him as a "simple revolutionary." Jesus openly rejected political and temporal power as well as any kind of direct leadership. His primary power is of the Word on the conscience and secondarily on what is done, and the movements of conscience trigger those options. More than finished doctrines, Jesus brought values that serve for all times and which will actually be corrosive on all negative values, idols, and absolutizations. Jesus cannot be pigeonholed into specific models or programs or we run the risk of privatizing or ossifying Him. He is found in the most notable ideals of all authentic revolutions. He was accused of "being political" and his followers will not be free from this accusation. Jesus was tempted to leave this ambiguity as all true Christians will be tempted; but to fall into that temptation will defeat the most dangerous and profound message for the oppressive powers than that of any revolutionary. The Christian message is more thorough than any political proclamation.

The church and Christians must follow these guidelines to not cut the transcendence of the Word and we ought to use mediations more prophetic than political, if we don't want to water down the message and make it short-term and partisan.[34]

Note the insistence in this argument that when Jesus was reduced to a political program, the true nature of the Word is missed as well as its political repercussions, and there were significant political consequences. Managing this tension between evangelization and politicization defined the ministry of Rutilio. "The tremendous political message—without getting into politics—of Christ, is to bring the Christian to engage in being politically conscious, but not authorized in the name of Christ and his faith to impose 'a determined or set political program.' On occasions, Christ could fall into ambiguity, but we must not forget that Christ did not want to leave that ambiguity, and that position cost him his life and led him to the cross."[35] What did this mean? What tension and ambiguity was Rutilio addressing?

To equate a particular political program or party with Christ's will was to make that program or party an absolute—and thus a god (an idol). This did not prohibit concerned Christians from proposing possibilities in the social and political realm—they simply could not advocate them

---

[34] Ibid., 19.
[35] Ibid.

as Christ's plan. Rather than advocate particular programs as absolute, what should endure are the values which Christ promoted, such as the intrinsic value and dignity of all people, especially those economically and socially marginalized, and a focus on true religiosity as service to others rather than the simple fulfillment of cultic obligations. Whether he was denouncing the law and the way it was applied or defending a woman "caught in the act" of adultery, whether he was healing lepers or forgiving prostitutes, all of Jesus' actions made those with whom he was engaged more fully human—and it is this value which should be the goal of any political model or program. So, propose social, political, and economic programs and ask as they are implemented and evaluated, does this model, program or policy make *all of us* more or less fully human? *There* the kingdom is built or impeded. There *is* a public dimension of the faith, and an essential one, but the way that dimension is perceived, proposed, implemented, and evaluated is always ambiguous and must include the question, is this or is this not what God wants?[36]

The opposite extreme must also be avoided—the privatization of Christ for our own adoration. "Whoever in the name of Christ and the community is the spokesman for the message of the kingdom, following the line of the same political theology cannot privatize Christ, his Word, or the options triggered by it. They must always leave room for criticism and healthy pluralism, in the name of service and the common good."[37] Thus, for example, sacramental adoration which stays purely personal or private militates against the spirit of Vatican II.

To summarize, two distinct avenues in evangelical method have been critiqued and removed from consideration. The first gave a primacy to the political and risked the danger of politicizing Jesus by making absolute particular parties, models, and programs. The second privatized the faith by ignoring the public dimension of the kingdom of God and Jesus' proclamation of it in favor of personal piety, cultic participation, and uniformity of belief. The question then became how could the team deepen the evangelization begun in the first stage?

---

[36] *Lumen gentium*, no. 31, articulated that this was the specific work of laypeople in their vocation to serve the world: "It is the special vocation of the laity to seek the kingdom of God by engaging in temporal affairs and directing them according to God's will."

[37] Grande, "Aguilares: An Experience of Rural Parish Evangelization," 19.

Deepening Evangelization through Courses

Far from starting from scratch, the mission team now had "thirty burgeoning communities animated by more than three hundred Delegates of the Word."[38] The goal was now to harness and direct this solid foundation by preparing the Delegates of the Word to take on new responsibilities "and avoid the multiplication of intermediaries between the community and priest." Critical to this was planning and attending a series of workshops and courses for the delegates to educate, conscienticize, and form themselves more deeply.

The key to this ongoing formation was to adapt "to the reality in which they and their community live; that it be a response to the demands and challenges posed by the communities in their growth." Again, the focus here was not merely on the communication of disembodied truth that was universal and eternal but rather how that truth could best be appropriated and lived out by a particular people in a particular place. For this reason, the team chose not to send the delegates out of the community to a level above the parish (a diocesan level) for their continuing education—at least not right away. The concern was that "it will make them jump to levels that are difficult for peasants to assimilate."[39] While ongoing formation and education was essential to the success of evangelization in poor, rural areas, it had to be done carefully. If they were pushed too soon or too far, the results could be negative. Classes at the parish level were not necessarily the next step: "This will take them out of and separate them from their own community; it will saturate them with undigested data, and they will not know what to do in their community. In the best of cases they will repeat without assimilating, but in no small number of cases the complexity is frustrating. We have arrived at this conclusion from experience and through other known pastoral experiences."[40]

The team opted for short sessions of formation, at most one day in length, with homework and reflection as their basis. The team structured their information to be practical and immediately applicable to the communities inhabited by the students. Grande explains that "the method will be dialogical, in groups and larger sessions, divided in sections where they will analyze their experience, codify these analyses from the personal to the community level and from these to national and universal levels." Here

---

[38] Ibid., 20.
[39] Ibid.
[40] Ibid.

we have a classic application of the inductive method of evangelization.[41] The core and center of this entire formation deepening was the Word of God. The goal was to make this Word of God part of their reality, and "if it is part of their reality, it can be encompassed as part of salvation history and, as such, it can illuminate their history with a vision of faith."[42] Note the inductive, integrated, and base-level method that emerged from within a community to change their own reality, and thus all of reality through the lens of the Gospel.

The courses for the delegates needed to be carefully planned and offered. Their characteristics were (1) that they be given in the parishes which unite the zones (only in rare exceptions should they be offered at a level above the parish [diocesan]), (2) they should be short and in small doses, (3) they should always respond to the community needs faced by the Delegates of the Word, (4) they should be oriented toward practical and communal work, (5) they should always follow active models of participation, and, finally and most importantly, (6) they should always be grounded in the Word of God.[43] In addition to these characteristics, a variety of courses were offered to appeal to various backgrounds, age groups, and learning styles.

To be taken after the courses in or near their communities, the following courses were examples of those above the parish level that may be suitable for delegates:

a) Experiential Laboratory of Peasants: five peasants, two lay leaders from the city, and two priests from the team attend. It takes place in San Salvador and is rich in experiences and in future applications.

b) Course on Agricultural Cooperatives: two peasants, two people from the city, and one priest attend; later more peasants and women can take this course. COSALCO in San Salvador organizes it. They will be initiating this approach to building agricultural cooperatives in the parish and in the small villages.

c) Mini-IPLA (Latin American Pastoral Institute): a peasant and a priest will attend for five weeks and it will be offered in San Salvador.[44]

---

[41] Cf. chapter 2 and the difference between inductive and deductive methods of practicing theology.

[42] Grande, "Aguilares: An Experience of Rural Parish Evangelization," 20.

[43] Ibid., 21.

[44] Ibid.

In each case the purpose of the course was to cover concrete topics that could immediately be applied to the community. Of particular interest for the team and Rutilio was learning how to use agricultural cooperatives. In a country with vast inequality in land ownership and thus agricultural production, one effective way to respond was collectively through the organizing of cooperatives. In a context where death by hunger was not uncommon, this ministry was in direct service to life! In this way, poor farmers who were helpless as individuals could pool their resources and collectively be able to afford the various components of agricultural production (seeds, fertilizer, etc.). In like manner, a better price could be had at harvest time if groups of farmers sold their product together in bulk. Of course, this undercut the profit margins of major agricultural producers—and this threat to profits eventually led to serious and violent conflict.

Within parishes, especially the rural parishes, the team instituted a program called the "community vaccine." The program "vaccinated" the communities from the corrupt politics of El Salvador and allowed them to truly exercise their democratic rights. The Gospel would introduce the community to the meaning of collective responsibility and values that were Christian. "Before the political climate ahead becomes really virulent, the communities need to be strengthened so they cannot be manipulated, and they need to be formed with a civic spirit that ought to animate the people, not manipulate them or allow them to be manipulated."[45] The concern here was about the "politics of usual," where small communities were given foodstuffs or promised whatever they needed (usually roads, running water, etc.) in return for votes.[46] This course took place in the parish in two parts and was three hours each in duration. The priests directed it through a reflection on the parable of the Good Samaritan. Groups responded to various questions designed to illicit their political situation as well as what they understood to be "political in their context." All of this was animated by the Word of God.

Part of the course also included civic education. "They are given the Constitution of the Republic and pointed toward the articles which support the political rights and duties at both the individual and community level."[47] Other forms of learning were also included, such as acting out scenarios and using theatre as a teaching tool. By staging scenarios and

---

[45] Ibid.

[46] I have personally witnessed in Latin America the delivery of rice, beans, and oil to families in exchange for promises to vote for a particular candidate.

[47] Grande, "Aguilares: An Experience of Rural Parish Evangelization," 22.

acting them out, all people, regardless of literacy, understood and appropriated the lesson. At the close of the course there was a plenary session with a definite completion as well as agreements on how to proceed with concrete issues and courses of action.

Another level of coursework was known as "training courses," where forty-five Delegates of the Word were selected to be trainers for other prospective delegates. Grande explains, "They have to be like the arms of the missionary team, the link between the communities and the parish and the new Parish council."[48] Their preparation was comprised of thirty-five hours over five weekends and was held in the main parish center. The teaching of this group was done by two priests and two collaborators who developed, in a parallel manner, those topics which occurred throughout the Bible and in their own situation. These included the historical situation of structural sin and violence, the causes of the situation that was the degeneration of relations, the overcoming of this situation and return to the proper relationship, liberation when new structures were made that humanized and did not oppress, and finally a focus on the "Plan of God" that included new people as members of a new community.

The method used to teach this course was dialogical; the priests and their collaborators only directed the overall plenary session. The groups, the evaluations, and the smaller talks were all directed by the trainers who "should not try to be 'preachers' but animators who 'prepare the road and help others grow.'"[49] Again, various methods of delivery were used to convey information and to communicate a reflection on their reality. "The person—and more the case with rural farmers—do not only learn through ideas, but through the senses, emotions, etc." In all the methods used there was a three-part process that should be followed.

a) Decoding, to come to find *what they themselves say* in the Biblical piece, a fact of life, a song, a game. . . .

b) Relation to their reality: interpretation *for them* in their situation.

c) Projection for future praxis in their communities.[50]

In addition to specific and multilevel courses for the Delegates of the Word, there were also more specific courses for others in the communities. This directly deepened the overall evangelization of the community as

[48] Ibid.
[49] Ibid.
[50] Ibid.

well. Examples included baptism initiators who "give instruction on how to approach parents, give them talks on family life, and explain the four themes that are given by the archdiocese alongside other complementary plans in the parish." Catechists received instruction and methods that enabled them to explain to the children of their community the catechism of the parish. Youth leaders learned how to do formation and use methods to form a core group of young people. Even coordinators and secretaries learned how to execute the monthly meetings of the Delegates of the Word. Additionally, mobile teams were formed who "begin to engage the young people and adults who already form the core of the village and city communities." They provided an intercommunity service of animation for the delegates and their communities.

The final stage of these courses were all given at the basic community level and were not so much about the "multiplication of knowledge" but rather "community leveling." By community leveling, Rutilio and the mission team meant that certain skills, ideas, and perspectives needed to be shared by everyone in a community and not just by leaders or some leaders. Thus, community leveling was a way of standardizing knowledge and skills of evangelization while avoiding elitism. The first course in this final stage was a "course on the relation of human beings to the earth." It was directed by eight university collaborators comprised of five Jesuit students, one seminarian, and two nearly ordained. They read a parable that was staged or dramatized in the manner of a short drama for the same villagers after a brief training. "The community analyzes and decodes various characters and the university collaborators record the verbal participation." The idea was to bring in a gospel text that illuminated what they drew out from the parable. The intended objective of this course was "an awareness of their reality and conscientization for the villagers as well as the realization of academic work for the students from the University of Central America. In the second place, they want to lift the universal vocabulary and related themes for adults for the next set of literacy courses." So in this course both rural villagers and prospective Jesuits were conscientized about Salvadoran reality.

A second course in this final stage was a literacy course offered by university collaborators with various villagers in three communities over forty-five days. The villagers, who belonged to these communities, continued and extended the education when the collaborators could not do so. The material and themes were prepared in the parish and in this way a better literacy class was offered.

A third course in this final stage covered the creation of cooperatives. Part of this course was given in San Salvador by the formation team of

CONSALCO, a Salvadoran buying cooperative. Talks were given in various hamlets and villages to inform people how to organize such an option as well as its benefits.

Finally, the last stage of courses was for a group of delegates who comprised a "permanent formation" group and whose area of focus was to connect the reality of base communities with parishes and diocesan offices. Jesuits in training accompanied and directed their formation and thus served as a link to the broader Catholic Church.

Culmination of the Deepening

For Rutilio and the mission team, the culmination of the second stage of evangelization took place in two multi-community celebrations—one was in the *Fiesta del Maíz* where the "coexistence and creativity of the community" was celebrated.[51] The other was a festival-tribute to the archbishop, which included the recognition and commissioning of the Delegates of the Word.

In the Festival of Corn, the corn and its production were chosen as the theme and symbol of the rural peasant. The preparation and creativity for the party, how it was made unique and special, came from the most basic levels of the community. The criteria for the events included that "everything will be community, nothing individual; the money factor would not detract as a determinant; it will be a party of both denunciation and hope."[52] The festival was first celebrated at the village or hamlet level and later at the parish level, which included various communities. Each community brought a collection of corn for the communal "corn meal," and the only charge was for the processing of the corn. Each community brought their best ear of corn, the best ornament created from a corn plant, and the best song about the work and harvest of the corn.

Each community put forth a godmother and godfather who served as a model of service and work in the community. The female was responsible for presenting the work of her community's women in the festival, while the male did the same on behalf of the men. Competition was avoided and emphasis was given to sharing and celebration. The gathering was lively with everyone participating and singing songs containing strong messages and protests. Its purpose was to provide a happy time for all.

---

[51] Ibid., 25.
[52] Ibid.

The festival-tribute to the archbishop was to honor his fifty years of service and the culmination of this day was the eucharistic service. About four hundred Delegates of the Word gathered in the pews and after the greeting and blessing, two delegates gave the homily. The first delegate spoke on how they were "delegates of God in service to the community."[53] This homily affirmed their call from God to serve. The second part of the homily was titled "We Are Church, Responsible for the New Person for a New Community." This part affirmed their call from their community in order to serve it. The two parts together, called by God and invited to serve by their communities, established them as "ministers" in the theological sense. Following the homily, the bishop accepted their profession of faith, "accepted their commitments and 'confirmed' them in their community functions."[54] Now they were lay ecclesial ministers. The purpose of this ceremony was to validate the call and ministry of the Delegates of the Word by the highest authority in the Salvadoran church, thereby bestowing legitimacy on their work as they formed new communities. Note that these lay ministers were always in communion with their bishops and even commissioned by them.

Conclusion

After offering the description of the second stage of evangelization in Aguilares and its surrounding communities, Rutilio concluded his article with a number of mistakes that he thought were made by his team, despite its goodwill. They included:

- Activism and immediate answers with little critique and reflection, losing an objective view and lucidity in planning.

- "Holy impatience" to force the pace and jump over stages, and subsequent flattening of values that need to be purified and transformed, not subdued or even less suppressed.

- To seek efficacy and efficiency in the short term falls into elitism and takes away from the basic levels of the community. We do not walk WITH the people if unconsciously we make it so the people cannot walk with us, and if they do not, only the elite will walk with us.

---

[53] Ibid., 26.
[54] Ibid.

- Imbalance in evangelization does not allow Christian values to be assimilated and settled in the community.

- Conscientization and maimed Christian politicization can easily rest in vindication and immediacy.

- Danger of falling into paternalism or more so into populism, creating leaders, not of service, but of oppression.

- With all these doubts we must ask: Do we educate, do we teach them culture or are we domesticating and transferring our own alienation? Do we comply with the Pauline motive "For freedom Christ has set us free"?[55]

Constructively, Rutilio and the team learned what worked and how. First, the team existed to enter into this pastoral opportunity as a *"Kairos of Salvation." Kairos* signifies a unique moment in time when people can be saved through the Holy Spirit working within an integral evangelization. The team relied on the analysis of human resources "from the base to the top and the diversification of the same." Rutilio clearly said that "we have to walk the road *with* them, not only *for* them or *from* our reality." From this the goal was clarity about the situation of the people and how it humanized or dehumanized. The method was through teamwork where everyone's strengths and weaknesses balanced out and contributed. They needed to proceed through a clear set of priorities that conformed to objectives that they used multiple methods to meet. The speed at which this was accomplished depended on the people served, not the team. "The best approaches can burn themselves or the people they intend to serve if the rate and methods are not suitable for the context." Finally, in order to evangelize others Rutilio reminded his readers that they must be open to the constant conversion to their own evangelization and the cost of that when entering into the lives of the poor whom they served. He concluded: "The beginning was a challenge; it still is today, perhaps even more so. In any case it is encouraging that 'the road is made by walking' in order to announce to the poor the good news of the kingdom of God."[56] Where that road ultimately took Rutilio is the subject we turn toward now.

---

[55] Ibid., 27.
[56] Ibid., 28.

Questions for Discussion:

1. How did Rutilio understand the relationship between the community and its sacramental life?

2. What is paternalism? How is it connected to clericalism? How are these detrimental to the faith development of a community?

3. How did Rutilio understand the priestly ministry? Is this consistent with your experience in the US church?

4. What is objectionable about a privatized Christ according to Rutilio?

5. How were the Delegates of the Word "commissioned"? Why was this important?

6. What was "community leveling" and why was it important? Can you think of any contemporary examples?

Chapter 9

The Road to Martyrdom:
The Final Months of Rutilio Grande

Now they had seen that they couldn't get me to sell out. So the judge, the mayor, and the comandante sent a document to the Estado Mayor (the main Army headquarters) saying that the priest and I were setting the people up so that we could impose communism there. Then came the first time that the National Guard came to my house.

I remember that one day I was sitting in my house. I had just come from working, and I didn't have a shirt on. And a Guardsman came with a sergeant.

"Buenas Tardes!"

I told him to have a seat, and he sat down. After looking at a nursing diploma I had there, he said to me, "Are you Don Lito?"

"Yes, I am."

"Well, I've heard a lot about you. I've come to talk with you about something that interests me." Up to this point, he was still trying to be persuasive. "Are you the one who goes to meetings in the church?"

"Yes. I meet there with other people."

"Yes, we know that. Look, what is it that you teach in the church?"

"Me? I don't teach anything. I learn along with everyone else."

"How's that? There's nobody there who teaches?"

"No, there we all give what we have, and in that way we're all learning."

("Very clever, very clever," he said, under his breath, to the sergeant.)[1]

Throughout the first and second stages of evangelization in Aguilares, land and land reform continued to be at the center of local and national politics. Recall that because Rutilio embraced the pastoral liberation method, his focus was on community *faith* formation, not political organization. Of course, this faith and its formation would have social and political consequences, but that would come after leaders were trained and the community was united.

[1] Maria Lopez Vigil, *Don Lito of El Salvador* (Maryknoll, NY: Orbis Books, 1990), 55–56.

191

One organization at the center of all issues related to land and land reform was the Christian Federation of Salvadoran Peasants (FECCAS). FECCAS was formed in 1964 through the initiative of the National Union of Catholic Workers.[2] Officially it was named in 1969, one year after the Latin American bishops met at Medellín. It was originally founded "to defend the rights of the *campesinos*, and it had established a base in Aguilares prior to the arrival of Grande."[3] It was this type of organization that the bishops of Latin America had committed to strengthening and organizing better at their conference in Medellín (1968).

> The Second Episcopal Conference wishes to voice its pastoral concern for the extensive peasant class, which, although included in the above remarks, deserves urgent attention because of its special characteristics. If it is true that one ought to consider the diversity of circumstances and resources in the different countries, there is no doubt that there is a common denominator in all of them: the need for the human promotion of the peasants and Amerindians. This uplifting will not be viable without an authentic and urgent reform of *agrarian structures and policies*. This structural change and its political implications go beyond a simple distribution of land. It is indispensable to make an adjudication of such lands, under detailed conditions which legitimize their occupation and insure their productivity for the benefit of the families and the national economy. This will entail, aside from juridical and technical aspects not within our competence, *the organization of the peasants into effective intermediate structures, principally in the form of cooperatives; and motivation toward the creation of urban centers in rural areas*, which would afford the peasant population the benefits of culture, health, recreation, spiritual growth, participation in local decisions, and in those which have to do with the economy and national politics. This uplifting of the rural areas will contribute to the necessary process of industrialization and to participation in the advantage of urban civilization.[4]

In the case of El Salvador, the relationship between FECCAS and the church would intertwine over the issue of land reform. This began early on when a group of "young university intellectuals, among whom were

[2] Rodolfo Cardenal, *Historia de una Esperanza: Vida de Rutilio Grande*, Colección Teología Latinoamericana 4 (San Salvador: UCA Editores, 2002), 434.

[3] Tommie Sue Montgomery, *Revolution in El Salvador: Origins and Evolution* (Boulder, CO: Westview Press, 1982), 106.

[4] "Document on Justice," no. 14, emphasis mine, in *Liberation Theology: A Documentary History*, ed. Alfred T. Hennelly (Maryknoll, NY: Orbis Books, 1994).

some Jesuit students of philosophy and theology" offered to collaborate in the training of FECCAS leaders.[5] The Jesuit-founded University of Central America then became an instrumental partner at this time. "The José Simeón Cañas Central American University, founded by the Jesuits in 1965, contributed much to the process of change."[6] This was possible because the very purpose of the Jesuit University in El Salvador, from the beginning, was the transformation of El Salvador in keeping with the goals of Vatican II. This is very clear in the following description: "While the church at the parish level was beginning to [re]socialize the people from a religious perspective, a new national university was founded in 196[5] with the intention of teaching children of the ruling class about the social and economic reality in which a majority of their fellow citizens lived, creating a sense of responsibility for changing this reality, and giving them the education necessary to do so. That at least was the intent of the Jesuits who formed the intellectual and administrative backbone of the Central American University."[7]

Some of this collaboration was evident in the "Grand Missionary Tour" of Rutilio when he partnered young Jesuit intellectuals with Salvadoran peasants in the exploration and development of agricultural cooperatives. But the overlap of the pastoral and the political would come even more directly with the communities that had self-organized throughout the evangelization of Aguilares. Recall that over the two-year "Grand Missionary Tour," Rutilio and his missionary team "established ten urban and twenty-seven Christian base communities (CEB's), training 326 catechists and delegates for various responsibilities, including pre-baptismal instruction (37); catechists (38); youth work (18); musical groups (72); founding and encouraging new CEB's (58 of whom 17 moved on to continue the work in other communities); and assisting in various courses (29)."[8] Often the Delegates of the Word, who had been trained by the church, and specifically by Rutilio in Aguilares, assumed leadership positions in local political organizations. "In the rural areas many priests and religious

---

[5] Cardenal, *Historia de una Esperanza: Vida de Rutilio Grande*, 434.

[6] Jeffrey Klaiber, *The Church, Dictatorships and Democracy in Latin America* (Maryknoll, NY: Orbis Books, 1998), 173.

[7] Montgomery, *Revolution in El Salvador: Origins and Evolution*, 107.

[8] Ibid, 105. See also Rutilio Grande, "Mártir de la Evangelización Rural" ("Martyr of Rural Evangelization"), *Collection: The Church in Latin America* 2 (San Salvador: UCA Editores, 1978), 70–73. (Before, during, and shortly after the civil war, many books were written by a group of anonymous editors at the UCA who remained anonymous for reasons of personal safety.)

women offered courses for training catechists and 'Delegates of the Word.' The catechists and the delegates were often the leaders of the peasants' unions."[9] This relationship between Christian base communities and social and political organizing is well documented.

> Despite differences in style and scale, CEB's in both rural and urban areas helped a large number of Salvadorans to develop a critical understanding about the larger political situation, identify their interests, and acquire organizational skills. From there, CEB members often became involved in organizations such as FECCAS and the UTC, which drew many leaders and activists from base communities in areas like Chalatenango and Suchitoto. Despite the participations of many members, most religious communities maintained a religious identity distinct from popular political organizations.[10]

This overlap between ecclesial leaders and political and social leaders was inevitable. The pastoral strategy of both Vatican II and Medellín was to develop lay leaders who would transform the world in the direction of the kingdom of God. "It is the special vocation of the laity to seek the kingdom of God by engaging in temporal affairs and directing them according to God's will."[11] In light of such a statement, it would have been impossible to separate one's faith and commitments from the social, economic, and political world one inhabited. This became evident very quickly in Aguilares. Only eight months after the missionary team had arrived, on May 24, 1973, workers in a nearby sugar mill went on strike. It was a peaceful strike, and the workers received a raise from management, though it was less than they had demanded. Montgomery described it this way: "The strike was not organized by the parish, but many of the workers were members of the CEB's and some of the leaders were Delegates of the Word. This produced in Grande a tension with which he would live for the rest of his life. 'He saw clearly that his mission was to evangelize and not political organization, but at the same time he understood that conscientization in a situation of injustice and oppression would necessarily lead to organization.'"[12]

---

[9] Klaiber, *The Church, Dictatorships and Democracy in Latin America*, 173.

[10] Anna L. Peterson, *Martyrdom and the Politics of Religion: Progressive Catholicism in El Salvador's Civil War* (Albany: State University of New York Press, 1997), 59.

[11] *Lumen gentium*, no. 31.

[12] Montgomery, *Revolution in El Salvador: Origins and Evolution*, 106. See also Grande, *Martyr of Rural Evangelization*, 83–85.

Oppression of FECCAS

Although FECCAS would continue to grow in Aguilares, it also expanded rapidly throughout the country. In the eyes of the oligarchy, the Jesuits in general and Rutilio in particular were intimately connected to the success of that organization.[13] Because the various parishes in the Aguilares area offered support for the 1973 strike, even though it did not organize it, "The local landowners, through FARO and ORDEN, centered their attention on the Jesuits and their work in the parish and the university."[14] The Agricultural Front for the Eastern Region (FARO) was an organization representing the interests of wealthy landowners that specifically targeted FECCAS as well as the Union of Workers in Rural Areas (UTC).[15] The Nationalist Democratic Organization (ORDEN) was a right-wing peasant paramilitary organization formed by the Salvadoran military (with US assistance) in the late 1960s to combat communism through a village-level "paramilitary network."[16] Both became violently involved in the push back against peasant organizations such as FECCAS and UTC, and thus the popular church in El Salvador.

In Aguilares, FECCAS established itself as an independent power. They did so upon the same base as the church, working with oppressed peasant farmers. Most farmers performed both subsistence farming and farmed for salary for wealthy landowners. Because there were few full-time agricultural workers, demand for labor was greater than the supply. This put any group that organized labor in a strong position vis-à-vis landowners. In the harvest of 1975 to 1976, two work slowdowns in the areas of La Cabana and Colima were put into effect, and various abuses at the *haciendas* (estates) of wealthy landowners were denounced.[17] Additionally, there was tension between "village patrols" made up of ex-military service members who were loyal to the ruling party (PCN).

Membership in these patrols was seen as a service to the ruling party in order to defend the country from internal and external enemies. These patrols initially were made up of people from both within and outside

---

[13] Montgomery, *Revolution in El Salvador: Origins and Evolution*, 106.

[14] Klaiber, *The Church, Dictatorships and Democracy in Latin America*, 173.

[15] Cardenal, *Historia de una Esperanza: Vida de Rutilio Grande*, 510. Klaiber also mentions this group in his chapter on El Salvador, "The Church, Dictatorships and Democracy in Latin America," 169.

[16] Phillip Berryman, *Stubborn Hope: Religion, Politics and Hope in Central America* (Maryknoll, NY: Orbis Press, 1994), 17.

[17] Cardenal, *Historia de una Esperanza: Vida de Rutilio Grande*, 439.

the community. Later, only people from outside the particular community being patrolled were employed, and the goal became to pull them from other communities "with no conscience."[18] The phrase "with no conscience" signified that organizers wanted patrol members to come from communities that had not been organized and who were not aware of their rights. Thus, patrol members were sought by the wealthy who would not succumb to community needs or the notion that the people ought to be organized in any way.

For their part, ORDEN countered the work of FECCAS by making resources available to select leaders in each community, which included access to credit and medicines. In one community, for example, a teacher was the designated contact for ORDEN. He acquired a lot of power because he received a salary from ORDEN and a salary from the school; he received money for the medicine he was given, as well as money for making his home available for meetings of the PCN. Additionally, he received loans for seeds, fertilizer, and insecticides which he then sold at higher prices to the local peasants. The message was clear. If you cooperated with ORDEN for your individual good, you were well taken care of, even if the community was not.[19] In some sense, this simply made the inequality and injustice of the local reality more reflective of the national reality at the time.

The various agricultural estates strictly managed the peasant workers. Work crews were organized by a foreman from each village. Workers were told to work fast and hard and not to be like those "strikers." If a worker was expelled from one work crew for organizing, complaining, or participating in a strike, it was very difficult to get work on another crew. The foreman usually replaced any problem worker with someone they knew was faithful to them, a "good person."[20] In this way, they controlled the workers. One man recounted his experience by explaining, "Only I could not get work, they wouldn't give me any. The reason was that about two years ago we had gone on strike and one of the village informers had denounced me, and this is why I couldn't find work." In certain communities a national identity card was required in order to work, which was difficult to acquire if one was not affiliated with ORDEN. Additionally, entire communities were displaced by some landowners with the help of the National Guard and the mayor's office in El Paisnal. In other places,

[18] Ibid.
[19] Ibid., 440.
[20] Ibid.

large tracts of land were required to be worked with no minimum wage. The abuses were numerous, widespread, and entrenched.[21]

The growth of FECCAS in the parish was not merely quantitative; it also indicated a qualitative growth in organizational capacity.[22] By November 1975, FECCAS was firmly established in nearly all the villages surrounding Suchitoto, Aguilares, and El Paisnal. The zones of very poor peasant farmers and small land holders were fertile ground for the organization. When there was opposition in a particular community to the labor organization work of FECCAS, the rich would line up against the organization and the poor would join it. The greatest number of affiliates, bases, and mobilizations of workers related to FECCAS were located in and around Aguilares. They were well-organized, strategically structured, and widespread throughout the area. The main problem was that "according to the constitution in force, these organizations were banned."[23] The response to such illegal activity would come largely at the hands of ORDEN through people being kidnapped, tortured, and killed.

According to Cardenal, ORDEN was essentially an internal espionage agency with a network of agents throughout the villages of the country. In addition to spying, it promoted small community development projects and made access to health and education services easier for its members to use. During electoral periods, ORDEN became a paramilitary organization for the official government party with the goal of intimidating local peasants. Faced with the expansion of FECCAS in Aguilares, ORDEN strengthened its bases there. According to a communiqué to its members in Aguilares, members (who numbered about thirty) were ordered to observe and try to infiltrate meetings of FECCAS, which were condemned as "totally communist."[24] The members were advised to stay in close contact with the National Guard.

FECCAS and the Parish

While FECCAS and the parish of Aguilares were completely separate and structurally autonomous one from the other, FECCAS received support and protection from the church as the repression increased. This happened for the obvious reasons of previous church involvement with

---

[21] Ibid.
[22] Ibid, 442.
[23] Ibid., 443.
[24] Ibid., 444.

training leaders for FECCAS and in the shared goal of land reform, labor rights, and poverty reduction. FECCAS also latched on to the church for protection, because it knew the movement could end prematurely due to government repression. From the perspective of the Salvadoran government, "the parish of Aguilares and FECCAS were considered one and the same."[25] This is why there were tensions between the two organizations on a daily basis.

Interestingly, ORDEN and FECCAS also broke down along denominational lines—Protestant and Catholic. According to Cardenal, FECCAS tapped the leadership of Delegates of the Word and catechists for its activities in various villages, whereas ORDEN encouraged Protestant biblical fundamentalism. According to one of Cardenal's sources, "A Protestant never became a member of FECCAS."[26] ORDEN encouraged a particular interpretation and use of the Bible, emphasizing such themes as furthering the work of the community as what God wants (abstract and general), and not taking what is not one's own (for example, land).

The influence of the Gospel was also clear on the directors of FECCAS. Under this influence they spoke of giving their life for others. FECCAS began with a deep and "fundamentally Christian spirituality which later changed to a Christian-revolutionary spirituality, which eventually formed a revolutionary-Christian spirituality."[27] Each phase signified a crisis of growth and an attempt to integrate the Gospel into their work of agrarian reform. In each phase, FECCAS was autonomous from the church in its structure and in its political philosophy. Nevertheless, the church influenced it as well. For many, entry into FECCAS was a type of conversion experience attested to by language such as, "I entered the organization when I really saw what was clear to everyone else." Another became a member "when I woke up and saw the necessity for a change."[28] This political conversion was similar to what many experienced in religious conversion as is clear in the following: "both see a light and wake up, both have a determination to give their lives for it, one for Christ the

---

[25] Ibid., 458.

[26] This distinction continues to this day, as many *biblieros* or Biblical Christians support the right wing of Salvadoran politics. It was pointed out to me by a former FMLN combatant in the civil war that many high-ranking military officers became Protestant ministers following the war. For more on the importation of especially US Protestant sects into El Salvador from the 1980s forward, see Phillip Berryman, *Stubborn Hope: Religion, Politics, and Revolution in Central America*, especially chap. 5, "Making Disciples."

[27] Cardenal, *Historia de una Esperanza: Vida de Rutilio Grande*, 461.

[28] Ibid.

other for the community in a constant struggle. For the first, the Church makes possible the change, while for the second, the organization does. For both, they abandon vices. Both conversions demonstrate an interesting parallel. The political conversion was deeply radical. The decision to give one's life is tremendously more radical when the repression became more acute every day."[29]

Because of this experience of conscientization in light of their Christian faith, support for socialism and the struggle of the lower classes surged. This was not only true in El Salvador, but also throughout Latin America. While this may be shocking to North American sensibilities, recall that in 1967 a group of bishops led by Dom Helder Camara (Brazil) authored a "Letter to the Peoples of the Third World," which received worldwide attention for its endorsement of socialism in their context.[30] Needless to say, all of this put tremendous pressure on Rutilio in his effort to lead *first* with the Gospel.

Accusations grew from outside the community that specifically targeted Rutilio. They began with leaflets in the Aguilares area dated July 17, 1975, published by the "Conservative Religious Front." They accused Rutilio and other members of his missionary team, including priests, of being agitators and haters who encouraged class warfare. According to the leaflet, they had thrown their faith in God and love of God in the trash. Rutilio responded to these leaflets and tried to clarify—again—his situation and his activities. The leaflets actually gave him the opportunity to proclaim the fundamental principles of the one and true Jesus, very different from the Jesus worshiped by the conservative Catholics who authored the leaflets.[31]

According to Rutilio, the message of Jesus was understood best by those who believed that God had created the world for everyone and not exclusively for a few. He also negated the opinion that he belonged to, or worked for, any particular political party. He stated that an affiliation with a political party was neither permitted nor necessary in order to defend who and what he was defending in the name of Jesus. He noted with emphasis that some people "have a God and His will which permits the abuse of the poor and the exploitation of the majority, who try to

[29] Ibid.

[30] Hennelly, ed., *Liberation Theology: A Documentary History* (1997), 48–57. It is worth mentioning that at the time of this writing, one of the most productive economies in South America was socialist Brazil.

[31] Cardenal, *Historia de una Esperanza: Vida de Rutilio Grande*, 462.

grab all that God has left for all human beings: read the Bible well, and slowly. You will find it subversive. Overall, you will find Jesus of Nazareth subversive, and maybe at some point so will the existing political party in our suffering country."[32]

Rutilio's love for the people he served was so great that he stated with certainty, "I fear absolutely nothing in defending your interests, even if it were to cost me life itself. To offer one's life for the love of one's neighbor is equal to what Jesus did, and he said a person can do no greater act."[33] Shortly after this statement, he gave thanks for martyrs from the church of Honduras who shared the same fate as Jesus. He then stated that the people should hate no one who attacks them. As proof of their love for their oppressors, people need to be ready to give their lives for the conversion and salvation of their oppressors which is in every case, "recognizing their injustices for the good of this, our country."[34]

A particular target of Rutilio in his response to this leaflet was the conservative sector of the Catholic Church in El Salvador. Recall that "conservative" had different connotations than it does today in the United States. Being conservative indicated an interpretation of the Christian faith that compartmentalized one's faith exclusively to religious observance and a concern for personal morality and spirituality. Such a faith rarely moved into the economic, social, and political realms as demanded by Vatican II. Rutilio argued directly against conservative theological errors in order to unmask a God which he believed they had created in their own image. Thus he stated, "We now see that there is a God made by human hands and kneaded with the blood of innocent brothers, which these so-called CONSERVATIVE CATHOLICS are worried about: it is the god of money and its interests. They wake up thinking in the name of money, the all-powerful god. They go to bed thinking in the name of money, the all-powerful god, even though what follows from this are thousands of filthy, emaciated, anemic, and poor peasants. Hypocrites! Stop calling yourselves conservative Catholics, because you are lying."[35] Rutilio was implying in his charge of hypocrisy that a self-defined "conservative" Catholic would conserve the teachings of the church—including Vatican II, papal encyclicals, and the teachings of their own leaders, the Latin American bishops at Medellín.

---

[32] Ibid., 463.

[33] Ibid.

[34] Ibid. Archbishop Oscar Romero states very similar ideas in his homily at the funeral of Rutilio.

[35] Ibid., 464.

There was little doubt that Rutilio was responsible for many of the successes in Aguilares. All of the parish pastoral and organizational activity was affected by his presence and hard work. He was instrumental in his efforts both to evangelize and to conscienticize the people of Aguilares and its surrounding area. For the landowners and foremen of wealthy estates, as well as their owners in the capital, the evangelization and conscientization in Aguilares was the equivalent "to planting hate and spreading socialism."[36] Cardenal points out that independent of Rutilio's constant explanations and stated good intentions, both of himself and the missionary team, his work could not be perceived in any other way, because all of it went against the established order of Salvadoran society.[37] Rutilio and the mission team had begun to delegitimize this order by removing one of its strongest bases of self-justification—the religious. Now the religious were against the prevailing order and, even more, encouraged peaceful resistance against it.

For this reason, Rutilio's political effectiveness diminished as his ministry grew. Throughout the remainder of his ministry, he insisted he was a proponent of no political party, even when official government lists named him as both a revolutionary and a subversive. As a religious leader, he believed he could not stay out of the politics of the common good. According to Cardenal, Rutilio believed "this was supported by the eternal values of the Gospel, which coincided with the fundamental values of humanity and for this reason, was not the legacy of any group or faction."[38] At the same time, Rutilio was aware of his role in both the ambiguity and radicalism of the priesthood. "To the established order, he had left the legal game of traditional political parties, and in doing so, Rutilio had become a dangerous subversive."[39]

While the parish in Aguilares believed in the rights of all people, especially the poor peasants they worked to conscienticize, they did not want to be associated directly with one political organization. For this reason, beginning in 1975, the parish and FECCAS embarked on a proposal to emphasize their "relative autonomy" from each other.[40] Under this new emphasis, the mission of the parish consisted of accompanying, illuminating, and motivating political action in the community according to the

---

[36] Ibid., 470.
[37] Ibid.
[38] Ibid., 471.
[39] Ibid.
[40] Ibid., 482–83.

faith. For this reason, the parish mission could not be identified exclusively with the objectives and ends of an agrarian organization, even if it confessed to be of Christian inspiration. The primary mission of the parish had to remain the Christian base communities, which existed as seeds of Gospel values and sources of inspiration for the work of the church.

In November of that year, Rutilio announced the formal separation of FECCAS from the parish and its status of relative autonomy. He even rejected a request to have the National Congress of FECCAS meet at the parish, as he did not want the organization and the hierarchy of the church to be confused by anyone. The tension that Rutilio experienced between the parish on one side and political organizing on the other was difficult for him. According to Teresa Whitfield, "A lengthy document prepared by other Jesuits in his support assessed the experience of Aguilares and found doctrinal justification for the mobilization of the *campesinos* in the documents of Vatican II and Medellín. But the justification made Grande's position no easier to bear: Grande felt himself so caught between total respect for the *campesino*'s right to organize and his worry about what was happening to the parish that at one point he offered his resignation to the archbishop."[41] The work of the parish instead became the offering of a variety of courses in order to continue educating its people about their own context in light of their faith. These offerings included a course on the "national reality in light of the faith." The parish chose the professors, and the courses were open to anyone in the parish, according to their respective levels of conscientization.[42]

As the work of the parish proceeded, pressure from the church hierarchy increased for the parish to more visibly separate from FECCAS. The same archbishop, who saw in Rutilio a vocation to the priesthood when he was twelve years old, was now asking him to avoid confusion with political organizations and to reign in the younger Jesuits who were creating concern with their political work.[43] At the same time, the archbishop and the papal nuncio were pressuring Rutilio with respect to his pastoral work in Aguilares. Salvadoran President Molina along with the conservative bishops of El Salvador (with the exception of Rivera y Damas) stated that priests were responsible for the subversion of the villages against the government. Only Bishop Rivera y Damas looked favorably upon FECCAS.

---

[41] Teresa Whitfield, *Paying the Price: Ignacio Ellacuría and the Murdered Jesuits of El Salvador* (Philadelphia: Temple University Press, 1995), 65.

[42] Cardenal, *Historia de una Esperanza: Vida de Rutilio Grande*, 483.

[43] Ibid., 495.

FECCAS responded by giving a presentation to the bishops about its work, all the while quoting the pastoral letters of Archbishop Chavez.

The same tensions that occurred at the parish level between FECCAS and the parish of Aguilares now emerged at the national level. Rutilio passionately defended FECCAS to the archbishop, arguing that the organization was consistent with Gospel values, the documents of Vatican II, the documents of Medellín, and, especially, the emphasis of the church to encourage agents of change. Thus, even while Rutilio was arguing for and working toward a more explicit separation of FECCAS from official parish ministry, he was also defending the organization before the highest levels of the church. All of this ambiguity and confusion would peak when the first phase of land reform was voted upon and passed by the Salvadoran National Assembly in the summer of 1976.

Land Reform, Final Months, Martyrdom

When the first phase of land reform passed on June 29, 1976, it created a forceful confrontation between the church and the state. The dispute lasted three months, after which the government substantially "modified" its decree on land reform on October 30. This retraction was notable for creating new social movements aimed at furthering land reform. The UCA (University of Central America) took a strong stand for the original June reform while ANEP (National Association of Private Enterprise) reacted with extreme virulence against the proposal.[44]

In summary, the land reform proposal was fairly modest. Recall that in 1961, 81 percent of arable land in El Salvador was held by six families. The first phase of land reform would redistribute agrarian property greater than eighty acres only in the zones of Usulután and San Miguel where some of the largest and most productive cotton farms in the country were located. The legislation did not affect Aguilares, and the global scheme of the reform was far from radical.[45] It was acknowledged early on that it would take decades to carry out the complete plan for land reform throughout the country. The first phase alone was supposed to take ten years and only upon completion of the first phase would the second phase begin.

The initiation of the first phase of land reform resulted in a level of repression against the church by the state that had never been seen before.

[44] Ibid., 508.
[45] Ibid., 509.

As noted, in October the National Assembly modified the original decree by renouncing the right to expropriate land. Because of this change, the only mechanism left was to allow landowners to sell their land at market prices. Land reform would now make the landowners even richer.

In the area around Aguilares, FARO formed. This organization represented landowners in the area and worked militantly against any organizing done by FECCAS. According to their literature, FARO existed to resist land reform, especially the reform passed by the National Assembly in the summer of 1976. As the various factions and organizations coalesced either for or against land reform—and there were many—the church found itself caught in the middle. For example, when various groups marched in the thousands through San Salvador in favor of land reform or opposed to land reform, they would often request a Mass to conclude their demonstrations at the National Cathedral. Archbishop Chavez asked that priests not concelebrate at these Masses and thereby not take explicit sides with organizations at the center of the debate. This was difficult for many priests who had actively worked for land reform through support of the intermediary organizations encouraged by the bishops (including Chavez) at Medellín.

At the priest senate meetings of the diocese of San Salvador that year, Rutilio argued that the bishops could not stand off to the side in this very important issue confronting their people.[46] "You have to be blind not to realize the urgency for peasants in different parts of the country, which continues to grow in a progressive awareness by force of circumstance, and given the specific circumstances . . . the government itself is faced with a severe challenge with these events and just read the speeches of President Molina . . . he has said things as a result of pressure from the masses, like it or not."[47]

Rutilio defended the goodness of the intermediary organizations (called for at Medellín) and urged the archdiocese to take the problem seriously and encouraged the church to contribute its support to the challenge of land reform. Archbishop Chavez agreed that the fundamental rights of these organizations coincided fully with Gospel values and were consistent with the conclusions of the 1974 Synod of Bishops at the Vatican where Paul VI released his groundbreaking work on evangelization titled *Evangelii nuntiandi* (Proclaiming the Gospel in Our Time).

---

[46] The Priest Senate was a body of priests who represented the opinions and values of the priests ministering in the archdiocese. Foreign priests were allowed to represent as well if they lived and worked in the archdiocese.

[47] Cardenal, *Historia de una Esperanza: Vida de Rutilio Grande*, 513.

Rutilio went on to share, in front of his fellow priests, his own experience of conflict related to land and his mission work in Aguilares. "He knew well the risks and failures of an authentic evangelization."[48] Through the UCA, the church did support the first phase of land reform, but it was vigorously attacked by both the right for supporting any land reform and by the left for supporting such a moderate vision of land reform.

Martyrdom

Two homilies of Rutilio, one from August 1976 and the other one month prior to his murder in 1977, offer a glimpse of how he preached and reacted to events as they unfolded. In 1976 during the third Festival of Corn, while discoursing on the meaning of Mary's *Magnificat*, Rutilio acknowledged the network of spies within the community, as well as the wealthy landowners who sought to preserve their wealth. The following is from his homily:

> And who are those who have no fear of God? Those who have reported here on our father and our brothers have no fear of God. Those who get up in the morning crossing themselves (he makes the sign of the cross while speaking) have no fear of God.
> In the name of coffee! In the name of coffee! In the name of Coffee! In the name of sugarcane! In the name of sugarcane! In the name of sugarcane!
> I have said before, but it must be repeated *ad nauseum*. To the powerful who climb down from their high places; to the self-sufficient, because you have gods here! And to the humble who picked them up; the humble who climb up to them. To those who have hunger they should be full of all goods, and to the rich and wicked of heart who don't want anyone to have porridge, for them nothing more. Those who want everything for themselves but do not want to share with their brothers in the Eucharist of fraternity . . . to these barbarians, right? We say: "He has brought down the powerful and sent the rich away empty-handed," because they are Cains, because they are cruel, and because they are ingrates of ANEP (the National Association of Private Enterprise).[49]

---

[48] Ibid.

[49] Rutilio Grande, "Homilía en el Tercer Festival del Maíz," *XXV Aniversario de Rutilio Grande. Sus Homilías*, ed. Salvador Carranza, Miguel Cavada Diez, Jon Sobrino, and Centro Monseñor Romero (San Salvador: UCA Editores, 2007), 63, translation mine. As indicated already, ANEP was an association in El Salvador strongly opposed to

Rutilio returned to his theme of unmasking opponents of land reform when he accused them of idolatry. The most important thing in their lives, the ultimate source for their identity and action in the world, was not their neighbor but their money. To the community gathered for the harvest festival, Rutilio did not simply ask them to pray; rather, he encouraged them to collaborate with God's will, based on Gospel values, to better the world in which they lived. This affected even how they perceived the act of prayer as is clear in the following: "There is a song out there that says, 'it is not enough to pray.' Be careful! We have not said that 'there is no need to pray.' It is not enough to pray! The mere intellection, the understanding, the mere word is not enough. As if to see if it is actual money that I have, the Word is verified *in action*, as it is said according to the Bible."[50]

The focus on practice emphasized a movement beyond traditional prayers of petition but did not signify, in any way, a lack of faith. Rather, it was the acknowledgment that human response through faith-in-action was necessary in order to cooperate with the coming of God's kingdom (Thy kingdom come! Thy will be done, on *earth* as it is in heaven). Rutilio emphasized both practice and the spirit with which one carried it out when he stated in the following:

> Dear brothers and sisters, this is our identity: we are Christians *if we follow the Lord*.
>
> The motivations that Jesus Christ had, the values of the Gospels, are our profound motivations. These internal motivations that he had, we want to have these in our journey, although it costs.
>
> When we organize ourselves, when we get into a village organization, these motivations are the motor of our journey through the parish and through the communities of the country. These profound motivations of the Gospel: we want a new world. All who go out as a result of the global work of the parish should carry the label of a Christian, not only as a cover. This must be the deep root of their validity and of their being, of the overall work of the parish, of our community, and of the numerous communities in the countryside and the city. All of you, the one who speaks and all those perched here, we are all responsible together. Because of this, the message of Corpus Christi (Body of Christ) and of all the great fiestas is: *Chris-*

---

the land reform. See Berryman, *Stubborn Hope: Religion, Politics and Revolution in Central America*, 87, 195.

[50] Grande, "Homilía en el Tercer Festival del Maíz," 63.

tians, we are the parish!, not the bricks and walls of the temple. We are all responsible.[51]

In Rutilio's final homily given in the village of Apopa in February 1977, one can sense the culmination of the conflict over land reform as well as the heightening of tension with wealthy landowners and the government. The background to this homily was the expulsion of the Colombian priest Fr. Mario Bernal. Prior to his expulsion, violence from right-wing groups and left-wing organizations began to increase. Mario Bernal was expelled from El Salvador on January 29, 1977, after five years of ministry in Apopa. Bernal had a weekly radio program on Radio Vanguardia that the government disliked. Rutilio gave a very important homily in protest of Bernal's arbitrary expulsion as well as a Christian testimony on behalf of the vicariate of Quezaltepeque in response to this action.

After announcing a welcome to all the various communities who had been invited to protest the expulsion of Fr. Bernal, Rutilio put forth the sacrament of the Eucharist as the embodiment of what he hoped for in a new Salvadoran reality.

> We meet here about the emergency of the priests, and we had the precise agreement, with the awareness of the faithful in our parish, to have this demonstration of faith. It was very clear that we met at the gas station and from there departed in an organized manner all together and in solidarity while confessing our faith; we concluded with the Eucharist which is our main commitment and the symbol of what Father Mario Bernal preached and defended.
>
> The Eucharist is the symbol of a shared table, with a stool for each person, and tablecloths long enough for everyone. It is the symbol of Creation, which requires redemption. It is already being sealed with martyrdom![52]

This all-inclusive meal, the Eucharist, was the symbol *par excellence* for Rutilio that God wanted everyone to have a seat at the table of creation. He wanted this symbol of Jesus' final meal to influence and structure social relationships very concretely. What followed in his homily was a careful argument for what the role of the church should be in the context of El

[51] Ibid., 64.

[52] Grande, "Homilía de Apopa," *XXV Aniversario de Rutilio Grande. Sus Homilías* (2007), 73, translation mine. Rutilio's reference to martyrdom refers to church people killed in Honduras and other countries as they worked to implement the evangelization from Medellín.

Salvador, how that role should imitate the incarnation of Christ, and how it should perceive the world and its people. After a brief introduction of a church in service to the world, fragile but incarnated in history, the homily is divided into three distinct parts: (1) equality of the children of God, (2) the risk of living the Gospel, and (3) persecuted like Jesus of Nazareth.

Rutilio's Last Homily

Rutilio began his homily by introducing an understanding of the church based on humility: "We are aware of our fragility, of our sins and betrayals on the long road of history. We are a human corporation, the human element of the Church on the level of laypeople, on the level of directors, priests and bishops and popes. We have confessed our faults and this is the daily requirement of the personal and corporate conversion of the Church."[53]

Beginning his homily by stating the need for the conversion of the church, Rutilio could argue with conviction that a change in the church's perspective, and the tension this created, was necessary. He wished to avoid understanding the church as "a museum of dead traditions or of undertakers" and preferred to see change as a sign of fidelity to the Holy Spirit.[54] This was difficult for the wealthy and conservative oligarchy of El Salvador, both lay and ordained; the church had changed its teaching with respect to its mission in the world! Far from being unfaithful to the tradition, Rutilio argued this change represented an acknowledgment of the human frailty within the institution of the church, as well as fidelity to the Holy Spirit as it constantly reformed itself. That is why an understanding of the church in service to the world, and in a particular context, was so important to him. "We feel ourselves part of this Church that we love, and we always want to see it reformed through the power of the Holy Spirit, in the midst of weaknesses that it has; in the midst of evil, in the midst of the problems in the world."[55] The beginning of this conversion, the beginning of this turning toward God was the recognition that all human beings are equal in the eyes of the Creator.

Equality of the Children of God

If the kingdom of God could be understood as the dual unity of (1) God becoming fully present to human history in Jesus of Nazareth *and*

---

[53] Ibid., 75.
[54] Ibid., 74.
[55] Ibid., 75.

(2) human history coming to be according to God's will, then how human beings interact and structure human society was very important.[56] Either we structure society, and ultimately human history, in accord with God's will or we do not. Rutilio began with our relationships to each other, in light of our relationship to God. If all Salvadorans were really equal in God's eyes, then that equality must be reflected in how they organized their society. Those who did not recognize this equality effectively frustrated the plan of God in this world; Rutilio identifies these people collectively as "Cain."[57] He left little doubt as to whom he identified as Cain: "All people have a common Father. We are all children of such a Father, even though we are born of the womb of distinct mothers here on earth. All people, evidently, are brothers and sisters. Everyone is equal one with the other! But Cain was an abortion in the Plan of God, and groups of Cains exist. He is also a negation of the kingdom of God. Here in this country groups of Cains exist and they invoke God, which is even worse."[58]

This direct reference to those who did not see everyone as equal is a twofold critique of the "Cains." Their first error was how they misunderstood their relationship to one another in God's eyes—everyone as equal. Their second error was using that misunderstanding to oppress others. In so doing, they negated the kingdom of God wherein human history was supposed to coalesce in accord with God's will as exemplified in the ministry and message of Jesus. If the wealthy and powerful of El Salvador truly believed in equality (this would apply to the wealthy anywhere), then the earth's goods would be available to all on a reasonable basis.

This was, and continues to be, the foundation of Catholic social teaching, which militates against the type of inequality that had been the status quo in El Salvador for all of its history. Thus, in very concrete terms, God intended the goods of this world for everyone. "God, the Lord, in His plan

---

[56] I am indebted to Fr. Jon Sobrino for this shorthand definition of the kingdom God. See Jon Sobrino, *Jesus the Liberator*, trans. Paul Burns and Francis McDonah (Maryknoll, NY: Orbis Press, 1993), chap. 4. This interpretation of the kingdom of God would fit squarely into what is identified as "realized eschatology." The kingdom of God has come (in Jesus of Nazareth) but is not yet fulfilled completely. God's action brings the kingdom; human cooperation either accepts or rejects it both individually and collectively.

[57] Cain is understood here to act against God's will by taking the life of his brother Abel. When God asks Cain where his brother is, Cain responds, "I do not know; am I my brother's keeper?" (Gen 4:9). This action by Cain results in God's punishment and is yet another effect of original sin.

[58] Grande, "Homilía de Apopa," *XXV Aniversario de Rutilio Grande. Sus Homilías* (2007), 75–76.

for us, gave us the material world. Like this Mass material, with material bread and with the material cup that we raise in a toast to Christ, the Lord. This is a material world for everyone without borders. This is what Genesis says."[59]

The symbol of this material world for everyone is made clear with the institution of the Eucharist by Jesus. "So the material world is for everyone, without borders. Like a common table with tablecloths long enough for everyone, like the Eucharist. Each person has their own stool. And so everyone comes to the table, with a tablecloth, and brings something of their own gifts."[60] This understanding of reality embodied in a meal, and the fellowship that accompanied it, verified for Rutilio that God wanted love to be the key to the kingdom. And so he preached: "Love, the signal of the kingdom! It is the only keyword, which summarizes all the ethical codes of humanity, and is sublimated and held in Jesus. It is the Love of shared fellowship which breaks down and checks all classes of barriers, prejudice and has overcome the same hate. We are not here in order to hate! Even these 'Cains,' we love them. They are our enemies—evidently they don't understand!"[61]

What, then, was the suggested response of a Christian to "enemies"? According to Rutilio, they must love them, but this did *not* mean a lack of conflict. Christians should not advocate physical violence, as he put it, but they should not hesitate to employ "moral violence." Says Rutilio, "Love is conflictive and requires *moral violence* of believers and the Church as a body. I said that we do not come here with machetes. This is not our violence. Violence is in the Word of God, which is violent to us and violent to our society, and which unites us and brings us together, although it beats us."[62] This made perfect sense when society failed to structure itself according to God's will in El Salvador. Moral violence was the inevitable confrontation between the kingdom and the anti-kingdom which included the denouncing of that anti-kingdom as contrary to God's will. People or groups of people were told they were selfish, and oppressive and hypocritical. This was part of the Christian message, the prophetic part, and justification for this type of prophetic ministry came directly from the ministry of Jesus. It was just as unpopular in Rutilio's time as it was two thousand years ago.

[59] Ibid., 76.
[60] Ibid.
[61] Ibid.
[62] Ibid.

When faith and Christianity were reduced to sources of peace and tranquility, the prophetic Jesus tended to fade away. But if the gospels were read carefully and from the perspective of the poor, Jesus was a man in almost constant conflict. While Jesus loved everyone, he did not love them in the same way! He condemned riches and blatantly told the rich that they could not have two gods. Riches were first bad for the rich, second they were bad for the poor, and, finally, they came between the rich and a sincere dependence on God.[63] This message is emphasized in each gospel through the story of the rich young man. The rich never think they are subject to these criticisms, and just as the response to that message resulted in violence to Jesus, the response continued to be violent to a church that was faithful to that message in El Salvador. Jesus also condemned the fulfillment of religious law when it interfered with human fulfillment. This was obvious when Jesus put hunger as more important than sabbatical laws against picking corn or the needs of a man on the side of the road over religious purity (the Good Samaritan). Perhaps the clearest manifestation of his condemnation of faith reduced to religious legalism was the forgiveness of a woman caught "in the act" of adultery—something the Mosaic law punished with death. Rutilio wanted the church to embody the same conflict that Jesus confronted in his own ministry. Only then could the church know and realize its mission in the world.[64]

> My friends; As a Church Body, the Church and each one of us who make it up—like the brothers who preached with truth on the way of the procession—we are all prophets. As an ecclesial body we are continuers of the mission of Jesus Christ. This body which is the Church, and which covers entire communities, has a mission, like homework, to announce and make possible a favorable environment for the kingdom of God here, in this world. This body must embody the values of the kingdom of God in the realities of your country in order to transform it effectively, like the yeast that transforms the dough.[65]

The same risk accepted by Jesus in this conflict was inherent in being faithful to the kingdom and working toward its realization. It was here that the church incarnated Christ in, and through, its *action* for the world.

---

[63] See Jon Sobrino, *Jesus the Liberator*, chap. 6.

[64] I will argue later that this method is strikingly similar to Archbishop Romero's address given at the University of Leuven shortly before his death.

[65] Grande, "Homilía de Apopa," *XXV Aniversario de Rutilio Grande. Sus Homilías* (2007), 77.

The Risk of Living the Gospel

The expulsion of Fr. Bernal from Apopa was the historical realization of his confrontation with the anti-kingdom. But it was not only an individual who was expelled; it was something greater than that for Rutilio. "The reason we gather together today in Apopa, from all the corners of the Vicariate, including other communities from outside the boundaries of our Vicariate, is the case of Fr. Mario. It is an ecclesial event. The Church cannot remain silent. It cannot stay off to the side on this act. We are affected."[66] Because he was a priest of a community within the Catholic Church of El Salvador, his removal affected more than simply himself—it affected everyone he served as well. What was at stake in the expulsion of Fr. Mario was not simply someone's freedom of speech or the right to organize; for Rutilio, it was about something much greater.

> What is at stake here is the fundamental question of what it means to be Christian today, and to be a priest in our country and on the continent that is suffering the hour of the martyr. The challenge is to be or not to be faithful to the mission of Jesus in the midst of this concrete world that we live in, in this country. If you are a poor priest or a poor catechist in this country from our community, you are slandered, threatened, taken out secretly in the night, and it is possible they will bomb you. It has happened! If you are a foreigner they will take you out! They have removed many foreigners! But the fundamental question still remains.
>
> It is dangerous to be a Christian in our environment! It is dangerous to be truly Catholic! It is practically illegal to be Christian in our environment, in our country. This is so because the world around us is founded on a radically established *disorder*, to which the mere proclamation of the gospel is subversive. And this is how you have to be, you can't be different! *We are chained to a disorder, not an order!*[67]

The confrontation between church and the state in this instance was really a confrontation between the Word of God and the world. A faith without conflict was not possible. The root of the conflict was an unjust society structured by a powerful few and the human suffering that resulted from that structure. These structures were made and promoted by human beings, not by God, and they were the fundamental *disorder* that was confronted. For the church to reside in that society without confront-

[66] Ibid., 78.
[67] Ibid., 79.

ing the evil around itself would be to fail as a church in the world. Rutilio thus confronted his society, his fellow Catholics in the oligarchy, and the great inequality present in that context.

> The statistics of our small country are dreadful on the level of health, the level of formal education, the level of criminality, the level of subsistence living of the majorities, on the level of land holding. It is all bundled up with a false hypocrisy and lavish works.
>
> Woe to you, hypocrites, who call yourselves Catholics but inside are full of filth and evil! You Cains crucify the Lord who walks with the name of Manuel, with the name of Luis, with the name of Chabela, with the name of the humble worker in the field!
>
> It was rightly said in our Archdiocesan Pastoral Week that "Our people hunger for the True God, and hunger for bread." And no privileged minority in our country has a Christian reason for being, except to work for the large majority that make up the Salvadoran people.[68]

Naming structural sin in El Salvador required Rutilio to see the crucified Christ in the people he served, the crucifiers as those attempting to preserve their economic, social, and political power, and the purpose of the church as denouncing that evil. This direct attack on the wealthy minority would have direct and serious consequences.

Persecuted, Like Jesus of Nazareth

Acting upon the social and political reality of El Salvador from the perspective of faith resulted in Fr. Mario's expulsion from the country. The new mission of the church in the world would be misunderstood and even twisted by enemies who did not want to be confronted with their injustice. According to Rutilio, Fr. Mario "fully fulfilled the ministry of a priest within the constraints of the ministerial priesthood in the Church. He did not overshoot these functions. He was not a guerilla; he did not front for any organized political group."[69] Regardless, he was expelled for confronting the *status quo*, kept in place by those who had much to lose. Interestingly, Rutilio went on to confront the importation of versions of Christianity which would allow the wealthy to remain "Christian" without challenge. This importation of mainly North American Pentecostalism is

---

[68] Ibid., 80.
[69] Ibid.

well documented, and for Rutilio it represented a Christianity made in the image and likeness of the oppressor in El Salvador.

> I call attention to the avalanche of imported religious sects and of the slogans of freedom of worship, in this context, as they are walking and crying out in the street over there. Freedom of worship, freedom of worship! Freedom of worship in order to bring us a false god! Freedom of worship in order to bring us a god that is in the clouds, sitting in a hammock. Freedom of worship in order to present to us a Christ that is not truly Christ. It is false and it is serious.[70]

Unable to respond to concerns from the church, the oligarchy of El Salvador simply changed churches—much like the oligarchy of neighboring Guatemala did throughout the 1970s and 1980s.[71] By shifting their theology to a more abstract Christianity concerned with salvation in the *next* life, the wealthy and powerful could ignore the injustices in this world while they reduced their Christianity to personal moral decision making and church attendance.

Consequences would come down hard upon priests like Rutilio Grande, as well as the church on the whole. For Rutilio, this was a sign of consistency with the ministry of Jesus, which resulted in his own crucifixion and death. Rutilio saw very clearly that being faithful to the Gospel came with a cost. He would become the first priest of many in El Salvador to pay it. The following section of his final homily attested to the fact that he knew his own persecution, and possible death, were imminent.

> The God-Man, the prototypical human being, was accused of rebellion, of being a foreign Jew, of intrigues through exotic and strange ideas, contrary to "democracy" as it is said, contrary to the minority. These ideas are contrary to God, because the accusers are contrary to God; they are from the tribe of Cain.
>
> Surely, brothers and sisters, they will return to crucify him. And I hope that God frees me from also being, perhaps, in the cast of those crucifiers! Without a doubt, brothers and sisters, they will return to crucify him again, because we prefer a Christ of undertakers and morticians.
>
> Many people prefer a Christ of undertakers and morticians. They want a mute Christ, without a mouth, who passes by them walking

---

[70] Ibid., 81.

[71] See Berryman, *Stubborn Hope: Religion, Politics and Revolution in Central America*, chap. 7.

in the streets. Many prefer a Christ with a muzzle on his mouth. Many prefer a Christ made for our own whims and according to our own interests.

This is not the Christ of the Gospel! This is not the young Christ, of thirty-three years, who gave his life for the noblest cause of humanity!

My brothers and sisters; some want a god of the clouds. They don't want this Jesus of Nazareth, who is a scandal for the Jews and madness for the pagans. They want a god who will not interrogate them. They want a god who will leave those in the establishment peaceful, one who will *not* say these tremendous words: "Cain, what have you done to your brother, Abel?"

Do not take anyone's life. Do not put your foot on the neck of any person, dominating them, humiliating them. In Christianity one must be willing to give his or her life in service for a just order, in order to save others, for the values of the Gospel.[72]

One month later Rutilio Grande was murdered. On March 12, 1977, shortly after five o'clock in the afternoon, a Volkswagen Safari left a small town in El Salvador known as Aguilares. In the vehicle were three people—an elderly man named Manuel Solorzano, a fifteen-year-old boy named Nelson Lemus, and Rutilio. On the way out of town, near the train tracks, the vehicle stopped to give three small children a ride. They were leaving Aguilares and their destination was the town of El Paisnal, roughly three miles away, where Rutilio was travelling to continue a novena in celebration of the town's feast day. As the bell was tolling to gather the people near the small church situated in the central plaza of El Paisnal, they made their way along the narrow dusty road that connected Aguilares and El Paisnal. "Rutilio liked the people already gathered when he arrived."[73] As they passed the small village of Los Mangos, the children recall seeing groups of two or three men located on the banks of the small canals on either side of the road. Behind the VW was a small pickup truck that had followed them from Aguilares. In a low voice, Rutilio is quoted as saying, "We must do what God wants."[74] As the pickup came closer to the VW, a hail of bullets fell from the sky, impacting the car. Later, a doctor who examined the bodies indicated that Rutilio was killed by bullets coming from both the front and rear of the vehicle. The weapons and ammunition used

[72] Grande, "Homilía de Apopa," *XXV Aniversario de Rutilio Grande. Sus Homilías* (2007), 82–83.
[73] Cardenal, *Historia de una Esperanza: Vida de Rutilio Grande*, 573, translation mine.
[74] Ibid.

were common to the local police. The bullets from the front of the vehicle hit his jaw and neck and penetrated his skull. From the rear and left, he was shot through the lower back and pelvis. Altogether, he was killed by twelve bullets.[75] When the bodies were found it appeared that seventy-two-year-old Manuel Solorzano tried, in vain, to protect Fr. Rutilio as his body completely covered him. "Nelson sat quietly in his seat with a bullet in his forehead."[76] The three children who had been given a ride were screaming in the far back of the vehicle. A man whom they recognized ordered them to leave, which they did, full of panic. As they ran down the road toward El Paisnal, they heard one final shot.[77] Covered in blood and dirt, they did not stop running until they had arrived in El Paisnal.

Immediately, the news of these murders was transmitted to the new archbishop of San Salvador, Oscar A. Romero, as well as to the provincial of the Society of Jesus, who also resided in the capital. Three Jesuits from the provincial office, Archbishop Romero, and his auxiliary Bishop Rivera y Damas all travelled to El Paisnal. At seven o'clock, President Arturo Molina called the archbishop to offer his condolences and to promise a thorough investigation. Later, the newspapers would say that the archbishop had called the president first.[78] This discrepancy between the government and church accounts of what occurred continued to be a developing theme throughout the period of violence that followed (1977–1992).

Rutilio Grande and Archbishop Oscar Romero

> Rutilio Grande's death was to prove a defining event for the Jesuits of Central America and for the Salvadoran Church under the leadership of Monsignor Romero. For the Jesuits, the internal disputes that had so characterized the painful years since the meeting in December 1969 were silenced by a unity born of persecution. For his part, Monsignor Romero emerged from his past to lead a Church under siege, but a Church that was unified by what many began to speak of as "the miracle of Rutilio."[79]

Much has rightfully been written about the life, ministry, and death of Archbishop Oscar Romero. What has not been recognized in the English-

[75] Salvador Carranza, ed., *Una Luz Grande nos Brilló: Rutilio Grande, SJ* (Comisión de la Compañía de Jesús, 2007), 96.

[76] Cardenal, *Historia de una Esperanza: Vida de Rutilio Grande*, 574.

[77] Ibid.

[78] Carranza, ed., *Una Luz Grande nos Brilló: Rutilio Grande, SJ*, 100.

[79] Whitfield, *Paying the Price*, 104.

speaking world, beyond a brief mention or a politicized sound bite, is the impact of the life, ministry, and death of Rutilio Grande on Romero's thought and ministry.[80] I would argue that it is impossible to understand the ministry and sacrifice of Oscar Romero without the background of his close, personal friend whom he called "a brother."[81] This is evident from a brief look at the homily Archbishop Romero gave at Rutilio's funeral as well as the structure of one of the last talks given by Romero at the University of Leuven prior to his own assassination. In a way, those two short pieces bookend his time as archbishop and both speak to the influence of Rutilio.

Romero introduced his homily at the funeral of Rutilio with two themes that resonated throughout his time as archbishop—both in his actions and in his pastoral letters. The first theme, broadly considered, was the church and its proper relationship to the world. The second theme was the uniquely Christian contribution to development.[82] In both cases, the term "liberation" was used. Both were framed by the question, "What does the Church provide in the universal struggle for liberation from so much misery?"[83] His response, in many ways, was a summary of the life and ministry of Rutilio Grande.

The church could not simply be "absent in this struggle for liberation." It must enter into the fray on behalf of the marginalized and poor in a unique way, even when such activity could be misunderstood. Second, Romero argued by quoting Paul VI that the role of the church in this struggle was to provide the "inspiration of faith" and a motive of "fraternal

---

[80] There are *exceptions* to this: They would include Douglas Marcouiller, SJ, "Archbishop with an Attitude: Oscar Romero's *Sentir con la Iglesia*," *Studies in the Spirituality of the Jesuits* 35, no. 3 (May 2003), as well as most of the material in Teresa Whitfield's *Paying the Price*. The most complete summary of Rutilio's life and work in English is the first chapter of William O'Malley's *The Voice of Blood: Five Christian Martyrs of our Time* (Maryknoll, NY: Orbis Press, 1980), 3–63. The best theological and pastoral treatment of Rutilio Grande is by Dean Brackley in his chapter in *Monsignor Romero: A Bishop for the Third Millennium*, ed. Robert S. Pelton, Robert L. Ball, Kyle Markham (Notre Dame, IN: University of Notre Dame Press, 2004). Nearly the entire chapter on Rutilio is unreferenced by the "anonymous Salvadoran author of the life of Rutilio Grande," vii. It was clearly written by someone with access to his homilies and letters.

[81] Oscar Romero, "Homilía en la Misa Exequial del Padre Rutilio Grande" (Homily in the Funeral Mass of Fr. Rutilio Grande), *Colección Homilías y Diario de Mons. Oscar Renulfo Romero*, 2nd ed. (San Salvador: Imprenta Criterio, 2000), 1, translation mine.

[82] For the development of these themes in a variety of ways, see Oscar Romero, *Voice of the Voiceless: The Four Pastoral Letters and Other Statements*, trans. Michael J. Walsh (Maryknoll, NY: Orbis Books, 2004).

[83] Romero, "Homily at the Mass of Fr. Rutilio Grande," 2.

love" for liberators. The social teaching of the church was thus offered as a gift of prudence and the basis of commitments which emerged from a motive of love.[84]

When Romero argued for the church's role in liberation, it was in *contrast* to other movements "without spiritual horizons." The social doctrine of the church had both horizontal and vertical dimensions, just as love of neighbor and love of God went together and could never be separated. Thus, as already argued in *Gaudium et spes*, *Populorum progressio*, and Medellín, the pastoral liberation that Rutilio fought for could never be reduced to simply the economic, the political, or the social. It was an integral liberation which sprang from faith but deeply engaged the economic, social, and political realities of this world. In like manner, Romero reminded the people at the funeral that even the funeral itself was a "gathering of faith," though undoubtedly he knew and hoped it had wider social and political implications.

Romero understood the death of Rutilio as a result of the confusion between the social teaching of the church—a teaching that should be the *source* of all political and social action for believers—and a political doctrine "that hinders the world." Nevertheless, he exhorted the priests at the funeral to recognize the message of Rutilio as being "most important to us." He asked that priests embrace this message in light of their faith and work together so as not to be divided by "dangerous ideologies not inspired by faith." Romero saw the dangers of a purely Marxist starting point for political and social organizing, and he clearly understood that the role of the church should be separate from this. What made the church distinct from other ideologies was precisely the argument made by Rutilio in his final homily at Apopa—love was the key.

Rutilio embodied this Christian form of love, according to Romero, through his accompaniment with those he served in a posture of humility and determination in the face of their suffering. "Rutilio was a priest who was with his people; he walked in their community in order to identify with them, to live with them, not to be an inspiration of revolution but to be an inspiration of love, a love that inspires us my brothers and sisters."[85] According to Romero, the love of God inspired the action of Rutilio. "My dear priests let us embrace this inheritance." Romero concluded his homily by stating clearly and firmly that the church had no enemies and that revenge was not the proper response to the death of Rutilio by criminals.

[84] Ibid., 2.
[85] Ibid., 4.

He then thanked all the collaborators of Rutilio who worked for Christian liberation. Finally he stated that, yes, there was a solution. "Let us understand this Church, be inspired by this love, and live this faith for I assure you that there is a solution to our great social problems."[86]

When one compares the three sections of Rutilio's final homily in Apopa with Romero's address at the University of Leuven where he articulated the three benefits of the church making a preferential option for the poor, it is difficult not to see Rutilio's influence on Oscar Romero. In Rutilio's final homily he addressed first the equality of the children of God, second the risk of the living the Gospel, and third the persecuted like Jesus of Nazareth. Similarly, the three benefits to Romero for the church making an option for the poor included a greater awareness of sin made possible through experiencing it with the people the church served; a deeper appreciation of the incarnation of Jesus Christ through an imitation of God's downward movement into human history; and, finally, a deeper faith in God and Christ because of the church's active participation of loving action in the world.[87]

Both Rutilio's homily and Romero's Leuven address begin with a substantial section on the church in service to the world which share striking similarities. Both speak of taking on the defense of the poor as well as undergoing persecution for taking on this defense. Finally, both emphasize that "no one has greater love than this, to lay down one's life for one's friends" (John 15:13). It would not be too strong to state that Romero lived out what he had seen embodied in the life, ministry, and death of his friend Rutilio Grande. For this reason we can be sure that both Rutilio and Romero realized the final sentence of his Leuven address: "And I also believe that by putting ourselves alongside the poor and trying to bring life to them we shall come to know the eternal truth of the Gospel."[88]

The successor to Archbishop Romero, Bishop Rivera y Damas, offered this thought on the profound influence of Rutilio Grande on the life of Romero: "One martyr gave life to another martyr. Kneeling before the body of Fr Rutilio Grande, Monseñor Romero, on his 20th day as archbishop, felt the call from Christ to overcome his natural human timidity

---

[86] Ibid., 5.

[87] Romero, "The Political Dimension of the Faith from the Perspective of the Option for the Poor," *Voice of the Voiceless*, address by Archbishop Romero on the occasion of the conferral of a doctorate, honoris causa, by the University of Leuven, Belgium, February 2, 1980, 178–86.

[88] Oscar Romero, "The Political Dimension of the Faith from the Perspective of the Option for the Poor," in Hennelly, ed., *Liberation Theology*, 302.

and to be filled with apostolic courage. From that moment on Monseñor Romero left the pagan lands of Tyre and Sidon and marched boldly towards Jerusalem."[89]

Questions for Discussion

1. How was FECCAS supported but separate from the Catholic Church in Aguilares?

2. How was ORDEN's interpretation of the Bible different from Rutilio's understanding of the Gospel?

3. What is the "moral violence" of the Gospel called for by Rutilio?

4. What is the correct relationship of the social teaching of the church to political life in any given context?

5. How did Rutilio Grande, SJ, influence Archbishop Oscar Romero?

---

[89] Jesús Delgado Acevedo, *Monseñor Oscar A. Romero: Biografía* (San Salvador: Universidad Centroamericana, 1990), 3. This quote comes from a presentation by Julian Filochowski titled "Eucharist and Martyria—the Witness of Oscar Romero" (conference on Global Catholicism, DePaul University, Chicago, IL, April 18, 2012).

Part 4

Lessons for the Church
in North America

Chapter 10

What Rutilio Grande, SJ,
Can Teach the Church of North America

An amazing amount of attention goes to concerns regarding one's own life in God, one's development as a person, the obstacles in the way of realizing one's full potential. We put great emphasis on an individualistic, highly psychologized—not to say narcissistic—approach to spiritual matters. In this culture, I came to believe, spirituality seems to be basically "all about me."[1]

A life of faith and hope and love rises in contradiction to the values of the Commodity Form in our culture. Faith, hope, and love are the three human activities deemed most impossible by the cognitive and behavioral standards of commodity consciousness. In Catholic tradition, one believes that these three human acts are "theological virtues"—the highest exercise of our human personhood, wherein we participate in the very life of God. Thus, not surprisingly, the anti-humanism of our culture is at the same time a lived atheism.[2]

There are so many ways the Catholic Church could use the insights and methods of Rutilio Grande to better evangelize our own North American context. Of the many ways Rutilio's work could be used, it would be helpful in this final chapter to focus in on three specific areas: (1) embracing social analysis as part of pastoral strategy that allows for more effective evangelization in a particular context, (2) a healthy model for the collaboration of lay and ordained in parish ministry, and (3) rediscovering a truly social dimension of faith for the North American church. The following argument is meant to be suggestive insofar as it takes the methods used

[1] Joseph Nangle, *Engaged Spirituality: Faith Life in the Heart of the Empire* (Maryknoll, NY: Orbis Books, 2008), xv.

[2] John F. Kavanaugh, *Following Christ in a Consumer Society*, twenty-fifth anniversary ed. (Maryknoll, NY: Orbis Books, 2006), 147.

by Rutilio and the insight gained by him and tries to apply it in a very different context and time. I conclude by arguing that Rutilio's ministry and ultimate sacrifice is relevant for our church here in the contemporary United States.

Social Analysis and Evangelization

In 1965, *Gaudium et spes* stated that in order for the church to be of service to the world, "We must be aware of and understand the aspirations, the yearnings, and the often dramatic features of the world in which we live."[3] According to Pope Paul VI's encyclical *Evangelii nuntiandi* ("On Proclaiming the Gospel"), evangelization is central to the work and life of the church: "the Church evangelizes when she seeks to convert, solely through the divine power of the message she proclaims, both the personal and collective consciences of people, the activities in which they engage, and the lives and concrete milieu which are theirs."[4]

A careful study of this quote illustrates the necessary link between the personal/collective consciences of people, activities, lives, and a "concrete milieu." Or, put another way, the church cannot form the personal and collective consciences of people without a firm grasp of the context within which it is evangelizing. More recently, John Paul II argued that "the Church values sociological and statistical research, when it proves helpful in understanding the historical context in which pastoral action has to be developed and when it leads to a better understanding of the truth."[5] Rutilio knew this and this is why he spent so much of the first missionary tour in Aguilares simply *listening*.

Recall that even though he was born and raised in the area he would one day evangelize, Rutilio began his work with the mind-set that the worldview of his mission team was not the same as the people whom they were serving. Separated by their relative wealth, privilege, and formal education, it was first necessary to attend to the reality within which the people of El Salvador were immersed and the effect of that reality on their personhood. Before the truth of the Gospel could be shared, the truth of the situation had to be grasped. For this reason Rutilio and his team began with listening tours and spending significant time in people's

---

[3] *Gaudium et spes*, no. 4. The document encourages the use of the sciences to do this in no. 62.

[4] Pope Paul VI, *Evangelii Nuntiandi*, no. 18.

[5] John Paul II, *Familiaris Consortio*, no. 5.

homes. Further, they utilized surveys that collected data and employed qualified people trained in sociology and anthropology who analyzed and interpreted that data. In addition to direct contact through listening to people and surveys seeking relevant data, he used national census data in a way that allowed him to understand the "macro" issues of El Salvador. These issues included everything from land distribution to income inequality to wage pressures on working-class peasants. Can and should the church of North America use the same method to evangelize people here? What might the results be?

Omaha: A Case Study

In 2002, Omaha Together One Community (OTOC), a consortium of faith communities, authored an excellent study of census data titled "Omaha Census 2000: The Shrinking of the Middle Class." Using data provided by the US Census, the authors of this report indicated that national wage decline began in 1973 and has resulted in greater income disparity and a shrinking middle class throughout the United States.

According to the OTOC analysis, in 1970 the median family income in Omaha, Nebraska, was $10,208 ($46,339 adjusted for inflation to year 2000), and in the year 2000, median family income was $50,821.[6] This demonstrated that there was roughly a 10 percent growth in the median wage, similar to the national average. But a quick view of a color-coded census map of Omaha showed that while some sections of the city did quite well, traditionally poor and racially distinct north Omaha (predominantly African American) and south Omaha (predominantly Hispanic) did much worse.

For example, census data showed that certain sections of town had heavy concentrations of children under seventeen with both parents working full-time, while other areas (such as west Omaha) had a much lighter incidence of this. While there were more two-parent families working, consumer debt was also exploding. Thus, although wages increased 10 percent on average, the benefits of that increase were not shared equally. Some people in some areas benefitted greatly while others saw few or no

---

[6] According to the authors of this study, "median income" is more accurate than "average income" (especially when Warren Buffett lives in Omaha). The median income variable includes two or more related people living together and does not consider single breadwinners. Further, it does represent the elderly but not those living alone, and it can include a single parent and child. The median income is not an average income but rather an income which has 50 percent of incomes above it and 50 percent of incomes below it.

benefits. Therefore, there were many people both above and below the median income, resulting in a greater income disparity within Omaha.

The OTOC analysis went on to ask, *so what?* Why does income inequality matter? What they assert is very important for an organization that wants to influence the consciences of its people in a particular milieu. According to the authors of the report, economic disparity leads to a variety of problems, including political disparity, social isolation, more consumerism (to "keep up with the Joneses"), an increase in health problems, and mortality. Finally, increased divisions between rich and poor lead to increased mistrust and decreased social capital.[7] Each of these negative effects should be carefully considered.

Political disparity manifests itself because the need for different programs and their costs will be interpreted differently depending on one's geographical area. The poor tend to vote less (because they have less time, energy, and resources for political involvement), so people in poor communities lose out on the impact of political decisions. Greater movement to the suburbs by those fleeing poor areas of town leads to another set of problems, including congestion due to development, which is almost always ahead of infrastructure and road capacity. In addition, housing units further away from the city center have higher infrastructure costs (more tubes, roads, wires, etc.) and can result in the devaluation of central city homes. Soon, poor areas of town begin to have lower high school graduation rates as a result of a decline in median income while unemployment rates in the same areas begin to increase.

Commuting to the suburbs has its own problems, as more time in the car leads to less personal interaction and more privatization. Those left in downtown areas now begin to see a concentration of social problems, including teen pregnancy, unemployment, drug abuse, and depression. The income disparity between those in the suburbs and those in the city leads to greater problems still. Such disparity increases consumerism because moving "up and out" of the city areas brings with it an entirely new set of expectations and comparisons. Luxuries become necessities and basic housing costs climb because builders focus on higher profits per unit in "premium" communities. This is not only hard on those trying to keep up but also hard on those unable to keep up. As the authors of the

---

[7] The amount of literature on the social effects of income inequality is vast, but one reference used by the presenters included Ichiro Kawachi and Bruce P. Kennedy, *The Health of Nations: Why Inequality Is Harmful to Your Health* (New York: The New Press, 2002). See especially chapters 5–8.

census study state, as "a small portion of families get significantly richer, the bar of consumption rises and everyone has to try harder to keep up with the Joneses. The cost for basic commodities such as housing climb steeply; local construction companies focus on high-profit multi-million dollar units, and basic affordable housing falls out of the market."[8]

Inequality leads to other problems. Richard Wilkinson, an international epidemiologist who researches the effects of inequality, states it clearly. "The pattern we've found in our research is extraordinarily clear. More unequal countries, the ones with the bigger income differences between rich and poor, have much more violence, worse life expectancy, more mental illness, more obesity, more people in prison, and more teenage births. All these problems get worse with greater inequality, because it damages the social fabric of a society."[9] This reading of reality would indicate that inequality is certainly a significant social issue as it affects many health indicators of humans.

In Omaha, income inequality affects the capacity of everyone to form and sustain a meaningful community. Social capital decreases and mistrust increases when communities are separated geographically and live within significantly different social realities. More time working to sustain a consumerist lifestyle means less community involvement in nonsocial or economic activities.

After considering this brief but accurate social analysis of one North American city, we can ask how might the evangelization of the church be affected? Because the social fabric that Catholics inhabit deeply affects the issues they care about—from abortion to poverty—knowing and understanding the social context can help guide pastoral strategies to evangelize. For example, would certain policies reduce the number of abortions in Nebraska when survey data tells us that of the roughly 2,400 abortions performed in 2011, over 30 percent were done for "socioeconomic reasons"?[10] Is being prolife simply about changing the legal status of access to abortion or is it about reducing abortions by supporting struggling women and families in concrete and effective ways? Nearly all of the effects of income inequality relate to the "life issues" that deeply concern the church. To continue our example, church members have no problem praying the rosary outside an abortion clinic—but would they

[8] Omaha Together One Community, "Omaha Census 2000: The Shrinking of the Middle Class" (slide 29).

[9] Theresa Riley, "The Social Consequences of Inequality," interview with Richard Wilkinson, *Bill Moyers* (web site), May 13, 2012, http://billmoyers.com/2012/05/13/the-social-consequences-of-inequality/.

[10] "Nebraska: 2011 Statistical Report of Abortions," Department of Health and Human Services of Nebraska, Office of Health Statistics (2012), 3.

vote for concrete policies that would relieve the economic distress of those same women seeking abortions? Should the church focus on the causes of behavior or simply condemn the act?

Building on the insights and methods of Rutilio Grande, a more effective evangelization of Roman Catholics in North America would include a clear and honest understanding of social reality and a faith response to that reality. Consumerism provides an excellent example of how this could be done. In his book *Christ in a Consumer Society*, John F. Kavanaugh, SJ, argues that perhaps the greatest moral threat today, one that forms consciences and deeply influences our behavior, is the embrace of what he calls the "commodity form."[11] This is the dominant form of culture in our celebrity-centered, competitively driven, consumer society.

> The consumer society is a formation system: it forms us and our behavior. It is also an information system: it informs us as to our identity and as to the status of our world. Its influence is felt in every dimension of our lives, and each dimension echoes and mirrors the others. The individual's "lost self" is paralleled in the dissolution of mutuality and relationship. The personal and interpersonal breakdown is reflected in the social and economic worlds through a general socialized degradation of persons, through a flight from human vulnerability, especially found in marginal people, and through a channeling of human desire into the amassing of possessions.[12]

What is at stake here is the "American way of life" and the question posed is whether North American Catholicism will substantially challenge it. Speaking from personal experience, I can state unequivocally that I have never heard a homily related to how we understand our "socioeconomic" selves or the purpose of money in relation to Christian discipleship—beyond the typical appeals to fill the Sunday collection plate. In light of that, I can't help but recall a message from Rutilio's final homily in Apopa: "Many people prefer a Christ of undertakers and morticians. They want a mute Christ, without a mouth, who passes by them walking in the streets. Many prefer a Christ with a muzzle on his mouth. Many prefer a Christ made for our own whims and according to our own interests."[13]

---

[11] Kavanaugh, *Christ in a Consumer Society*.

[12] Ibid., 4.

[13] Grande, "Homilía de Apopa," *XXV Aniversario de Rutilio Grande. Sus Homilías*, ed. Salvador Carranza, Miguel Cavada Diez, Jon Sobrino, and Centro Monseñor Romero (San Salvador: UCA Editores, 2007) 81.

The continual refusal to engage the social and economic basis of our moral decision making has direct consequences for how we reasonably approach the "life issues" the church is so concerned about. We would rather discuss them—from abortion, to the death penalty, to immigration, to poverty—as if they are simple individual moral choices. The reality is that those issues can never be effectively addressed apart from an understanding of our concrete social reality and the decisions made in that context.

As a university professor who receives the results of years of Catholic school and parish formation in the students I teach, I can state with certainty that the current strategy to catechize students through a relentless focus on teaching doctrine simply does not work. Students want to know how and in what way their faith relates to their lives and the decisions they will make *in the world*. This never comes up when the focus is on memorizing doctrinal truths and repeating prayers—pastoral strategies that have changed very little over decades. Our students need theology as it mediates the faith to a given context, whereas catechesis simply delivers the truths of the faith.

This severance of faith from life, the natural result of catechizing without context, is then extended into a compartmentalization of faith outside of "real life." This explains why the number of abortions, divorces, and other social maladies are virtually identical between Catholics and non-Catholics. We aren't really any different from mainstream society because we are not evangelized in an integral way—it is simply nonintegrated knowledge. An integrated evangelization would begin by situating people in their social context and demonstrating the importance of faith commitments through a thorough understanding of *that context and its effect on human beings*.

Collaboration of Lay and Ordained in Parish Ministry

In the final section of his paper titled "Redeeming Catholicity for a Globalizing Age: The Sacramentality of the Church," Paul Murray articulates what I think is an important contemporary truth regarding the Roman Catholic Church.[14] He stated (and I paraphrase here) that *the major tension* in contemporary ecclesiology is the strained relationship between what

---

[14] Paper presented at the Leuven Encounters in Systematic Theology (LEST) VI: "Believing in Community: Ecumenical Reflections on the Church" (Leuven, Belgium, November 2007): 7–10.

he called the "centralizing tendency of Rome" and its relationship with the "far-flung poles" of the church. He sees this playing out especially through the issues of enculturation and the role of the laity.

Edward Hahnenberg recently argued at a national symposium on lay ecclesial ministry that "The emergence of lay ecclesial ministry over the past 40 years stands out as one of the top three or four most important ministerial shifts in the past 2,000 years."[15] So, given that lay ecclesial ministry is both a source of tension in the Roman Catholic Church and one of the most important ministerial shifts in history, we would do well to reflect on how global Catholicism throughout the world is managing this reality.[16] One place to look would be Rutilio's great optimism and inclusive approach in relation to lay ministry in the work of evangelization.

One of the striking aspects of reading through the record of Rutilio's ministry, both in teaching at the seminary and in his evangelization of Aguilares, was his insight that effective ecclesial ministry occurs only through a healthy collaboration between priests and lay leaders within a given community. Furthermore, those leaders must be recognized as leaders *by the community*, not simply by the priest. This model has great potential for the North American church.

Recall that during Rutilio's first experiment in El Paisnal, he sought out leaders who would form the base of what he hoped was a religious awakening that would transform the community. He chose the *adoradores* who practiced the traditional piety of eucharistic adoration and who lived soberly and cleanly. What resulted was a community fractured by small groups devoted to piety with an emphasis on rules and doctrine. No hoped-for social transformation occurred.

Rutilio had a second opportunity to work with laypeople from local communities during the Aguilares mission team experience. He notes the importance of local lay leaders, as well as their self-selection by the community.

> Now, there is no community without responsible leaders. Here, the conflict lies. Where to begin! Do we begin with the formation of the community or with leaders? If the matrix of the community

---

[15] Edward Hahnenberg, "The Vocation to Lay Ecclesial Ministry," *Origins* 37, no. 12 (August 2007): 178.

[16] For two years (2005–2007) I served as academic director of Creighton University's study abroad program in the Dominican Republic. As an academic, this was an exceptional opportunity to actually experience what I had been studying and teaching about for years—the Latin American church in one particular context.

does not exist, from where, how and for what are leaders going to originate? Who is going to choose these leaders? Will there be true leaders or those who only have a vocation to be a sacristan? How and where will they be formed? How will the people accept them? We have wanted to leave the answers to these questions to the overall mission meeting, as we have already noted. Create a process which integrates and evenly develops the three dimensions of the Mission: evangelization, community, leaders.[17]

Notice how his approach completely changed after the failure to identify effective leadership in El Painsal. He doesn't have to be the one to choose the leaders because he knows that working with the acknowledged community leaders will make for more effective ministry. Instead of choosing the leaders for a community, now Rutilio and the team offered very clear leadership *criteria* but encouraged, even required, the people to choose from among themselves who would best fulfill that criteria. Thus he stated: "From the first day, an emphasis is made, implicitly and explicitly in all that is done, that a person is held and known to be qualified if they are perceived as doing 'service,' and not as domination. This approach intends to avoid all elitism and paternalistic power players who wish to 'grow the others.'"[18]

As the mission developed a formal process was put forth which allowed for the emergence of leaders chosen by the people of God who collaborated with the priests to evangelize a community. Shared leadership was the model embraced.

In the final days of the mission the lists of potential leaders can be reduced to the highlights for attendance, activities, interventions, etc. The next to the last night the community election is held. The criteria for the election are put forth: service, commitment, initiative, responsibility, sacrifice for others, and availability, etc. The same community suggests the names; those named are asked to indicate their availability, the pros and cons, and according to this the community approves them and gives their vote, which must be of the majority. As such they are designated as *Delegates of the Word of God in service to the community*.[19]

---

[17] Rutilio Grande, "Aguilares: Una Experiencia de Evangelización Rural Parroquial" ("Aguilares: An Experience of Rural Parish Evangelization"), *Búsqueda* 3, no. 8 (March 1975): 25, translation mine. See appendix of this book for the full translation.
[18] Ibid.
[19] Ibid., 26.

What emerged from this call by the community was the formal designation of lay ministers by the leadership of the church. And it wasn't
leadership to simply assist or help the priests; Delegates of the Word
were intended to remain and help sustain a community after the mission
team had moved on. "The mission will leave a parish promoted in such a
way that laypeople with one or two priests can move forward." This was
important to Rutilio and the mission team from the beginning. Without
laypeople assuming the kind of role encouraged by Vatican II, his ministry
never would have been possible. This was clear when Rutilio wrote that
"one of the objectives is that the layperson takes their responsibility and
place in the Church and that the priest, only by substitution, does what
can and should be done by the layperson." So while the initial work is
initiated by the ordained, that work fails if it cannot be continued by laypeople. "We believe the first push should come from the priest, in order to
provoke a movement that can be taken by laypeople and the communities,
leaving the priest as a companion and animator of the faith."[20] A priest
accompanies a community and supports the spirit that works within and
through the people of God; he doesn't determine or dominate that spirit.

The inclusion of laypeople meant not only their participation in community leadership and evangelization but also their formation and training with ordained collaborators as well. In the second stage of the mission,
Rutilio explained his hopes for the ongoing and permanent formation
of lay collaborators under the category of "permanent formation." His
hope was stated in the following: "After the initial awakening that creates
union and mobilization, a group of people continues forming with periodic
meetings in the base communities and in the parish center; they are reflection groups which at the parish and above the parish level participate
in meetings with district officials from the Church as well as inter-parish
meetings as committed laypersons in the Christian and pastoral work they
do. Jesuits in training accompany and direct their formation."[21]

As one can clearly see, laypeople were essential to the ecclesial vision of
Rutilio; in fact, without them, a leadership from within that would allow
the people of God to apply the Gospel to their context and thus transform
it toward the kingdom of God would have been impossible. Rutilio never
tired of reminding the people he served that they had a critical role in the
evangelization of their own communities—and not to rely on the pater-

---

[20] Ibid., 22.
[21] Ibid., 27.

nalism so often expected of priests in Latin America. In his last homily at Apopa, he stated this in a particularly clear manner:

> Now, my dear brothers and sisters, friends, allow me, after we have heard the Good News of the Word of God in the gospel, in this reading, to say a few things to you. We are part of the Church formed by lay people—the majority of the people of God are you all. And if we are perched here in the bleachers, our ministry has no purpose without the function of your ministry. Ministry comes from the verb "to minister," which means to serve the people of God.[22]

As the former director of a lay ministry master's degree program, I can say without exaggeration that lay ministry is still only *tolerated* in many dioceses of North America.[23] Rarely does a community choose or "call" its own leaders, and I am not familiar with any lay ministry programs that form lay ministers alongside ordained ministers. Anecdotally, during my first year of directing the degree program, one of my students was informed by a newly ordained priest that the term "lay" and "ministry" did not belong together in the same sentence. I am aware of some pastoral institutes and theologates associated with religious orders where a collaboration in education may occur (for example, Boston College and the Graduate School of Berkeley at Santa Clara), but for the most part, there is little true collaboration between lay and ordained in terms of formation and education. Such collaboration would presume a kind of equality within the people of God, a kind of shared leadership, which simply does not exist in the North American church at the moment.

Diocesan seminary programs have continued to form and educate seminarians within a monastic model. By that I mean future priests are formed away from others in a quasi-monastic setting (all male, celibate seminarians). They study and socialize with each other, but then they are put in parish contexts where the majority of their ministry and time is spent working with laypeople. Some religious orders serve as exceptions to this, including the Jesuits and Franciscans. But there are other models of formation and collaboration (especially in Latin America) that, if appropriated, would

---

[22] Grande, "Homilía de Apopa," *XXV Aniversario de Rutilio Grande. Sus Homilías* (2007), 74.

[23] I served as the founding director of Creighton University's master's in lay ministry program from 2002–2004, part of which required me to collaborate with the archdiocese of Omaha and its staff in the implementation of this program and the vetting of those permitted to study within it.

allow for more effective evangelization in the North American church.[24]
What both topics to this point in the chapter suggest—first through the need
for more social analysis in light of the faith and second through a different
model for effective collaboration between lay and ordained—is the need
to recover the meaning of Vatican II and the importance of Catholic social
teaching. Let us now look at a third method of applying Rutilio Grande's
insights and methods to the church of North America.

The Social Dimension of Faith

One of Rutilio Grande's favorite sayings was that the "Gospel has to
grow little feet." He dearly wanted to take a Gospel that had been "spiritualized," or one that was too abstract for the faithful common people
he ministered to, and make it real. But before that could be done, he
had to say something about the ground upon which the Gospel would
walk. Rutilio never tired of beginning his homilies with an overview of
the contemporary social and political situation around the people he was
speaking to. Even though he was from the same area as the people he
served, he continued to use the social analysis skills he learned in formation. He was literally building the groundwork upon which he would
then situate the Gospel. This isn't only key to effective ministry; it is also
important theologically. The Franciscan priest and author Joseph Nangle,
OFM, puts it this way:

> If God has become one of us, then all human beings enjoy almost
> divine dignity. And we who prosper on this earth need to pay atten-
> tion to the ones who do not—otherwise, God is mocked. I believe
> the incarnation helps all of us here and now to face the fact that
> our world is upside down and needs to be righted. I'm convinced,
> therefore, that a living practical faith in God's incarnation serves
> as the indispensable grounding for an engaged, outward-oriented
> spirituality lived in the heart of the empire.[25]

Nangle argues in his chapter "The Incarnation" that a Christian spirituality will always include three dimensions—the individual, the interpersonal, and the social. North American spirituality, he argues, gives

---

[24] For an article outlining the very effective lay ministry program instituted in the
Dominican Republic, see Thomas Kelly, "Lay Ministers of the Future: Lessons in Trust
and Collaboration from Latin America," *Bibliotheca Ephemeridum Theologicarum Lovaniensium* (proceedings of the LEST V conference, Leuven, Belgium: Peeters Press, 2009).

[25] Nangle, *Engaged Spirituality*, 12.

significant time and energy to the first two and very little to the third. This neglect of the social emerges from a Christology that is nearly Gnostic. By that I mean the vast majority of students I teach at the university level have no problem discussing the divinity of Christ but have no idea how to understand the humanity of Christ. This "vertical" Christology, as I would call it, almost completely ignores the horizontal dimensions of Jesus' life and ministry—except insofar as they point to his divinity. For example, there is an inordinate focus on miracles—not as an example of God moving toward the poor and marginalized in love, but as an example of "divinity" narrowly construed. This one-dimensional perspective on Jesus is then mirrored in a one-dimensional spiritual life, with an overwhelming focus on the self and its spiritual needs. Jesus of Nazareth was fully human, fully divine, and one person. Emphasizing the social dimension of Jesus' ministry would help us reclaim an orthodox Christology where the humanity of Jesus is not ignored.

The personal dimension of the faith is critically important; each of us must have and develop this part of our spirituality. As Nangle says, "There is no mystery in this natural process of moving from birth through childhood, adolescence, and on to adulthood; what is remarkable is that God in Jesus experienced it as well."[26] While this dimension is important, it can never be the only dimension we develop, otherwise, as noted sociologist Robert Bellah states, "What is at issue is not simply whether self-contained individuals might withdraw from the public sphere to pursue purely private ends, but whether such individuals are capable of sustaining either a public *or* a private life."[27] So while this dimension is essential, it is never the only one developed.

The second dimension, the interpersonal, is also important, "The best of interpersonal relationships gives meaning, challenge and purpose to each of our lives—as they did to Jesus' life." This has become more of a focus in contemporary spirituality as, according to Nangle, "that entire network of the others whom we know in the course of life—all form part of *our* life in God, *our* spirituality (the plural here is important)."[28]

But our spirituality is not complete until we recognize the importance of the social dimension. "There are forces surrounding every one of us that shape our lives for better or worse: family, neighborhood, housing,

---

[26] Ibid., 12–13.

[27] Robert Bellah, et al., *Habits of the Heart: Individualism and Commitment in American Life* (Berkely: University of California Press, 2008), 143.

[28] Nangle, *Engaged Spirituality*, 13.

education, socio-economic realities, civic government, and religious traditions. This was true for Jesus, and it's true for every person born into this world."[29] This social dimension of spirituality allows one "to understand the structures of society that unavoidably shape each of us." The result of this is a deeper awareness of the world around us and the need in that world. "People are helped or hurt by social realities," and thus Nangle came to realize that "a true spirituality has to be aware of this fact." [30]

Most North American Catholics do not hear much about "structures" or "systems" from church leaders, in part, because they are not trained in the use of social analysis to understand their reality, and in part because they see the world's problems in terms of the kind of individuality with which they understand themselves. But the lack of this dimension leads people to perceiving moral social issues through the lens of individualism—and the explanation for every moral evil is poor personal decision making. Poverty is a choice of irresponsible people; abortion is simply about the decision of a mother and should thus be made illegal, etc.[31] In each case, an issue that requires an understanding of "structures" is reduced to personal responsibility. This may also explain why the social issues the North American Catholic Church chooses to focus on are all issues reducible to individual decisions—abortion, contraception, homosexuality, stem-cell research, end of life decisions. What is missing here is the social dimension of spirituality—a dimension that Nangle argues is critical to Christology. "Whether I was right or wrong, I came to believe that this social dimension was the most significant reality in the life of Jesus. His consistent responses to the historical, often unjust, structures of his time and place stands as a major thrust in his life and ministry and turned out to be the principal reason for his capture, torture, and death."[32]

Not only is a fuller understanding of Christ possible through a greater emphasis on the social, but a fuller understanding of the work Christ left to us becomes more clear as well—helping to welcome and build the kingdom of God. In fact, according to Vatican II's Dogmatic Constitution on the Church (*Lumen gentium*), the social dimension of the faith is the work and purpose of lay participation in the church!

---

[29] Ibid., 14.

[30] Ibid., 14–15.

[31] For an excellent article on the *failure* of current Catholic prolife strategies, see Richard W. Miller, "Pro-life Moral Principles and Pro-life Strategies: Expanding the Catholic Imagination and Response to Abortion," *The Journal of Peace and Justice Studies* 19, no. 2 (2010): 2–26.

[32] Nangle, *Engaged Spirituality*, 15.

It is the special vocation of the laity to seek the kingdom of God by engaging in temporal affairs and directing them according to God's will. They live in the world, in each and every one of the world's occupations and callings and in the ordinary circumstances of social and family life which, as it were, form the context of their existence. There they are called by God to contribute to the sanctification of the world from within, like leaven, in the spirit to the Gospel, by fulfilling their own particular duties. Thus, especially by the witness of their life, resplendent in faith, hope and charity they manifest Christ to others.[33]

Because it can never be enough to focus only on my personal spirituality or our interpersonal spirituality, there must also and always be a social dimension of spirituality that allows me to see how to order the affairs of the world according to God's plan. For example, individual believers are very comfortable reading Scripture for a meaning that is personal, even private. At times, one can hear of interpersonal meanings emphasized at Mass. But when have you ever heard the social meaning of Scripture accentuated? What would the story of Jesus and the rich young man mean in relation to contemporary US consumer society? The Good Samaritan? The rich man and Lazarus? All of these parables have important, even critical, social dimensions that are rarely developed in how they are understood. Pope John Paul II offers an excellent example of someone who first perceived sin in individual terms but later came to understand, and even emphasize, broader types of sin.

Although the idea of structural or social sin has been accepted and articulated formally in Catholic social teaching since the 1971 document Justice in the World (*Justitia in Mundo*), John Paul II was initially "wary of this idea." Citing the work of Adam DeVille, Kenneth Himes, OFM, illustrates that John Paul II's thought evolved on this point. Initially, "The pope noted that sin could be understood as social in the sense that each individual sin affects others, however indirectly."[34] In a 1984 apostolic exhortation titled Reconciliation and Penance, John Paul II described a type of sin as descriptive of "certain relationships between various communities."[35] This description moves from a wariness about social structures to an acknowledgment that they may, in fact, affect people in

---

[33] *Lumen gentium*, no. 31.

[34] Kenneth R. Himes, "Liberation Theology and Catholic Social Teaching," *Hope and Solidarity*, ed. Stephen J. Pope (Maryknoll, NY: Orbis Press, 2008), 237.

[35] Ibid.

much the same way that communities do. Of particular concern to the pope was the sense of individual accountability that could be lost in the language of social sin. In his 1987 encyclical titled On Social Concern (*Sollicitudo rei socialis*), he stated the following:

> If the present situation can be attributed to difficulties of various kinds, it is not out of place to speak of "structures of sin," which, as I stated in my Apostolic Exhortation *Reconciliatio et Paenitentia*, are rooted in personal sin, and thus always linked to the concrete acts of individuals who introduce these structures, consolidate them and make them difficult to remove. And thus they grow stronger, spread, and become the source of other sins, and so influence people's behavior.
>
> "Sin" and "structures of sin" are categories which are seldom applied to the situation of the contemporary world. However, one cannot easily gain a profound understanding of the reality that confronts us unless we give a name to the root of the evils which afflict us.[36]

Finally, in the 1995 encyclical On the Gospel of Life (*Evangelium Vitae*), this acknowledgment of structures of sin was confirmed with the designation of certain contexts as revealing a "culture of death."

Given that there is a relationship between my individual choices and the context in which I live and move and find meaning, the social dimension of our faith is not optional; it must be central to a lived Christian discipleship.

When we begin to understand the context in which we live, tragic realities such as abortion will be understood as emerging from a highly competitive culture that is unfriendly to families and uncaring for the poor. We will then be able to ask ourselves some very difficult questions. For example, how can the abortion rate be so much lower in secular European countries where it is legal than in Catholic Latin American countries where it is illegal?[37] Will changing a law change a culture? Why is the Catholic abortion rate the same as other denominations or non-denominations?

---

[36] John Paul II, *On Social Concern*, no. 36.

[37] Richard W. Miller, "Pro-life Moral Principles and Pro-life Strategies," 6–7. Says Miller, "As of 2006, Belgium, Germany, and the Netherlands have the lowest abortion rates in the world. Abortion is not only legal and widely available in these Western European countries, but it is also generally paid for by their national health care systems. Contrast that with the South American countries Peru, Chile, and Brazil, which have some of the highest abortion rates in the world, despite the fact that abortion is illegal in these countries."

What more can the church do to actually change the number of abortions right now?

A deeper understanding of our social reality, both in terms of our spirituality and our obligations, can then lead to a more effective collaboration with the kingdom of God. Most importantly, this would make us a more effective force for life on every issue, both individual and social! This is the work of the church, including both lay and ordained members, to welcome the kingdom as it continues to break into human history and to transform the world in light of it.

Conclusion

In his book *How Latin America Saved the Soul of the Catholic Church*, Edward Cleary, OP, emphasizes a number of themes and contributions from the church in that part of the world. His chapters include the following titles:

- Successfully Bringing Millions of Laypeople into Service in the Church (chap. 2)
- Embracing Diversity: Encounters with Non-Christian Religions (chap. 4)
- Emphasizing the Poor and Vulnerable (chap. 5)
- Transforming Theology from Hyperintellectualism to Concerns of the People and Care of the Earth (chap. 6)
- Emphasizing Evangelization and Empowering 1.2 Million Lay Catechists (chap. 7)
- Choosing Human Rights and Dying for Them (chap. 8)
- Peace-Keeping and Mediating (chap. 9)
- Sending Missionaries with a Message of Solidarity (chap. 10)[38]

A cursory glance at the writings and homilies of Rutilio demonstrates that many of these chapters are embodied in his life and death. The question of whether we have anything to learn from the Catholic Church of El Salvador, and specifically the life, ministry, and death of Rutilio Grande, hinges upon what we believe the purpose of the church to be. If we limit that purpose to weekly Mass obligation, sacramental services, and comfort

---

[38] Edward Cleary, *How Latin America Saved the Soul of the Catholic Church* (Mahwah, NJ: Paulist Press, 2009), iii.

for our times of need, then the lessons from Latin America will never be heard. This me-centered therapeutic approach to Christian spirituality so indicative of a heavily consumerist and individualistic mentality rarely looks beyond the self and its needs.

What the North American church needs is for the Gospel to grow feet within and to walk amid the messy reality of life here and now—and in doing so, move us more closely toward serving the poor and vulnerable. It is only in this downward movement of compassion, a movement that imitates the incarnate Christ we serve, that the Gospel can liberate us from the worst of our culture.

Rutilio shows us a way to do this. Ever faithful to the Vatican II vision that the church serves the kingdom of God, Rutilio embodied a model of evangelization that engaged people in the midst of their lives, people who struggled to live the Gospel in their context. By including a greater reliance on social analysis, a healthier collaboration of lay and ordained, and a stronger emphasis on the social dimension of the faith, the North American church can become a more effective other-oriented servant of the kingdom. And when we do, the Gospel will grow feet here as well.

Appendix

Aguilares:
An Experience of Rural Parish
Evangelization

A translation of: Rutilio Grande, "Aguilares: Una Experiencia de Evangelización Rural Parroquial," *Búsqueda, Organ of the Pastoral Commission of El
Salvador* 3, no. 8 (March 1975): 21–45.

Presentation:

The experience of the evangelization of Aguilares, as a pastoral process,
is very much conditioned by the space, time, and people involved. Even
within the same experience there exists different variables to consider
which cannot be ignored. Thus, little can be theorized and less applied to
other places, even if they are similar.

In this regard, to speak and more to write of "experience" is very premature. It would be better to keep searching and remain quiet!

These notes are rather the foundation for a global assessment that we
have in mind and want to do soon.

With the prayers of the Archdiocesan Pastoral Commission we agreed
to surrender this to *Búsqueda*, because we neither more nor less claim this
to be our experience.[1] Take this as a contribution to the diocesan process
as a kind of trial, a seeking of new ways to do pastoral ministry. These are
uncertain steps, a mumbled word, open to an encounter and to dialogue
with those who want to continue searching.

---

[1] *Búsqueda* was the "Organ of the Pastoral Commission of San Salvador, El Salvador," a journal in which various bishops and pastors shared a conversation about their
pastoral efforts in the particular areas.

With all these limitations we present the most salient features of the experience we began a little more than two years ago.

The development will follow a chronological process, outlining the most important steps, emphasizing the points that are judged to need more pastoral attention.

I have divided the exposition into two large parts following the stages that we can distinguish in our work:

1a. Stage: Grand Missionary Tour (September of 1972 to Pentecost of 1973)

2a. Stage: Strengthening (From Pentecost of 1973 to the Festival of Corn, August 1974)

An addendum will include a series of charts, tables and diagrams that can shed some light on and clarify the previous exposition.

1a. Stage: Grand Missionary Tour

1) The missionary team and its projection

At the foundation of this experience there is a fundamental option by all the members of the team for a pastoral ministry focused on the marginalized majorities. Such majorities are crystallized in the suburban and rural masses. The marginalized peoples are located there and these people are El Salvador.

That primary option was maturing since the year 1972, the date in which Father Rutilio Grande finished his course at IPLA in Quito. Favorable circumstances for that option presented themselves and came to fruition in the work of a team.

The archbishop welcomed these aspirations and gave them his approval. The archbishop soon appointed us to the parish of Aguilares which had no pastor at that time.

The priests Rutilio Grande and Chus Angel Bengoechea made a one-week retreat in Santa Tecla in order to plan and organize their arrival to the parish. After looking more closely at a theory of reality through a typology of urban and rural poverty, they were sent to ask the question, "What would the Lord Jesus do in a similar situation?" They drew some tentative conclusions in terms of their goals:

* **Motivations**. In light of the concentration of clergy among the urban minorities (the wealthy), it seemed urgent to insert us into the marginalized majorities, THE POOR PEASANTS, the great reservoir of religious

people in the country.[2] To begin purely pastoral work as a team opened up new forms of pastoral ministry for the Jesuits of Central America who were focused almost exclusively on teaching in the city.

* Pastoral Goal.—EVANGELIZATION in order to recreate a church of living communities of new people with pastoral agents conscious of their human vocation who become promoters of their own destiny and who bring change to their reality along the lines of Vatican II and Medellín.

* Attitudes.—First, we had to be conscienticized by their reality [of the majority] through a sensitization and awareness of their world which would bring us to incarnate and identify with their problems.[3] We did not want to instrumentalize or domesticate their religiosity without animating them to be co-creators of a dynamic, prophetic, and de-centralized community in order to arrive at a promotion that will detect agents of change, key men and women, pastoral agents, and multipliers.

* Method.—Personalizing, dialogical, creative and critical, based on the pattern of action-reflection-action, that would theologize their reality starting from the solidarity of love, faith and hope in this person, here and now. To make a person say their word, be responsible and engage in the historical process of re-creating new individuals and communities.

* Criteria.—Priority is given to evangelization and conversion before the sacramental and cultic. Announcement of the new person who denounces those who exploit and is aware of exploitation. We want a mobile church, not a church that waits for the people to come to it, or brings the church to the people, but to be the church of the people.

* Goals.—Removal of their own mindset and life [fatalistic surrender to poverty and their situation] in order to welcome and accept outsiders.[4] Awareness: to realize the surrounding problematic through reflection and structural analysis. Conscientization: a constant critical attitude in a dialectical unity of "action-reflection" in service to continuous historical commitment.[5]

---

[2] Parenthesis mine. The minority to which the authors refer are the wealthy of San Salvador.

[3] Inclusion mine.

[4] Inclusion mine. I believe Rutilio is referring to the fatalism in which a person is resigned to reality as it exists.

[5] *Concientización* translated as conscientization is a phrase used by Paulo Freire in his seminal work, *Pedagogy of the Oppressed* (New York: Continuum, 2006). The significance is captured in the following: "A deepened consciousness of their situation leads people to apprehend that situation as an historical reality susceptible of transformation" (85).

 * Tactics.—Separate money from the sacraments and worship. Give priority to the marginalized and to the community over the individual. In conflicts, be with the oppressed. Avoid the traps and the compliments of the powerful who want to monopolize us [the clergy].[6]

 * Duration.—Reasonable period of some years, avoiding the extremes of the past: merely the installation of a work of the Society of Jesus or the short-lived excitement of a popular mission. The mission will leave a parish promoted in such a way that laypeople with one or two priests can move forward.

 * Participation.—One of the objectives is that the layperson take their responsibility and place in the church and that the priest, only by substitution, does what can and should be done by the layperson. Our aspiration is that the mission team be relieved by diocesan priests; and is therefore open to all collaboration, participation and integration with priests, laypeople as well as religious.

2) Most Notable Early Achievements

 With these provisional approaches, on September 24, 1972, the two initiators of the pastoral team and the experience "are sent" to the parish: Rutilio Grande, SJ, and Chus Angel Bengoechea, SJ, Days later two others are summoned: Benigno Fernandez, SJ, and Salvador Carranza, SJ.

 The fastest way to get to know a reality is to plunge into it. Therefore, after initial contacts and trials, a plan was decided upon and a deadline fixed to enter fully into the work.

 Up to January 15th, feast of the Lord of Mercy, Patron of the city and parish, the team would work intensively in the city. After this date they would work intensively in the rural villages. With the rains, they would return to the head office.

 In this manner in over eight months of time—relatively short—the team would have a good initial push and would obtain ample knowledge of the parish and its peoples.

Rutilio was educated in this method at the Latin American Pastoral Institute in Quito, Ecuador, in 1968.

 [6] Inclusion mine.

Missionary Tour:

1) **Urban Area**—The city is divided into ten zones with many other missionary zones. Each of these zones is worked for two weeks. Average attendance of sixty people.

2) **Rural Area**—"The Mission" is offered to all those who request it. Requests are studied and fifteen mission centers are selected. In each one of these centers a priest and his associates will remain for fifteen days. These mission centers are developed until June 10th, Pentecost, the date upon which the rains begin. The average attendance in these centers is 150 adults.

Missionary Method

Our ministry took the name of "missions" for the resonance and connotation that kept the correct meaning of our work among the people and for the evangelical meaning it had for us. In practice, we will not see much resemblance to traditional missions, especially if we consider the methodology adopted and the purpose behind it.

The path or the area of "the religious way" was chosen as a starting point for the various reasons explained below.

1) **Prior to the Mission**

A general offer of the mission was made by the mission team and, when accepted by the people, we responded quickly. Opinion polls of the people in the zone were completed, asking which places they would choose to have a mission. In principle, all dependence on powerful people was eliminated in terms of sites, lodging, etc., that could monopolize the missionary and remove their freedom of speech as well as the freedom of the people being missioned.

A large mixed commission from a particular zone has to come to the parish to formalize their request and give some general survey data about the area, its people, its problems, and its conflicts. They put forward their needs to the mission, those who want baptism, marriage, and other sacraments. With them other details are specified and it is the responsibility of various other commissions to create the best environment for the mission.

The exact date of the mission is made following a preliminary visit to announce and prepare for it. It is important to finalize details like decorations, benches, lighting, etc.

2) **Mission**
A general description of a day of mission: Family visits in homes. The priest and their associates spend some time and eat in each home.

This is the way to approach the community and particular problems within it. With the data collected in these visits and other data more systematically obtained in the continual dialogue with qualified elements there, the team will begin to create an anthropological record of the place: fiscal, economic, social, political, cultural, and religious reality. These will be the basic themes generated that can be treated in corresponding decoding of selected bits of the New Testament. With the associates reviewing activities, data is compared, contrasted and codified, and evening sessions are planned.

In the first hours of the afternoon, have a session evangelizing the children with an appropriate methodology. Later a large session with adults will commence.

Main Event of the Mission Day

Continue to follow the data so that after 15 days a rudimentary outline can be developed that embraces a celebration of the Word of God. From the first moment, the maximum participation of the community must be sought. A three-fold objective is pursued through this:

—the beginning of self-evangelization

—the beginning of community

—the beginning of self-selection of Delegates of the Word[7]

Steps in the Central Session:

—Greetings, songs of the message which create an attractive and confident environment. (The children can play a great role in creating this environment, before removing them in order to accommodate the adults.)

—Present the New Testament to all who wish, even if they can barely read. Training in how to use and understand the same New Testament. Search the text, select passages according to the problems raised by the anthropological record.

---

[7] *Delegados de la Palabra*, or Delegates of the Word, was the unique form of lay ministry in El Salvador at this time. While catechists focused on the teaching and delivery of one sacrament, Delegates of the Word functioned more like organizers and animators of a community. They led community worship services and were trained to assist people in reading the Word of God and *applying* it to their situation. See Tommie Sue Montgomery, "The Church in the Salvadoran Revolution," *Latin American Perspectives* 10, no. 1, *Central America: The Process of Revolution* (Winter 1983): 71.

—Act of reconciliation of the community, sign of peace, brief prayer, and a song to orient the Word.

—Invitation to proclaim the selected text; it is read two or three times by different readers, a man and a woman at minimum. Among the readings they can begin making notes, suggestions, and listing questions that surround the text.

—Work in groups; invite them to divide into groups of eight to ten people as a minimum in order to dialogue about the text proclaimed. Among themselves they should name **a reader** who should be reading the text verse by verse; **an animator** of the dialogue who encourages and moderates participation; and **a reporter** that takes down a list the group makes the whole time. Pursue maximum participation.

—**Plenary Session** (one or several simultaneously depending on the number of assistants). In order to be manageable and fruitful, the plenary session should have no more than sixty or seventy people. This is moderated by the priest and his associates. The moderator should fix in writing and be as close to the verbalization of the people as possible and systematize the summaries given by the reporters. Return to the full form of questioning the most significant points in order to deepen them through the opinions of the participants. All this should be complemented by the priest who will summarize the key ideas considered at the session.

—Communal prayer, announcements, farewell, song.

—Meet together for a brief review with those who participated the most in the various activities. Progress and problems in the session can be evaluated as well as participation. They are invited to the next sessions since they, themselves, will encourage other people to participate more.

Although the method in broad strokes is easy to grasp, the plot and background are more delicate. All of this is intended to encourage the motivations and teaching attitudes of Paulo Freire in his educational projects which seek conscientization and liberation with the marginalized.

Other Elements of the Missioning Process

In a mission, the priest and his associates draw upon all contacts, personal, familial, various groups, and the community—for all have something important to offer the immediate end of understanding as much as possible about the reality of the environment, which will become evident in the anthropological record of the place. Further, the entire team should reflect on that material in order to try to capture the world of the peasant in its total reality and vision, in its conception and expression.

The names of those who strongly participate are especially noted, and the same dialectical method should be explained to them. These people are emerging as natural leaders, the natural animators, who are evaluated each night of work to correct and assimilate better the dialogical method. They will encourage the various groups meeting in these sessions and they will be accountable for the progress of the mission. Thus it will happen easily that the community will elect, at the end of the mission, its own leaders according to the criteria of responsibility, dynamism and animation. The two weeks of mission activity will help men and women of initiative, mobility and influence come forth from the community.

From the first day, an emphasis is made, implicitly and explicitly in all that is done, that a person is held and known to be qualified if they are perceived as doing "service," and not as domination. This approach intends to avoid all elitism and paternalistic power players who wish to "grow the others."

Self-Selection of Leaders

We think this point is of capital importance. The institution of the church has become fossilized in the clergy. We lament the fact that we don't have true communities. And for good reason this leads us to question whether we really have a church.

Now, there is no community without responsible leaders. Here, the conflict lies. Where to begin! Do we begin with the formation of the community or with leaders? If the matrix of the community does not exist, from where, how, and for what are leaders going to originate? Who is going to choose these leaders? Will there be true leaders or those who only have a vocation to be a sacristan? How and where will they be formed? How will the people accept them? We have wanted to leave the answers to these questions to the overall mission meeting, as we have already noted. Create a process which integrates and evenly develops the three dimensions of the mission: evangelization, community, leaders.

It is certain that we will have to put the accent on either evangelization, community, or leaders. But we always have to keep in view the other dimensions and order them toward each other without disassociating them or distancing them.

We believe the first push should come from the priest, in order to provoke a movement that can be taken by lay people and the communities, leaving the priest as a companion and animator of the faith.

To detect these key men and women that the community will designate as their delegates, we look at their work in the same community. Leaders will emerge after the mission process who, from their concrete actions, will demonstrate a commitment to others because they give widely and respond to others with commitment and community service.

We note the different moments of this selection process.

—**Before the mission**: there are the lists of those who have asked about the mission; of those who have mobilized the parish to make formal preparations; of those who provide ideas, initiatives, etc., in the interview with the priest; of those who made commitments and have responsibilities; of those who made practical things like decorations, locations, benches, lights, etc.

—**In the mission**: From the first night, attendance should be taken of those involved in doing or, above all, saying something in public. This is important even though people are not used to it and are ashamed to speak. From the first evaluation it was noted that the work of the coordinators of the mission would be not so much to speak or do, but to "encourage others to do, to talk and to participate." They were encouraged to be leaders, not preachers; to seek **with others** for the truth, unity, action and organization.

This takes into account, above all, those who provide improvements, changes, and constructive criticisms. They are committing to work with people, to engage and involve all the people.

Some evaluation of the plenary session on the progress of the mission also helps the engagement process. This would require an appropriate dynamic to be used.

Halfway through the mission the idea is launched: "after these fifteen days of mission will everything remain as it was before this brief flare up?" And so it begins to be clinched:

THEN BEGIN YOUR MISSION!

In the final days of the mission the lists of potential leaders can be reduced to the highlights for attendance, activities, interventions, etc. The next to the last night the community election is held. The criteria for the election are put forth: service, commitment, initiative, responsibility, sacrifice for others, and availability, etc. The same community suggests the names; those named are asked to indicate their availability, the pros and cons, and according to this the community approves them and gives its vote, which must be of the majority. As such they are designated as **Delegates of the Word of God in service to the community**. In practice this has resulted in one delegate for every four or five people. The predominance of men or women as delegates has varied in different places. The position and number of delegates always stays open to revision. The same service to the community will be given according to the measure of commitment.

As a beginning, it is preferable that the delegation be numerous in order to place the engine of the community within the community, open to augmentation from other delegates that are emerging after the mission, to diversify in the different services of the community and also in order to purge and self-eliminate if someone doesn't finish the work that the community has entrusted to them.

The final night of the mission the delegates accept publicly and individually the designation and the commitment to serve the community. From this moment on, they will be in charge of leading and caring for their community. They are not left alone, but are put under the tutoring of another older delegation, or a foreign partner or another community that will ensure the growth of the delegates as well as the community.

The delegates will be the link between their own community and the parish or greater community.

The new delegates should have a meeting in order to give some norms, criteria, and minimum schemes in order to begin to build the road with their community; in order to meet, evaluate, and become organized.

In the final celebration of the Word have the baptisms with a suggestive ceremony with catechesis about the commitment of the baptized which include commitments to the community. For example:

—The delegates elected by the community make a commitment, light a candle and pass them to

—the community that makes a commitment, takes the light and passes the light

—to the parents and godparents who are going to baptize and

—to those who are going to get married and finally to

—the parents of the children who are going to receive first communion.

On Sunday morning, those married and making first communion should receive the greatest possible number of New Testaments and confirm to them that they are to help "follow the mission."

During the fifteen days, have two or three eucharistic celebrations. The central act of the celebration of the Word will add to the second part of the Mass. These eucharistic celebrations have as their goal:

a) Avoid being labeled as "separate" by giving as much importance to the Gospel.

b) Avoid that they feel or say that "now these priests have changed everything, they don't even say Mass."

c) Deepen the sense of reconciliation as "change" and the sense of the Eucharist as a memorial and commitment with Christ.

Every night, while the priest is available, is the time for consultations, confessions, settling problems, etc.

3) After the Mission Visit

Initiating the community process is essential and delicate work requiring patience in accompanying it in its growth without ever abandoning it. In the beginning it requires constant and close supervision.

A) Accompanying the communities.

A priest directly assumes responsibility for the village and accompanies the peasants while visiting the communities, attending its meetings, dispelling doubts and confusion, and evaluating with the community on the one hand and with the delegates on the other, the progress of the community and of the delegation.

From the first moment we have counted on the help of foreign partners.[8] After attending a mission and initiating them in the method described, there were those who gave an irreplaceable contribution to the community after the mission, now that local priests were on other missions.

These collaborators were university students with Christian and social concerns and some seminarians, as in the case of Tavo Cruz, who was ordained and became part of the team and is today a fundamental piece of the same in the absence of Padre Chus Angel.

These collaborators coalesced with two communities of Jesuits who had lived successively in Aguilares, who had a house and studied at the same, and who gave part of their time to do pastoral ministry. The first community studied the Human Sciences at the University of Central America (UCA). This community actually did their theology based on the pastoral praxis in Aguilares and in the Center for Theological Reflection at the UCA. Various Jesuits in this group graduated in various disciplines.

The contribution of the young, interdisciplinary and pluralistic, even if not exempt from tensions, is very beneficial and positive for everyone, especially for the people of Aguilares. They have always tried, but cannot accomplish works that can develop the natives and help mediate the work of the missionary team. Their work is temporary and substitutive.

---

[8] I believe this refers to foreign missionaries of various orders who served in El Salvador during this time.

From this criteria were born the **Preparers**, who are peasants featured in the assimilation of this method and in leadership who prepare two celebrations of the Word every fifteen days with a priest in the home parish. They then return to centers in their zone in order to transmit what they have received and done, acting as a bridge with the parish.

Envoys of the Zone are sent to these various centers throughout the zone from each delegation (group of Delegates of the Word). These, in turn, communicate in the weekly meeting of their delegation, where they evaluate previous sessions of the community, prepare for the next, and plan new actions and share commitments.

The community meets at least weekly in order to celebrate the Word.

This dynamic which has been emerging from the experience is evident through evaluations. These returns are to be reflected upon at the basic level, of prioritization, of unification and a certain schematization. Even though we present this process in the attached (organization chart no. 3) we have to take it more as a dynamic process than as something already acquired or fixed.

B) Palpable Results in the Missionary Tour

—Great discovery of the Gospel by themselves: "we are now removing ignorance. . ." "We were in the dark. . . ." An appetite for the Word has been opened and they comment and make it applicable in their own way.

—The Gospel and the situation in which they live come together quickly: "we are bringing the gospel from the spiritual to the material," they say in their naïve verbalization.

—They begin to rise out of their magical consciousness: "what can the poor actually do . . . ?" "to be conformed to the will of God," and they have begun to realize there is no will of God that things have been the way they are.[9]

—They have confidence in themselves: they lose the widespread complexes, the shame, the disability, and discover they can express themselves.

---

[9] *Conciencia mágica* has been defined as "a state of mind that attributes human events a 'superior power that dominates them from outside and to which it is necessary to submit docilely. This type of consciousness is dominated by fatalism." See Montgomery, "The Church in the Salvadoran Revolution" 73, footnote 11.

—They begin to realize that many social ills come from not "being united" and they have begun to acquire a sense of community.

—They start to distinguish what is primary in their religiosity and what is more secondary: "what are we doing with this?"

—They are experiencing the possibility of change and betterment from their religiosity.

—They begin to meet, to mobilize, and to see what they can do.

—The reception of sacraments as repetition and sacramentalism decreases, but the sense of the same as change, commitment, and vital signs increases.

End of the First Stage

On June 10, 1972, Pentecost, the birth of the Christian community, a great celebration, is held in the main parish of the emerging communities in order to ask for and celebrate the new spirit of the communities which serves humanity and human beings who serve the community.

Community entries are received that bear signs with various unique gospel texts. The popular solemn Mass is celebrated, animated by sets of guitars from various villages. The homily is a greeting to the *people of God* consisting in the first part of encouragement, to give them confidence, and to dissipate difficulties. The first accusations against them will be of "Protestantism," of moving to the material and not the spiritual, of communism, of politics, of illegal meetings that are bad and the National Guard will come and tie their hands and take them away, and what will happen with internal conflicts of power, threats and fear. The same accusations were made against Jesus and will be made against all true Christians.

After the principles of the missionary team are declared in its pastoral action, they are distributed through printed papers:

1—Before everything else, we are MISSIONARIES for the entire community; it is said we are SENT to proclaim the Gospel cleanly and simply, without pretense or other personal interests, according to the mandate of Jesus to his apostles: "Go and proclaim the Gospel to all peoples."

2—According to this, under no pretext will we administer any sacrament to those not adequately evangelized, for we gravely betray the Gospel and our conscience if we do.

3—We have nothing to do with political groups of any class or party. We owe everything to the community.

4—Our only POLITICS are to be faithful proclaimers of the Gospel which has to do with all human activities aligned with God in order to transform the world.

5—We will denounce with energy and without pretense all sorts of injustice and abuses against the human person, wherever they come from whether they are private individuals or groups.

6—Our goal is to build together with you, A COMMUNITY OF BROTH-ERS AND SISTERS, COMMITTED TO BUILD A NEW WORLD, WITHOUT OPPRESSORS OR OPPRESSED, and ACCORDING TO THE PLAN OF GOD.

After the Mass, we have a popular cultural-religious party of Christian brotherhood and coexistence. The numbers, the songs, the presentations caused a deep impact as a prelude to a new awakening.

This is the end of the first stage.

Second Stage: Consolidation

Back to the base: Diagnosis

After Pentecost the team, with its collaborators, begins a period of re-flection. This reflection is based on the intense activity of the first stage, on the experience and the accumulated data, and even more on the re-flections every Thursday morning during the mission. The data will be analyzed, codified and globalized in order to propel us into further action.

This reflection includes:

1) Evaluation: Bringing together disparate data to be examined criti-cally. An interpretation and systematization of the same data is made and deficiencies are seen which are acted upon consequentially.

2) Maintenance: The accompaniment, the animation and the deepening of the Gospel is studied in every missionary community as well as the qual-ity of the preparation of Delegates of the Word and community animators.

3) Planning: A pastoral work projection for the second stage is completed: new frontiers of work, correction of errors, and growth of programs to meet the work to be diversified in the same communities: with children, young people, adults: marriages and Delegates of the Word.

Three important areas of action have concerned us:

a) Sustenance in order to purify and transform the traditional pastoral work of sacrament and cult at the parish level, in a way that does not remove or extinguish the values through which it is promoted. The community will take responsibility for and participate in sacramental life. The base needs to be involved as cocreator so the community will not fall into clericalism or paternalism. Untie the economic maintenance of the church from the sacramental and cultic. Pursue a greater autonomy of the communities from the support of the priests.

b) Growth of living communities, not so much quantitatively but qualitatively. For this, our primary attention goes to the Delegates of the Communities, to the diversification of their functions; how they can be formed without falling into elitism or distancing themselves from the base.

c) Open new frontiers in the city that do not lead to a desperate activism or the employment of people from outside the community. The ideal pursued is to create conditions and form people in a way that in the remote future they can be responsible for pastoral duties with one or two diocesan priests.

Parish Reality

The analysis of accumulated data and experience together with other technical means supplied by the university about land, resources, etc., leads us to a better knowledge of the reality in which we move.

Geophysical Enclave

The Lord of Mercy Parish in the city of Aguilares, was erected in the year 1952 as a break-off from Guazapa which bordered it on the south. Linda is to the north with New Conception and Tejutla, the Lempa River is in the middle. It is located to the east of Suchitoto whose civil jurisdiction included the three most western villages. To the west, with the parishes of Tacachico and of Quezaltepeque, we served two small villages of the latter. Included in the parish were the thirteen villages in the jurisdiction of El Paisnal. At the same time, the village of La Toma belonged to Aguilares until the year 1932 when it changed rapidly into a town and eventually became the city it is today.

Currently, the parish covers approximately one hundred seventy square kilometers, covering the northern part of the Department of San Salvador, marked by the rivers Acelhuate, Lempa and Sucio, to the northeast of Cuscatlan and a narrow strip bordering the Department of La Libertad.

The plain of Aguilares is three hundred meters above sea level, with small mountainous zones, rugged foothills, and rocky areas. The tropical climate is very hot and humid, with significant variation between day and night during the winter months.

The Troncal Norte is the only paved road crossing the plain from the south to the north. The old railroad follows the same direction, but before it arrives at the Lempa River it takes a western turn, following the river until Santa Ana, along a route of large historical estates. Suchitoto joins Aguilares through an unpaved road with daily service by various buses. The same thing happens in Suchitoto, from where there is a road gradually opening that goes through Tacachico and leads to Santa Ana.

Population

The parish comprises around 33,000 inhabitants spread through the City (10,000); El Paisnal (2,000) and the rest are scattered through the villages of the previously mentioned municipalities, more than three pertaining to Suchitoto and two to Quezaltepeque.

Socio-Economic Reality

Aguilares, recently elevated to the designation of a "city," is only forty three years old since its founding. A large part of the adult population was not born here. In the continual internal migrations that characterize our overcrowded country, people from a variety of backgrounds have settled here.

The population consists of a nucleus of small commercial business people, simple skilled professions, and peasants who are piling up in the peripheral areas leading to new neighborhoods and settlements that lack the most basic urban services [like water, sewer, electricity, etc.].[10]

The markets on market days change Aguilares from Thursday through Monday into a chaotic confluence of diverse occupations and backgrounds.

The Village: the plain is dominated by the large landowners of the area with more than thirty five large estates. The "rule of sugarcane" mercilessly eats away the little flat land that still remains. The humble peasant has to perform a continuous miracle to convert the stony rented ground, which does not serve the landowners, into a corn field. The emerging livestock industry also uses this impoverished land.

The three great mills of La Cabana, San Francisco, and Colima, with some other sub-centers of less importance, temporarily absorb the peasant labor of the region which increases during the harvest with workers and truckers from other areas.

[10] Inclusion mine.

Social Stratification

—The dense number of property owners who are residents in the city, whose intentions are perhaps paternalistic, collude with landowners and fatten themselves through this collective plot, at the cost of the worker.

—Among these landlords we can distinguish those who exploit the sugarcane as a unique activity and in the traditional way, and those for whom the mill is one but not the most significant business interest within the agricultural-industrial, trade and banking activities that manage the country.

—The medium and small landlords, residents here, tax the profits on the mills. Some of them are dedicated exclusively to agriculture, but more frequently they are supplemented by business in the city. They reproduce the previous scheme locally.

—Peasants have their huts and small pieces of land in order to cover their sustenance and they work temporarily in the mills. Some have their shops taxed from trade with the city.

—Peasants rent the rocky ground that cannot grow sugarcane for their own small farms. They hope their harvest can pay off their debts from renting the land and buying the seeds and fertilizer.

—Many people settle in an area without the ability to buy land or find more permanent work, they basically are slaves, as the sugarcane does not require the labor of other crops. These are the most exploited and they are subject to the whims of the owners as the outdated Land Laws do not cover layoffs or years of work. The evictions are becoming endemic, because nobody wants to have unwanted people on their farms who could cause conflict.

Worker-Boss Relationship

It is clear domination and exploitation. The Job Code does not respond to the real situation of the worker. Nearly all of it refers to the permanent worker, and jobs, outside of the rare cases of the employers, are considered temporary. The same emergency measures like minimum wage and other tasks are scoffed at daily because their interpretation always aligns with the interests of the employer. There is the appearance of law, but there are numerous tricks which make it ineffectual. There is no reason to protest because everyone knows there is a surplus of labor. The ministerial inspections easily filter into the offices of the employers. If you come to speak with a worker, it is not surprising that he feels self-conscious and fears reprisals such as being fired or other abuse that will deepen his previous situation. Workers realize that even the fines put on the operation from the inspection will come from their own sweat.

While the peasants are not organized, as they could be under the law, the owners have more weapons and the workers will always lose and continue to be exploited. While land tenure and property ownership is not touched by the existing code, the only valid law will become the law of those who are strongest.

For the rest, the urban market is responsible for depleting what the peasants have gained in the harvest season and putting them into debt, plunging the rural worker into a situation of incredible misery.

Family Situation

The family is unstable, with high fertility and mortality rates and broken homes. Malnutrition and sickness are the mortal enemies of human beings. Housing is poor, small, dirty, and miserable. The absence of electrical light, water, and sewer give these hamlets a primitive aspect where they remain unknown by the outside world.

More than fifty percent of our population is under the age of twenty-five. Given the quantitative and qualitative indices of actual schooling it is not easy to reduce the level of adult illiteracy, a reality that no institutional program exists to change.

The best intentions according to reformists can help little with their attempts to patch up our people oppressed by all these influences; they remain enslaved by these personal and environmental ills, marginalized progress, and historical things done in the country; they become conformist, without any recourse, and no hope of overcoming these realities; they are easy victims of sexism, alcoholism, prostitution, and a high level of criminality.

If this could be said of human beings in general, it is the female peasant who suffers when the men project their actions and frustrations upon them.

Cultural and Religious Reality

Socio-culturally our people are oppressed as well. They have no voice, nor expression; they do not know how to "say their word." The expressions they do have come from the subculture imposed by the city, the radio, and propaganda.

The fact that Aguilares is a center for people from very diverse backgrounds relegates all the cultural and religious traditions of their place of origin to second place. Tradition weighs little in Aguilares, which results in an ambivalence for the pastoral process. Even if it were possible to facilitate change, because one doesn't need to overcome traditional barriers, the people lack the matrix that can feed and sustain their popular religiosity. Remove this popular religiosity and there is no other option but to be absorbed by the semi-pagan environment.

Politics and its expression is for the majority something murky, not a clean thing. Political events are forms of entertaining people in order to get votes, rather than an expression of their will or aspirations to achieve a better situation for everyone.

They accommodate law enforcement and their patrols with fear and servility when they arrive at a place, and avoid having to deal with them. They will obey and follow an oppressive leader or chieftain which tends to merge with economic forces, reinforced, at times with the politics of prestige. They can barely emerge from paternalistic or populist motivations.

Religiously we incorporate in our people the scheme of oppression: exploited-exploiter. The priest has some knowledge and magical powers with which he is able to manipulate everyone. God is a capricious king with whom we must be content. His will is blamed for all that exists and happens and is something with which "we must still comply in all things." To Him they go for certain needs and at certain times, like a pharmacy or a benefactor.

In the rural areas, traditionalism, magic, individualism, the rites of passage, and fatalism are religiously predominant. One lives the religious sphere through alienating traditions. Their Christianity is nothing more than semi-magical devotions, without content, with some peripheral and confused notions highlighted by a great pastoral abandonment and the absence of almost any evangelization.

Only through a miracle of God or through that which deprives them, tradition, are they able to be confessed "Christian." Even if some have profoundly Christian values, categorically they don't know what being a "Christian" is. This is of grave concern to us pastors, for before the aggressiveness of the sects and the exacerbation of secularism of all kinds, of every wind that blows and even the minimum demands of true Christianity, they stop being Christians. For these reasons, it is the hour of evangelization and of mission and no wonder it is heard at every step: "they have deceived us but now they are helping us understand our reality."

Diversified reality

In all the reality studied we have tried to look for the diversity of levels, necessities, goals to achieve, and answers or actions we ought to undertake. We summarize here only the pastoral reality that is our own.

Pastoral reality

All can be said to be Christians through baptism, but nearly all are without evangelization. Catholicism prevails, as does popular religiosity, with its true values and false values.

After the missions we can say that a great group of twenty to twenty-five thousand people are without evangelical impact. A group of around five thousand has some questions. For some two thousand the Gospel means "something." And we could call about four hundred people "committed" in some manner.

As our people are in the center of the coordinates between God and world, time and history, we can affirm with the language of conscientization from Paulo Freire that the great majority have an immersed or quasi-immersed consciousness, magical and intransitive of their reality, from which they cannot distance themselves in order to objectify and criticize that reality. This reality dominates and crushes the human being who becomes an object rather than a subject and ruler. This person does not make history and without being this maker of history, they can hardly be liberated. Only a small number of people have an emerging consciousness or are in transition to one, even if it is naïve; they are being evicted of their oppressors—landowner, priest, God—there is a widening of the horizon of perception and awareness that the problems of the world raise, but their consciousness is not easily manipulated now, nor does it have the capacity to respond. They are becoming the subjects of their own liberation and begin to make history. They are the people in Exodus who are ready to receive the Easter message from the New Man, brother of human beings and Lord of history and the universe. These will be those who are able to build a new, open society in which there is room for the word and for criticism, for dialogue and responsibility, to be the managers of their own destiny and creators of history.

Prospective Reality

To translate this reality to the pastoral project, we can say that in the parish is a Kerygmatic level, of an option for Christ and his message. Only very few are at a level of catechesis, of personal change, of initiation and confirmation on the road of the faith. There exist indices, qualitatively encouraging even though low in number, of the dimensions and expressions of community (*koinonia*) and of the responsibility before human beings, the society and the world (*diakonia*).

The baptismal commitment is something general and merely of traditional experience. Even those who are most advanced have no global vision or even a minimum scheme within which to anchor their faith. They are drawing out elements of the Gospel which are valid but without a framework within which to understand and apply them. Christ and Christianity are reduced to a series of topics or recipes with a general commitment to be better; the expressions of Christian life are nothing more than moralizing or a tangential encounter with Christ or the Gospel; and in terms of cultic expressions, they do not exceed the superficial or the semi-intelligible. All this does not invalidate that they are very close to the spirit of the Beatitudes.

1) Urgent Work

This background imposes the following mission:

—Our mission is to GO TO ALL THE PEOPLES from the parish and to make present the reign of God.

—MAKE THEM "MY DISCIPLES," *kerygma*: to opt for Jesus, this is the evangelization to re-Christianize.

—BAPTIZE THEM. . . .AND TEACH THEM, *koinonia*: make a community of faith; this is catechetical-liturgical evangelization.

—DO EVERYTHING I HAVE COMMANDED, *diaconia*: a commitment to change the world, this is the evangelization of actual experience.

While we cannot separate the three functions of the pastoral program (prophetic, cultic, and teaching) in our pastoral formation here and now, it appears that we need to put the emphasis on the prophetic and use the other two, to help this one.

Moreover, both in the cultic (*koinonia*) as in the promotional (*diakonia*), we should put the emphasis on the beginning of all evangelization: the *metanoia* or change of personal attitude toward the kingdom. If the insistence was solely on the community or toward promoting change, it could become politicized, and that Christianity would run the risk of being weak because of a weak base. In this temptation we are not immune. In the underdeveloped village in which we move, it would be sad that the faith—our specific mission—remained underdeveloped because we promote the other dimensions more.

We think that to PREACH THE WORD without reductionism will involve the other dimensions and will be the touchstone which will purify the truth of the prophetic.

According to this, it agrees with the fourth principle that we proposed to the people of God (cf. p. 14) "Our only POLICY is to be faithful proclaimers of the Gospel". . . . to suitably and persistently pronounce and denounce.

The prophetic ministry will be that which proclaims, provokes, accompanies, confirms, presides, celebrates, and verifies faith in Christ and his Gospel as bearers of a dynamism of values able to lead to a new heaven and a new earth, through a different society of human communities, new and free people. This is the horizon for which we want to create the conditions of possibility under the outcomes of the goals and objectives mentioned above.

2) Approaching our Priestly Identity

As a team of priests we wanted to find some agreement and convergence before the glaring crisis of priestly identity. Between the priest who only performs sacraments and the priest who only works in politics, there is a spectrum of priests for everyone. Between these two extremes we try to find our position.

Derived from the prophetic-priestly-kingly character of the people of God, the presbyterate is ordained to serve with the ministers of the Word, through worship, and animation, charisms instituted by God for the community and mediated by it.

These ministers emphasize prophetic service or evangelization, as both Jesus and the Apostles did. If anything, we should be "professionals" in the manner of Christ, Paul, etc., in the ministry of the Word.

Woe to me if I do not preach the Gospel! This Pauline urgency has to be ours. But, what do we understand by EVANGELIZATION? LEAVE THE MEETING WITH GREAT NEWS, PROCLAIM THE NEW PERSON, our PASCHAL person, the whole person found in all situations and circumstances.

This person has basic features:

a) Values

—austerity, poverty, generosity in what they have socioeconomically.

—profoundly religious in his culture.

—dedication, endurance, and sacrifice in their political potential.

—the Beatitudes become vital and concrete in the person, though they don't know it.

b) Anti-values

—dependent, alienated, oppressed.

—socio-culturally they are not what "should be" nor what "must be."

—they have yet to make explicit or dynamic those radically evangelical values and able to conscienticize the new person, paschal, liberated and liberator, always in exodus to a new land.

We cannot exchange our alienations from the society of our origin. To leave aside values without putting other better values in their place that can support and energize them to "be more," will frustrate them and lead to greater alienation. Today they only have their religion and their machete; remove their religion from them and all you have is the machete. . . ! Therefore, this "to be more" is not based primarily in ownership, knowledge, or power, which are not liberating and even less salvific, but rather, in those realities attendant to true liberation.[11]

This is how we are going to meet people today in the here and now as alienated but requiring the Good News—evangelization—to be consciousness-raising and politicizing as necessary dimensions, but only insofar as they are related to full evangelization. We must always have evangelization include and transcend consciousness-raising and this in turn, include and transcend political consciousness-raising. This leads us to study the ways of evangelization and to choose one.

The Ways of Evangelization: secular and religious (not wanting to say which way is the more Christian). They are not mutually exclusive concepts; on the contrary, both need to be included so that the goal is truly Christian. If the religious is included in the cultural, the religious way will break open a dimension in nothing alien to the secular. In other words, as we can divide one method from the other, we will always end up covering the other side if it is true evangelism, for our goal we can have no dichotomies: either be evangelized or be deceived.

We,

—under the weight of the religious in the popular soul,

—through the radically Christian values of our people,

—for the efficacy and practical viability in our environment, tactically CHOOSE the religious way, even though strategically we agree with the objective of the secular way. We believe that this, other than responding to other contexts more secularized and more religiously reluctant, has

---

[11] This is clearly a reference to the Ignatian value of "Magis" or the more. This is taken from the phrase *Ad majorem Dei gloriam* (Latin for "the greater glory of God"). This reflects the aspiration to do and give more to Christ.

not been sufficiently experienced by the peasantry. Nor does the secular way offer guarantees of its veracity. Further, it involves some suspicion of activities that have overtones of consciousness-raising, politicization and even the mere gathering of the people.

The religious way of evangelization cannot be dismissed as ineffective or already exhausted. We believe that what has failed in our popular Catholicism is precisely the evangelization which has tried to Christianize it. Our experience during these two years, rather than contradict this truth, supports our option in the majority of cases.

Moreover, diocesan priests and the traditional church support this option, for they want the New Testament, the traditional pastoral activity of the church, the evangelization of Jesus, and of Paul to be interpreted this way. It is certain that the secular way has found a place with the Jesuits and in the pastoral activity more recently in the secularized world. Professorships, trades and work have been used to convey the Christian message. But the results are put into question by a sector of the population that is more numerous than the pastors.

Both the secular and the religious ways want to respond and be supported by a pastoral conception which derives from a certain vision of the church, which is, in turn derived from a Christology. At the end of the day for all Christians, Christ is the Way, the Truth and the Life.

Christ is mutilated when he is reduced to an object of devotion such as when guerilla slogans refer to him as a "simple revolutionary." Jesus openly rejected political and temporal power as well as any kind of direct leadership. His primary power is of the Word on the conscience and secondarily on what is done, and the movements of conscience trigger those options. More than finished doctrines, Jesus brought values that serve for all times and which will always be corrosive on all negative values, idols, and absolutizations. Jesus cannot be pigeonholed into specific models or programs or we run the risk of privatizing or ossifying Him. He is found in the most notable ideals of all authentic revolutions. He was accused of "being political" and his followers will not be free from this accusation. Jesus was tempted to leave this ambiguity as all true Christians will be tempted; but to fall into that temptation will defeat the most dangerous and profound message for the oppressive powers than that of any revolutionary. The Christian message is more thorough than any political proclamation.

The church and Christians must follow these guidelines to not cut the transcendence of the Word and we ought to use mediations more prophetic than political, if we don't want to water down the message and make it short-term and partisan.

Practice

The tremendous political message—without getting into politics—of Christ, is to encourage the Christian to engage in being politically conscious, but not authorize or impose in the name of Christ and his faith "a determined or set political program." On occasions, Christ could fall into ambiguity, but we must not forget that Christ did not want to leave that ambiguity, and that position cost him his life and led him to the cross.

Our situation has characteristics very similar to the time of Jesus. Whoever in the name of Christ and the community is the spokesman for the message of the kingdom, following the line of the same political theology, cannot privatize Christ, his Word, or the options triggered by it. They must always leave room for criticism and healthy pluralism, in the name of service and the common good.

Current Situation Here

Because of the sociocultural and religious state of our people; because of the messianic expectation of change for a different world; because of the vindictive attitudes in our depoliticized or badly politicized environment; because of the level of Christianity and conscientization; because of the violence of the prevailing structure; because of the same option the team made: for tactical reasons, we ought to be very critical of whatever conscientization and politicization that may implicate our evangelization.

As a team, maybe we take the slower route, but even with this way we are not free of risk and danger. This leaves room for the diversity of gifts of team members, according to their different charisms. Whenever there is a pastoral decision, it is even more important to consult the team.

We do not intend to remove the Gospel from our people and leave them only a machete, nor do we intend to allow them to fall asleep in their religiosity under the cover of and in the name of the same gospel. As a team we want to and came to "PUT YEAST IN THE DOUGH, NOT GIVE THEM BREAD."

2) Deepening

Pentecost of 1972 signaled the end of the first stage of the missionary tour and of the birth of a renovated church with more than thirty burgeoning communities animated by more than three hundred Delegates of the Word. The enthusiasm and the impact produced by everyone in the parish must be harnessed and must accompany this momentum to strengthen these communities and make the Gospel impact their lives. The invaluable work of the collaborators from the post-mission must be multiplied and overflow to the Delegates of the Word and the communities. This is the most favorable moment for the most conscientious and prepared Delegates of the Word to take on new responsibilities and avoid the multiplication of intermediaries between the community and the priest.

Create a temporary organizational plan (see the attached) and launch a work plan. The Delegates of the Word will be the operational platform, like the axel and motor, which will revitalize and grow communities. There must be a substitution and functional shift, for work which up until now had been done by the priest or collaborator. For this we must diversify the functions and services of the Delegates of the Word, and give them sufficient preparation and training so they can perform with efficiency. The stage for courses and workshops has come.

Courses

We intend for the formation of the Delegates of the Word to be adapted to the reality in which they and their community live; that it be a response to the demands and challenges posed by the communities in their growth. We believe that if we send them to courses above the parish level for a week or more, it will make them jump to levels that are difficult for peasants to assimilate. This will take them out of and separate them from their own community; it will saturate them with undigested data unrelated to their community. In the best of cases they will repeat without assimilating, but in no small number of cases the complexity is frustrating. We have arrived at this conclusion from experience and through other known pastoral experiences.

For these reasons we opt for sessions that are not very long, at most a day, with homework and reflection as their basis. We intend their understanding to be practical, in a form that allows them to apply it immediately to their communities. The method will be dialogical, in groups and larger sessions, divided into sections where they will analyze their experience, codify these analyses from the personal to the community level and from these to the national and universal levels.

The central nerve is the Word of God: if it emerges from their reality, it can be encompassed as part of salvation history and, as such, it can illuminate their history with a vision of faith. If the Word of God can illuminate the reality that we have in our hands, we can try to live that life according to the faith.

Characteristics of the Courses

—They are given in the main office of the parish or in central zones. Only as an exception have we sent Delegates of the Word to courses above the parish level.

—They are short and in doses.

—They respond to the needs of the community and the Delegates of the Word.

—They are oriented to the practical work of the community.

—They follow active models and encourage participation in the direction of the same.

—They are always grounded in the Word of God.

Diversification of Courses

1) Outside the Parishes

Only as an exception would we send them to these courses, but they are very important for future courses for the parish. For this reason a priest is always sent who can incorporate their experience into the parish courses.

a) **Experiential Laboratory of Peasants**: five peasants, two lay leaders from the city and two priests from the team attend. It takes place in San Salvador and is rich in experiences and in future applications.

b) **Course on Cooperatives**: two peasants, two people from the city and one priest attend; later more peasants and women can take this course. COSALCO in San Salvador organizes it. They will be initiating this approach to building cooperatives in the parish and in the small villages.

c) **Mini-IPLA (Latin American Pastoral Institute)**: a peasant and a priest will attend for five weeks and it will be offered in San Salvador.

2) Parish Courses in the Main Parish Office

For those from the city this will be offered midweek, while those from the villages will attend on Saturday and Sunday.

a) **Urban Catechists**: The city is divided into ten centers, in which catechesis will be held on Saturday. The catechists arrive at the parish on Friday, and a priest begins and prepares the lessons with them. They use the method of St. Anne's Providence (a church).

b)"**Community Vaccine:**" Before the political climate ahead becomes really virulent, the communities need to be strengthened so they cannot be manipulated, and they need to be formed with a civic spirit that ought to animate the people, not manipulate them or allow them to be manipulated.

— **Place**: the main parish center.

— **Length**: two doses of three hours; the Sundays for the Delegates of the Word from the villages and Tuesday for those from the city.

— **Directing**: the priests.

— **Method**: reflection over the parable of the Good Samaritan. Groups respond to various questions and detect what they mean and what they need to understand of the political.

— **Plenary discussion, completion, and agreements**.

— They are given the **Constitution of the Republic** and pointed toward the articles which support the political rights and duties at both the individual and community level.

— They are also presented a short story-parable which the community will stage; the community will then decode each character when the priest arrives.

In the parish Masses during these weeks, the Word should be focused on clarifying for the general public the posture of the Missionary Team on these issues that create so much confusion in the people during times of political campaigns that divide and disturb the communities.

c)**Courses for Trainers:** These courses by the mission team will replace the service provided by foreign partners, that is, to prepare and train other Delegates of the Word in the central zones. Through a consultation with the communities, forty-five Delegates of the Word are selected to go on to be trainers. They have to be like the arms of the missionary team, the link between the communities and the parish and of the new Parish Council. They will be given a preparation of thirty-five hours divided into five weekends in the main Parish center.

— **Animation:** two priests will prepare a course during the week. It will be run by a priest and two collaborators.

— **Content:** they are developing, in a parallel manner, those topics which occur throughout the Bible and in their own situation:

a) Historical situation: structure of sin and violence.

b) Causes of the situation: degeneration of relationships.

c) Overcoming of this situation: return to the proper relationship.

d) Liberation: make structures that humanize and do not oppress.

e) Plan of God: new people as members of a new community.

— **Method:** emphasizes the active and the dialogical. The priest or his collaborator should only direct the overall plenary session. The groups, evaluations, and smaller talks should be directed by the same trainers. This dimension is emphasized because they themselves are trained in this method and should not try "to be preachers" but animators who "prepare the road and make others grow."

Within the rate of assimilation for the rural farmers, the maximum efficiency should be sought. For this we took into account technical aspects of the total language, to better capture the entire person. The person—and more the case with rural farmers—do not only learn through ideas, but through the senses, emotions, movement. . . A song could be thrown out that is listened to, analyzed and interpreted by them, as a way of deepening or of providing rest and relaxation; group activities, slides, graphics, and games should also be used.

In the development of these themes this process should be followed:

a)— Decoding, to come to find **what they themselves say** in the Biblical piece, a fact of life, a song, a game. . .

b)— Relation to our reality: interpretation **for us** in our situation.

c)— Projection for future praxis in our communities.

d)— **a leveling course**. This is designated so for a double motive: this was promoted in each community and to other delegates who were selected as trainers to have a new function. The aim was also to achieve some uniformity in the plan or steps that the communities followed in the Celebration of the Word, because in the early days there was ample room for experimentation and creativity in one's own community. This was developed in the parish center,

on Sunday mornings, simultaneous with the courses of
the trainers.

— Animation: a seminarian and a collaborator.

— Objective: to evaluate the diverse experiences in the preparation
of the texts and in the development of the community sessions,
to take the plans that would be followed in the parish by the
trainers and the communities in their sessions (see attached).

e) **Course of the Delegates of the Word:** With the experience of
the training course, five courses follow for those who have sequen-
tially passed, nearly all the Delegates of the Word from the village.
They have similar characteristics to the trainers, although they are
mixed—male Delegates and female Delegates of the Word. This is
like the first level of formation for everyone. They are given homework to do during the week in their community with the other delegates that have already passed or who will pass the short courses. In
this way they will deepen what has been given in the course as well
as the other delegates who are living in the same environment and
problematic developed through the same course. This homework
is in the mode of a questionnaire that the participants must bring
answered to the course.

f) **Course in the City and in El Paisnal**: The communities of these
two centers followed a system outside of that followed by the farming villages due to their urban or semi-urban contexts in the case of
Aguilares and in El Paisnal. The two communities finally emerged
with the missions they had there during Lent. It was necessary to
incorporate them and unify them, however possible, with the movements in the farming villages.

In the respective parish centers, separate courses were given to all the
Delegates of the Word during fifteen consecutive afternoons.

— two priests, two Delegates of the Word, one trainer and one
collaborator were responsible for these courses.

— With a similar methodology to the other courses, three instruments that all Delegates of the Word ought to use were
emphasized in their training: reality, the Bible, method.

After these first-level courses in the parish center, they diversified the
functions of the Delegates of the Word, unified and planned the meetings:
the trainers, in the zones, of the Delegates of the Word and the communities.

Specific Courses:

In order to diversify the services of the Delegates of the Word, they will periodically meet to prepare for their diverse functions. They have as their objective: to share experiences of ministry, resolution of problems, and formation for their services to the community.

a) Initiators of baptism: instruction on how to approach parents, give them talks on family life, explanation and application of the four themes that are given by the archdiocese with other complementary plans in the parish.

b) Catechists: instruction and method that enable them to explain to children of their community the catechism of the parish.

c) Youth Leaders: formation and methodology to form a core group of young people. As a guide, give them an appropriate agenda with plans for discussion made in the parish.

d) Coordinators and Secretaries: formation for the execution of the monthly meeting of the Delegates of the Word.

e) Mobile Teams: give as first steps, four teams that will begin to engage the young people and adults who already form the core of the village and the city communities. Provide an inter-community service of animation and revision within the Delegates of the Word and their communities. Cooperate with the priest in short courses for base communities.

f) Talks on marriage preparation and the responsibilities of baptism are given periodically in the main parish office.

3) Parish Courses at the Basic Community Level

These need to be provided in the communities or in the central zones and the basic level of the community needs to participate more, not only Delegates of the Word as above, that we have indicated here. They are not so much courses in "multiplication" of knowledge as they are in community leveling.

a) Course on the Relation of Human Beings and the Earth: Directed by eight university collaborators (of them, five Jesuit students and one seminarian; two nearly ordained).

—Method: reading of a parable that will be staged in the manner of a little drama for the same villagers after a brief training. The community analyzes and decodes the various characters in the parable and the university collaborators record the verbal participation.

Bring in a gospel text that illuminates what they get out of the parable.

For this course they chose two core groups of villagers and intended multiple objectives: an awareness of their reality and concientization for the villagers and realization of academic work for the students from the UCA. In the second place, they wanted to lift the universal vocabulary and related themes of adults for the next set of literacy courses.

b) Literacy Course: The university collaborators work with various villagers to give the beginnings of the method to three hamlets over forty-five days. The villagers who belong to various communities will continue the instruction when the collaborators cannot do so.

The material and the themes are prepared in the parish.

The team of villagers will give the others two more courses, in other hamlets.

In reality, a better prepared literacy class will be developed than before.

c) Courses in Cooperatives: In the village and city a good group of people is selected who receive an initiation into making cooperatives. They choose some of them to go and improve their understanding and engagement in cooperatives in San Salvador.

Later they will give talks in the hamlets and in the neighborhoods of the city to prepare the opening in Aguilares of a *Salvadoran Buying Cooperative* that is directed by Pilar.

The continuation in the formation of cooperatives has been irregular for various reasons, but the principal reason has been the departure of Fr. Chus to Medellín, Colombia, to finish his formation, when he was incorporated in the formation team of COSALCO (Salvadoran Buying Cooperative).

In reality, the cooperative is found in the parish during a time of hope and of reflection.

d) Permanent Formation. After the initial awakening that creates union and mobilization, a good group of people continues forming with periodic meetings in the base communities and in the parish center; they are reflection groups which at the parish and above the parish level participate in meetings with district officials from the church as well as inter-parish meetings as committed laypersons in the Christian and pastoral work they do. Jesuits in training accompany and direct their formation.

4) Culmination of this Stage

In the process of consolidation two celebrations have been highlighted. The Festival of Corn and the festival-tribute to the bishop.

Festival of Corn

Encouraged by the celebration of Pentecost the previous year, a celebration is to be held for villagers intended to celebrate the coexistence and creativity of the community. This has good reception and resonance in the communities. Choose "the corn" as a theme and symbol of the rural peasant. The points of agreement and criteria for making the celebration different and original should come from the most basic levels of the community. They set the criteria for what will encourage:

—everything will be communal, nothing individual.
—the money factor will not detract as a determinant.
—it will be a celebration of denunciation and of hope.

The celebration will be prepared and held at the community level (the village) and later the best of it will be taken to the great celebration of the entire parish community. On August 18, with their corn at the front, they will determine that this is the moment for the gathering.

Each community brings a collection of corn for "corn meal" which will be communal and people will only be charged the cost of processing the corn.

They will bring those selected:

—the best ear of corn
—the best ornament based on the entire corn plant
—the best song, at the least the most original, that sings of the work and the harvest of the corn.

Each community will present a godmother, regardless of age, chosen as a model of service and work in the community. She will be responsible for all the work of women that is presented at the celebration on behalf of her community and she will present to the public the performance of her people in the competition, etc.

One man from each community, indicated by similar criteria as the godmother, will be in charge of all the contributions of the men at the celebration.

Everything that could be construed as competitive was avoided, leaving aside popular acclaim, the designation of the best, especially when they could not be quantified or qualified by a jury chosen from among them.

In the same way, the gathering has been lively with everyone participating; even the songs have had strong messages and protests, with great variety, creativity and widespread participation. Everyone enjoyed the celebration. Without doubt a success that will be surpassed in years to come.

Festival-Tribute to the Bishop

In order to celebrate the fifty years of service by our pastor and arch-bishop, the Delegates of the Word offered him a eucharistic service on 29 December. About four hundred delegates were arranged by delegations and occupied the pews of the church. After the greetings and offering, two delegates offered the homily. The first delegate from the village spoke on: "We are Delegates of God in service to the community." The next delegate from the city spoke on: "We are Church, responsible for the new person for a new community." Afterwards the bishop took their profession of faith, accepted their commitments and "confirmed" them in their community functions. At the end he gave them a "mission" and blessing, at the same time each delegate was presented to greet him.

This is the end of the second stage, and a new re-launching to follow in the work of the kingdom.

In Conclusion

What is outlined here requires critical reflection and verification through time, confirmed by the entire experience. It would be naïve on our part to affirm that this worked and that did not.

The ministry is primarily an application of the message of salvation to the whole person. It is a practice in which there are many factors that combine and seek to balance tensions that are not antithetical, but dia-lectical, and are creators of a new result.

One mistake could lead one to assume that one priest could not initi-ate a similar experience. Some cases in the same archdiocese prove this assumption to be untrue.

The fact that several priests and a constellation of collaborators have undeniable advantages, especially for the start, also has its counterpart. From there come, despite good will, dangers and failures that we observe. To have had abundant human resources poses serious questions for us. I will point out a number of the most notorious:

—Activism and immediate answers with little critique and reflection, losing an objective view and clarity in planning.

—"Holy impatience" to force the pace and jump over stages, and subse-quent flattening of values that need to be purified and transformed, not subdued or even less suppressed.

—To seek efficacy and efficiency in the short term falls into elitism and takes away from the basic levels of the community. We do not walk

WITH the people if unconsciously we make it so the people cannot walk with us, and if they do not, only the elite will walk with us.

—Imbalance in evangelization does not allow Christian values to be assimilated and settled in the community.

—A twisted conscientization and politicization without a Christian foundation can easily rest in vindication and immediacy.

—Danger of falling into paternalism or more so into populism, creating leaders not of service, but of oppression.

—With all these doubts we must ask: Do we educate, do we teach them culture or are we domesticating and transferring their own alienations? Do we comply with the Pauline motive "For freedom, Christ set us free. . . . "?

We glimpse these and other dangers, these tensions are also a horizon, which we always reach whenever we put these conditions on the manner in which we walk.

We dare to advance some guidelines of these necessary conditions in our case, but they can be helpful for others. They are applicable at various levels: personal, parochial, zonal, the vicariate level, etc.

1) **Where are we**: A clear vision of the reality together with and from the moment we live as a pastoral opportunity and possibility; as a "Kairos of Salvation."

2) **On what we can rely**: Analysis of human resources from the base to the top and the diversification of the same. We have to walk the road WITH them, not only FOR them or FROM our reality. We need to know upon whom we can rely and upon whom they can rely.

3) **Where are we going:** Clarity in the short, medium, and long-term objectives and goals. Without this clarity we are walking blind. We do not want to change them into snipers or into conservative fish of a state, who if they don't paddle, will be swallowed by the current.

4) **How we will walk**: From that which is stated above, it follows that there is certain unification; if it is not possible to work in a team, at the least there must be coordination. And to the contrary, if confusion in the people results, one destroys something while the other claims to build it up.

5) **Where do we begin**: We cannot cover everything. We have to establish priorities which conform to the objectives. We should not be content and think "we have already done something." Multiple methods will be

chosen, with tactics that radiate outward, through zones that indicate the church is awake.

6) **At what speed will we go**: All that has been said before will be conditioned to walk WITH others. At the rate they go, they can and should go. The best approaches can burn themselves or the people they intend to serve if the rate and methods are not suitable for the context.

7) **What plan**: All of this assumes great transitivity, mobility, reflective attitude, and critical dialogue; continual conversion will assist us very well in preaching, but it will cost us to enter that conversion. This should be perhaps, the beginning of any approach if we want to evangelize ourselves and evangelize others.

A Final Word

Throughout this process the impression could be given that the Prime Actor is a little withdrawn in the dark. We try to advance the Reign of God. "First God" is a popular saying of profound significance.

This Reign is among us; it must be raised up and done explicitly. This is our work and for this we are workers. But we do not want to consider ourselves useless before it begins. If we do not realize the work is His, we distrust God, and we will take ourselves too seriously. Following Jesus and putting our trust in Him, we establish relationships between peoples and communities: we prefer to consider ourselves useless after we did what we had to do.

We plan a general evaluation of the experience. Before this it is premature to advance results. After making a "pit stop" we will see whether to continue, straighten the path, set back, or seek a change. . . ! We only intuit that something has to change.

The beginning was a challenge; it still is today, and perhaps more so. In any case it is encouraging that "the road is made by walking" in order to announce to the poor the good news of the kingdom of God.

> Aguilares, El Salvador
> In the Parish of Our Lord of Mercy
> January 15, 1975
> By the missionary team
> Fr. Salvador Carranza, SJ

Index